W9-BAR-654

The Pursuit of Pleasure

ALSO BY LIONEL TIGER

Men in Groups
The Imperial Animal (with Robin Fox)
Women in the Kibbutz (with Joseph Shepher)
Female Hierarchies (edited with Heather Fowler)
Optimism: The Biology of Hope
The Manufacture of Evil: Ethics, Evolution, and the Industrial System
China's Food (with Reinhart Wolf)
Man and Beast Revisited (edited with Michael H. Robinson)

LIONEL TIGER

The Pursuit of Pleasure

Little, Brown and Company
BOSTON NEW YORK TORONTO LONDON

First Paperback Edition

Library of Congress Cataloging-in-Publication Data

Tiger, Lionel, 1937–
The pursuit of pleasure / Lionel Tiger. — 1st ed.
p. cm.
ISBN 0-316-84543-4 (hc)
ISBN 0-316-84544-2 (pb)
1. Pleasure. I. Title
BF515.T54 1992
171'.4 — dc20 91-21389

10 9 8 7 6 5 4 3 2 1

MV-NY

Published simultaneously in Canada
by Little, Brown & Company (Canada) Limited

PRINTED IN THE UNITED STATES OF AMERICA

Joyce Ravid

Contents

The Pursuit of Pleasure

INTRODUCTION

Cellos, Velvet, and the State

THE SEXUAL SPASM is the most physically pleasurable human event. How does a person become introduced to it? What meaning does it have? How does it fit into the larger picture of personal and communal life? Let me begin this book about pleasure by telling how a newly adolescent Montrealer first experienced willful orgasm.

Kindly do not think of passion, drama, seduction, betrothal, ardor. Be aware this was not sex with another person. At the time that seemed an adventure of stunning complexity and unlikelihood. Instead it was an act of solitary masturbation in the home of some relatives whose children I was minding while the parents were out for the evening. This was not an act that could be first undertaken at home. The anticipated trauma of stolen pleasure could not so openly happen at the central scene of the strict regime I was planning to challenge. I was not that brave.

Please understand that youngsters raised in the Canadian province of Quebec in the forties and fifties were surrounded by a tightly controlled religious and political regime that had its roots in prerevolutionary France (Brittany, as a matter of fact). It was widely considered the home of one of the most conservative Roman Catholic communities in the world. People under sixteen were not allowed to see movies, any movies — even Walt Disney nature films — except in schools, because commercial cinemas clearly could reveal to the young the sports and ambiguities of lives led differently from those with which we struggled in sexual puzzlement. The Jewish community in which I was raised, so vividly and robustly chronicled by Mordecai Richler, may have been bawdy and colorful for some, but for others, such as myself, it was tight, fiercely earnest about the value of work, and a hopeless school for pleasure let alone scandal. Censorship of all kinds was effective and pervasive, and there was a well-supported Morality Squad (this is true) in every serious police force.

Thus it was very difficult for a boy, this boy, to learn about the mysterious possibilities of the body. There were neither manuals of procedure nor classroom or laboratory opportunities for even devoted youthful scholars of the matter. I understood from baffled experience that the penis became erect and that it felt improbably good if manipulated. I knew its role in reproduction, if only at the level of macrotheory. My principal working clue about the specific task I was anticipating was the dirty talk of boys, particularly the grubbily clear password phrase "jerking off." Surely even a simpleton could adopt this as a guide to action.

And this jerking off I resolved to do. But when? Would I pass out? Would my face be red for hours afterward? Would my sex organ interfere with a seemly good-bye to my cousins or would I be huffing and puffing? Would I be incapacitated if my baby charges needed help? Timing was crucial. I waited until the babes were fully asleep and had issued no complaints or observations for nearly an hour. Then I calculated halfway from then to the time my employers were expected to return. That would be my moment!

But where? That depended on what would happen, and this I didn't know. I was reasonably confident some fluid would result. But how much? Would it conspicuously and obviously soil my clothes? Would there be a graphically telltale mess? Would it produce a pagan flare of a stain on the living-room wallpaper? Or leave a betrayingly carnal odor?

I found the perfect solution. I would do it naked in the bathtub! No soiled clothes. The tub had obviously ample storage capacity for anything I could foresee producing. The evidence could be removed with the twist of a faucet. It was a sanitary, prudent, and thoughtful solution to the dilemma created by my ardent confusion.

But how long would it take? And what if I lost track of time? I had to gamble I decided to wear my watch, *which was not waterproof*, in the bathtub.

The truth has to be told that I was a sexual success that night. I mastered myself during an act of theft from a gloomy culture that embargoed pleasure. The earnest student became an autoerotic autodidact. And the question of who has a right to pleasure and how much and why, and what communities think about all this and under whose control, has vexed and interested me ever since.

Why are high-school students induced to enjoy Elizabethan drama but in virtually no school system offered helpful hints on enjoying physical pleasure by themselves, at no economic cost, without fear of unwanted pregnancy, without interfering with someone else's schedule of homework? This is particularly interesting as a practical matter because masturbation presumably has a calming effect, especially on adolescent males. In practice, while male sexual intercourse usually causes an increase in bodily testosterone, which is associated with assertion and aggression, masturbation leaves the level of this influential substance unchanged. It may actually reduce the tension and sense of frustration adolescent males often experience.[1]

I am not altogether serious in suggesting that masturbation become an official part of the school curriculum. But I am serious about what its absence implies about the controversial matter of pleasure — about what people think pleasure is, about who may have it, about who controls it, about who celebrates it. There is no instruction in masturbation because there appears to be a belief or a fear or both that when adults license and approve of sexual pleasure, this literally leads to licentiousness. The community's values appear to depend on the apprehension that for the young it is more dangerous to have pleasure than not to. What should parents do when their adolescent child wants to have sleepover sex in the comfort and safety of home rather than more riskily and fugitively elsewhere? And what will the neighbors think?

There is a fierce endemic contest in many communities about who gets pleasure, which pleasure, when, with whom, and with what cost or tax. It is hardly ever a casual matter. We will review some human communities in which there is a frank embrace of sexual and similar pleasures. But far more often "Thou shalt not" looms larger than "Please enjoy" on the tablet of commandments and in the broader scheme of things too. Why is this?

It seems backward. What is the attraction of "no" and the fear of "yes"?

I begin with sexuality, but the matter goes far beyond it. For example, discussion of food during the schooling of the young for life focuses on the food groups, vitamins, and other issues of well-meaning gastric housekeeping rather than the pleasure of food, its variety of tastes and array of social functions, and the artistry and social enthusiasm it can reflect. For the first time, the French government is experimenting with primary-school courses designed to teach children about the techniques and history of French cuisine. However, the principal stimulus appears to be not the encouragement of delight but rather stern nationalistic assertion and an effort to withstand the incursions of foreign — largely American — fast food.[2] While people who study botany and zoology may enjoy flora and fauna, the emphasis in their work is on plant physiology, on classification, on technicality, not on the wonderful impact on the senses and the spirit of the feats of nature. Only recently have historians begun to inquire into the richness of personal, private, domestic life rather than about the formal movements of states and despots, generals and trade monopolies.

Economics continues to emphasize broad transactions of money and products. In contrast, there is little attention paid to the economics of the domestic, personal, affectionate, and aesthetic character of private lives. This is so even though it is on these subtle matters, which are often associated with pleasure, as well as with need, that economic activity finally depends. It has been estimated that some 60 to 70 percent of economic transactions flow through the domestic sphere. But this is the least well understood broad factor in economic life[3] — even though we know that when people cease to enjoy consuming at home, the overall economy falters.

When there is a depression, one important source is at home, in depression of the spirit.

Of course there have always been disciplines such as literature, musicology, and art history, and they have often been converted into earnestly solemn courses in Art Appreciation, Music Appreciation, and the like. The formality and impersonality of much academic scholarship and teaching decisively overwhelm the force of joy or the buzz of pleasure. The rigmarole of evaluating students, assessing scholars, and criticizing critics undermines the spirit of the events of art that initiate and nourish the entire endeavor. The fun goes out of it. It has been replaced by a kind of accountancy. However high an academic degree may be, on the centigrade scale it is usually at best lukewarm.

Tom Jefferson's Challenge

I will not merely offer the banal complaint that educational and similar systems should offer their members more vivacity, amusement, and gladness. While a carrot is not the most enticing pleasure I can imagine, it is undoubtedly more amusing than the stick. We know that children learn through play and that they play as vigorously as they babble and eventually learn to talk. In an important sense, fun and games are their work. All work and no play will not only make Johnny a dull boy but a stupid one.

Yet there may well be excellent and comprehensible reasons for the dourness of particular social enterprises. The American revolution was luminously innovative and influential in its emphasis on the political value of "the pursuit of happiness." This was surely a fresh consideration for practical political activists. But there are several subclauses. The first is that the original Jeffersonian formulation sought the "pursuits of happiness" — a very different and much more domestic and local matter than "pursuit" in general. As well, as it was finally settled in the American constitution "happiness" referred to political satisfaction rather than personal delight.[4] And it is not clear that happiness was and is seen as valuable as liberty, which involves a very special and protective attitude to individuals in social groups.

Therefore can we assert that pleasure is ethically comparable as a value to equality? Equality demands for its achievement a sustained social passion and an apparatus of thoughtfully planned social institutions. In contrast, perhaps pleasure is just a luxury, like velvet, or subtly smoked salmon, or Yo-Yo Ma playing cello. Perhaps, also, knowing how to discover and experience pleasure is a skill and an art form in its own right, one that has to be cultivated and is in no way a political right. Perhaps pleasure *does* make people lazy and indulgent. Perhaps masturbation at fourteen does lead with grim inexorability to conniving irresponsible decadence at forty. Perhaps the sexual bravado of the 1960s and 1970s did in fact yield people confused by the contrast between the ease with which intimacy could be enjoyed in a moment and the difficulty with which it might be sustained over a lifetime.

Sugar and butter are delicious to eat but generally bad for people. Is this a simple sign of a more complex truth?

Pleasure — the Drug

The subject is hot. Entire countries such as Bolivia, Peru, and Colombia are convulsed, enriched, and traumatized because they grow or process a substance — cocaine — that is then sold for staggering sums of money in American cities, which are in turn convulsed, impoverished, and traumatized. This is mainly because the human central nervous system converts certain chemicals into a sensory experience defined as highly pleasurable. Even if continued cocaine use soon becomes relentlessly addictive and destructive, which it does, the first episode often entails a persuasive aria of pleasure. Pleasure is the drawing card, even if it is crimogenic as well. And private pleasure becomes an intensely public matter.

At other times in history, different communities, such as that of China, and different substances, such as opium, were the subjects of the coiled embrace of pusher and addict. Frank, rank, convulsive addiction is a recurrent feature of countless communities. Colonial merchant empires and up-to-the-minute urban gangs exploit a clear human vulnerability to substances that produce a dramatic bang of pleasure.

Or the issue can rest on subtler events. Even the appeal of sugar and tobacco, which so powerfully stimulated the drastic growth of slavery, depended on the power of the body, the pleasure of the mouth, the vigor of human desire for sensual experience. Whole industries continue to rely on a cavalcade of changes in skirt length, pasta garnish, carpet style, tie width, exercise schemes, town plans. They reflect varying notions of what is desirable and pleasurable and what material objects and activities best define an enviable person.

So slumlords thwart the health and rights of tenants to better squeeze from their holdings the funds to provide a coveted Mother's Day lunch in a tablecloth restaurant serving costly protein, uncommon vegetables, and urgently rich desserts. The largest industry in the world is tourism, in which people from one part of the world visit another because they enjoy it. While countless people in the world have too little food to eat, countless others are too fat from eating too much — because they enjoy it. Electricity links hundreds of millions of people in a web of community bent on sports, games, fairy tales, music, dramas, political and social rituals — optional pleasures shared on an unprecedented scale. Privately, numberless people plant and tend and enjoy vegetation, often because of the pleasure of the senses rather than the economic benefit of their produce. Numberless people own members of other species for whom they care at some cost and often with considerable effort and impressive dedication. Just take a glance at the improbable variety and number of dog and cat foods in a supermarket — a sign of careful and generous affection. A Gallup poll of 1990 informs us that 68 percent of Americans give their pets presents for Christmas, 32 percent share beds with them, and 24 percent celebrate their birthdays. Apparently plants and pets provide people so much pleasure that we are willing to jump the boundary around our species. Some humans even seek out highly specialized forms of sexual pain that give them pleasure. Conveniently, sadists prefer the pleasure of inflicting it.

When the Tough Get Going, the Going Gets Tough

At the same time that pleasure mobilizes the world in endless ways, it is also one of the most controversial of the central elements of human life. It is denounced from pulpits and grandly associated with terrible punishments in interminable afterlives.[5] The priestly bulletin informs you that if you do certain things that give you pleasure you will baste in hell, whereas if you abstain you will inhabit the cool perfection of heaven. Sages pronounce on which pleasures are acceptable and which corrupt, which serve God or man and which benefit only the pleased and very possibly the devil too.

But this is not only the business of theologians. Governments too decide some pleasures are criminal, others questionable, still others highly taxable. Confidently, some governments assert that certain pleasures reveal political unreliability and even perversion — for example, enjoying homosexuality in Cuba or jiving to rock and roll in Burma or peering at pictures of naked humans in China. Such governments support earnest and unforgiving legions of guardians to supervise people's pleasures and monitor their sumptuary goals. It is an old story, the story of "art made tongue-tied by authority," as Shakespeare wrote in his sixty-sixth sonnet.

Children are not exempt, either, from debate about the questionable impact of pleasure. Phalanxes of educators have marched to a drum beaten by the rod from which children must not be spared. In earnest retaliation, smaller, more recently formed battalions prefer the goads of satisfaction, exploration, challenge — pleasures — as the guiding lights of education. Theorists of infant welfare argue over the wisdom of embracing children when they cry — won't they grow to associate pleasure and comfort with whininess? Won't they become "spoiled"? And hence won't they be generally unfit for the adult business of responding to the real world, which overflows with near-chronic perturbation? Or, instead, will infants who banshee without consolation conclude that the social world is mercilessly without succor and that hard skepticism is the inevitable colorless order of the day and the life?

Here is an issue this book will address: the relationship between individual experience and public policy. The attitude a person has to his own pleasure and pain may be readily extended to a broad notion of politics in the wider community. Is the cup of life half full of pain or half empty of pleasure? Do you cheer for the Stick Party, or the Carrot Party? Presumably, most people are generally unwilling to create political arrangements that maximize the pain of others.[6] But how many are sufficiently generous to seek political forms to maximize their fellow citizens' pleasure but not their own?

Is the lineup longer for the "No" party than the "Yes" party? Are some communities simply more fun than others? If so, why?

Pleasure — the Political Issue

It is necessary to put this in perspective. The study of pleasure is a necessary part of social science. But as I have noted, there has been much more serious consideration of how pain and associated deprivations can be avoided than how pleasure can be achieved and maximized. This is altogether sensible in the context of human evolution and history. There were (and are) so many perils and obstacles that must be overcome for life to go on. Attention to what seems like optional pleasure seems far less worthwhile and certainly less pressing, less legislatively immediate. For someone desperately thirsty during a drought, earnest natter about which Médoc of the eighties has a more elegant bouquet is an idiotic, insulting irrelevance. To campesinos in thrall to heartless Salvadoran oligarchs, conversation on the role of sentimentality in popular culture is a diversion from their need to confront implacable facts of economic deprivation.

The first obligation people have to themselves and those close to them is to ensure physical survival and to establish social arrangements that offer decency and continuity. In this book I take for granted that this priority must be respected — both in the practical ways one interacts with other people and as a citizen, and intellectually too. I hope it is understood clearly that I am writing about a category of human experience well above the more fundamental issues of persistence and health.

These issues unfold fundamental concerns. Pleasure matters. It has a reputation. A city such as New Orleans, which is thought to be a friendlier arena for pleasure than most, is called "the Big Easy." Discussions of popular culture often focus on how diligently producers strive to mix uplifting "art" with lowest-common-denominator "entertainment." A "hard worker" is more readily and generally esteemed than a "playboy." It appears to be impossible for governments to avoid taking some position on various pleasures, whether to prohibit them or tax them or restrict them or invest in parks in which to enjoy them. While perhaps ideally (as Canadian prime minister Pierre Trudeau announced) "the state has no place in the bedrooms of the nation," this stricture remains an eccentrically rare description of what actually happens in real-life regimes. How a community deals with pleasure is an important revelation of its political nature.

It is also revealing about our vastly complicated species. Here is another theme: to see if our evolution as a species and the role of pleasure in this evolution has an impact on our conduct as a community and as individuals. There is a tremendous amount of variation in human arrangements, a diversity that makes it difficult to issue confident generalizations — to talk about the species as a whole.

Nevertheless, there *is* a definite and common human race. There may be a way to understand the shape of the forest while retaining affectionate concern for the trees. For example, recall the English political philosopher Jeremy Bentham. In his time he was seen by European enthusiasts as "the Newton of the moral world" for his aggressive assertions about the theory that the best community created "the greatest happiness of the greatest number." His *Introduction to the Principles of Morals and Legislation* (1789) offers the famous ringing announcement: "Nature has placed mankind under the governance of two sovereign masters, *pain* and *pleasure*. It is for them alone to point out what we ought to do, as well as to determine what we shall do. On the one hand the standard of right and wrong, on the other the chain of causes and effects, are fastened to their throne. They govern us in all we do, in all we say, in all we think. . . ."

"Sovereign masters"! What a demanding phrase. Was Bentham right about the "sovereign masters"? And if so, what is this "Nature"? Bentham wrote before Darwin told us that evolution in the distant past had direct meaning for life in the immediate present. Now we know very much more than Bentham could about our history and prehistory. If we don't know where we're going, at least we have a clear idea of whence we came.

This sharply changes how we can consider pleasure and pain. It even compels us to reassess the kind of biblical description of pain that Job experienced, as well as its cautionary equivalents in other moral systems. It prompts us to reconsider in terms beyond moralizing what happens when pleasure becomes extreme, as in the legendary sagas of Babylon and Rome, and in the real and fictional lives of pleasure-meteors such as the Great Gatsby and Oscar Wilde. For them enjoyment went beyond its moment and its occurrence. It became almost a matter of principle. Most people do not live their lives with such dramatic emphasis on the pursuit of pleasure. But the extravagant tales of apparent joy of hedonists may be informative.

Pleasure — the Threat

This book should have value for individuals who attempt to evaluate their own experience and particularly their pleasures. Not that it is designed to provide self-help. But it should self-inform. This is chiefly because its subject is the broadest version of the self, the species. Its argument is that we humans of diverse histories enjoy similar pleasures — even though the literature about these pleasures is far less authoritative and respectable than the equivalent documents of despair, such as Job's. Though it is not true, the rumor exists that Eskimos have several hundred words for snow. I will be implicitly concerned in this book with the comparison between how we describe pleasure and how we describe work, because this may be a subtle revelation of our notion of pain.

Description of pain is, I believe, more rigorous and respectable and earns more points. There is a story about the assistants to Robert McNamara at the Pentagon during his work as secretary of defense during the Vietnam War. Evidently, he would appear for work quite early — six, six-thirty, seven o'clock was late. When his less eager assistants slid into the parking lot and suffered the rebuking sight of his car in its space, they touched the car's hood to estimate from its remaining heat how long before their boss had beat them to the salt mine.

Working hard and long was and is the mark of distinction. There remains great nuance in the descriptions of hard work, which is in general highly commended. Once, our academic department was visited by a representative of a national research agency for a routine evaluation of our facility and what we were doing with the ample research funds we had been awarded. Our imposed guest spent virtually his entire time with us announcing how hard he worked, how punishingly much he traveled, how many such visits he had to make, how demanding were the judgments expected of him, how pivotally significant was his function, how enervating was performing it.

This was puzzling and irritating. Impolitically, I asked why did he not quit the work and return to the university from which he had come. He was both deflated and angry. Clearly, I did not understand and did not appreciate the richly redemptive value of his activity. I had violated a given, almost a sacred given. I had failed to be awed by his *very hard work.* There was no equivalence between his portentous attitude to this work and his evident unwillingness to discuss his pleasure. It was virtually inconceivable that he would have launched into an equivalent aria about how *easy* his job was, how deftly and swiftly he completed each of the pitifully *simple* tasks his misguided and overgenerous employers assigned, and how gleefully *enjoyable* was each and every working day.

Two hundred words for work, and just a few simple grunts for pleasure. But why?

An elaborate suite of answers is required to understand this — an array that ranges in gravity from comments on specific laws about the closing hours of pubs to broader hypotheses. Let me issue an advance bulletin giving one such answer: *Powerful people enjoy it when they are able to define and restrict the pleasure of others.* Their enjoyment is not only mean-spirited. It is also a deep response that reveals something about the fundamental springs of human social order. Pleasure and its availability loom as a resource, rather like wealth. Its distribution is subject to certain forms and limits. These can range from the restricted hunting grounds of the European nobility to the sumptuary laws that determined which colors were reserved for which echelons of the population — royal purple for guess who? — to the epochal laws governing the right to domestic privacy and autonomy. In between are opportunities for social enjoyment such as clubs, sports facilities, even political groups, in which management of membership is often a privilege. The home is, of course, usually the least public of venues for enjoying pleasure. The ability to dominate people at home is an extreme case of assertiveness by power wielders.

Perhaps only censorship is more extreme. It is an effort to control the pleasure people have within that highly secret place, the skull. Think of it! Someone is trying to control the fun you have in the remarkable primitive privacy of your own head!

Pleasure — the Wide Screen

The definition of pleasure, the control of it, and the apparent pleasure enjoyed in controlling it are issues of plain magnitude and controversy. Few people lack opinions and sharp moral views about the place of pleasure in the well-lived life, what form it should take, and with what intensity it should be pursued. I will examine all this while maintaining a clear focus on the physiological elements of pleasure, the possible evolution of our human pleasure systems, and the specific social, economic, and political activities involved in sustaining human pleasure.

The issue is not merely attitudinal. Serious consequences flow from how communities determine the relationship between pleasure and austerity. Should people live simply now and save their money to invest for pleasure later? Is it sensible or absurd to borrow money for a vacation? Is it better to work harder than to play harder? In the struggle between the Athenians and the Spartans, the historic fulcrum of their contest was the moral quality of the respective societies. On one hand was the hard Spartan rigor involving athletic competition, military discipline, and an emphasis on postponement of pleasure. This was in contrast to the more elegant, discursive, and congenial urbanity of Athens. Do you know who won the war? Most people think Sparta did, perhaps because it is assumed their apparently less pleasurable lives made them fiercer fighters. And the Athenians were supposed to be effete and soft. And, true to stereotype, the Athenians lost.

There has been a long-standing and internationally significant competition between austere Marxist disciplinarians of both public and private life such as the Maoist Chinese and the often aggressively luxury-loving capitalists possibly best reflected in communities such as the Silicon and Napa valleys in California. Perhaps Marxism as a system is under successful attack and its mandate to guide behavior has evaporated. But its attitudes toward pleasure — fiercely prefigured by John Calvin and his ilk — find continued echo in many regimes. The competition is in good measure about whether people should endure discipline now to earn pleasure later or instead enjoy pleasure now as a way of enhancing the prosperity of their community. Does obedience to that central notion, "deferred gratification," pay off? Does the community benefit more from barbecue parties at the beach than after-hours study sessions in the Party Palace? If all work and no play makes Johnny a dull boy, does it also make him a limited employee and an unimaginative citizen? Does some play and no work make Johnny a cream puff of a force on the job and a cipher at town hall? And can it really be that a simple but effective reason for the emergence of industrialism in the North Temperate Zone was the discipline of having to respond to a variety of climates, some of them severe enough to obligate people to work to store food? And is it just coincidence that people preferentially take holidays where and when it is warm?

The breadth of these questions and their possible answers emphasizes the inevitable early problem of any book, to define its terms and reveal its ambition. About pleasure, this is a rather drastic obligation. Each individual owns a personal view of what pleasure is and may have real difficulty in appreciating or even comprehending the pleasures of others. Some people detest mushrooms while others hunt them avidly in damp forests. One person finds garlic totally irritating while another is convinced that you can never be too rich, too healthy, or add too much garlic to a stew. One person enjoys repairing an appliance while another would just as soon rush the confusing bits and pieces to the nearest dump. Tom tapes Bartók, Dick collects Dvořák, and Harry is totally reassured by the harpsichord.

Different communities define pleasure in quite different ways. Rich English aristocrats may prefer watching cricket matches over a two- or three-day span while English workers may crowd into soccer stadiums for intense afternoons of rapid competition. The Japanese frequent nightclubs that offer them a microphone and an opportunity to sing while a recorded orchestra produces the musical background. American collegians participate in hundreds upon hundreds of glee clubs. Some folks enjoy sliding down chilled mountains on skis and others covet hours of lying inertly on sandy beaches in warm places. Some patronize symphony orchestras in formal halls, while others seek out downstairs spots where jazz players improvise. Some enjoy soufflé desserts and others five miles on a track or country road. Some people enjoy all these things and more.

The difficulty of definition is part of the problem precisely because pleasure is so idiosyncratic, so private. Hence, its interest to governments and the church. Control people's pleasure and you'll control them. It is also of interest to jurists to protect rights in private pleasure by delineating it clearly. So sexual pleasure between a consenting twelve-year-old and an adult is wrong under any circumstances, whereas it is not between twenty-five-year-olds unless duress or illegal financial inducements have been used.

But this indeterminacy is also what is so fascinating about pleasure — not only to social commentators but to individual people. Every person has an agenda of worried private questions: Am I enjoying the right pleasures? Am I having as much fun as I should or could? Have I misunderstood what life — *my life* — entitles me to? Will I, when I am old, leaf dolorously through a catalog of the nights and days in which I failed to race for pleasure, in which I allowed my time to slide uninterestingly away? Is there a secret pleasure-ingredient in the lives of others to which I have either an allergy or a blind spot? Are some communities simply more pleasurable? If so, how do they accomplish this? On the other hand, is their pleasure-loving life practical and enduring? Or will they be visited by some compensatory misery, as, for example, some moralists have defined sexually transmitted disease and AIDS?

And what must governments do? Uphold the politics of joy with parks and dance festivals? Or advance the rule of rigor by licensing alcohol strictly, censoring films and plays, and honoring hard work?

But again, what is this pleasure? It is highly subjective, as I have already suggested. Sometimes it seems to be an empirical fact — for example, when you pet your dog or cat, it cuddles or purrs, and as for you, your blood pressure may well decline because you are relaxed and pleased to comfort your animal. Nevertheless, even the *Oxford English Dictionary* can do no better than insist on its personal, psychological quality. Here is its surprisingly simple definition: "The condition of consciousness or sensation induced by the enjoyment or anticipation of what is felt or viewed as good or desirable; enjoyment, delight, gratification. The opposite of *pain*." The authoritative compendium approvingly cites Edmund Burke's equivocal "Pain and pleasure are simple ideas, incapable of definition."

We will do better than that here, as we proceed. But for the moment it is enough to assert that pleasure is easily and widely assigned to the positive side of the ledger of experience. To paraphrase the comment of Justice Potter Stewart about pornography, while it is not easy to define, you know it when you see it. If this is true, it is in itself interesting, because it suggests a common human "emotional vocabulary" about pleasure, just as there is about pain and tragedy in their obvious forms — injury, death, mourning, terror, sharp hunger.

In fact, perhaps we can turn the uncertainty about the specific nature of pleasure into a useful question: *why* are we uncertain? One primary reason is that people in the industrial societies have focused fiercely on work and much less avidly on play. Large numbers of the people of the world live in communities that have successfully met the challenge of working effectively and productively. In fact they have been defined by the manner in which they work — industrialization. Not only industrious people, but industrial.

And yet is this trip necessary, this relentless round-trip to the office and the factory? Is there a fundamental natural reason to work hard rather than live soft? A glance at other species suggests that what people think of as "nature red in tooth and claw" is hardly the plight of other animals, as far as work is concerned. As scientists become more sensitive to the lives of the animals they study, it becomes clearer that seeming inactivity is a survival strategy all its own. In her quite thrilling review of recent material Natalie Angier comments ". . . [H]umans who feel the urge to take it easy but remain burdened by a recalcitrant work ethic might do well to consider that laziness is perfectly natural, perfectly sensible and shared by nearly every other species on the planet."[7]

This is of course a beguiling idea for which there is also some sturdy scientific persuasion. Yet it is a South-Seas-Island reverie in the context of the practical econo-politics of industrial communities. There remain sharp inequalities and countless opportunities for improving both drastically and subtly the economic conditions of countless industrial people. There is much to be done about industrial work and the resources it provides. But it is probably also time to begin to characterize communities not only or not even by how they work but by how they play. Not by efficiency but by enjoyment. Not by treasure but by pleasure. Not only by the warmth of clothes but by the intriguing way they drape. Not only by the number of dining tables sold but by what is said and felt around them.

ONE

Where Is the State of Pleasuria?

WE HAVE ALREADY seen the indeterminacy of pleasure. Pleasure is a point on a continuum. This makes it difficult to pin down and to define. It can range from the stunning fullness of the final minutes of Beethoven's Ninth Symphony to the precise good looks of the arrangement on a white plate of Tuscan beans, diced onions, basil leaves, and straw-colored olive oil. It can range from the broad bodily inner comfort that follows a calm hot bath to the exchange of "hello" with the mail deliverer on the way out the door. It can range from the oceanic triumph of soothing an ill infant to sleep to a rewarding glance at a boastful carving over the entrance to a Victorian bank. There is drastic pain on one hand and confident ecstasy on the other. Pleasure straddles the elaborate ground between heaven and hell, those fascinating if improbable symbolic dramatizations of a vital polarity in human experience.

Following the lines of the dichotomous definition in the *Oxford English Dictionary*, I wrote about this book to Ronald Melzack, who is Professor of Psychology at McGill University in Montreal and an internationally known expert on pain.[1] He replied: "All I find in common between pleasure and pain is that both involve the limbic system and both are complex as hell. I don't know of a good analysis of pleasure. Clearly one is needed."

The limbic system — the primitive bit — of the brain is the connecting link. Not the missing link — it is not missing at all! It is very real, very ancient, and broadly and decisively influential on an array of important behaviors and experiences. In considering pleasure we are concerned, certainly first and perhaps foremost, with a physiological matter — with erotic zones being touched, with sugar on the tongue, with a soft song within earshot. However, there is a fascinatingly different kind of pleasure too that is a confounding additional complication. Much pleasure occurs for reasons outside the body, having nothing directly to do with it. The body readily responds with apparent pleasure, even physical pleasure, to external stimuli that aren't physical at all.

For example, ideas have great power over pleasure. Assume that you are a scientist and you have been doing important and innovative work for twenty years. I tell you in a believable manner that you have just won a Nobel Prize. The idea will give you pleasure. Your physiology will be affected. You may experience a shot of adrenaline. You will smile involuntarily. You may throw your arms up in the characteristic triumph gesture of players who score goals or fighters declared champ. But the only thing that happened was that you were introduced to an *idea* that had a cascading set of effects on your body, even on some of its most basic and presumably "nonscientific" systems, such as digestion and energy. Pleasurable ideas quickly become part of the body, just as depressing information about a death in the family or some equally serious tragedy can immediately trigger a set of responses from a slackening in posture to a literal change in the chemical composition of urine (this is also a useful medical guide for diagnosing depression).

So when we discuss pleasure we must deal not only with the continuum between pain and pleasure but also between theoretical pleasure such as ideas, the arts, and conversation, and plainly physical pleasures such as food, sexuality, and climate. This complicates our investigation. But it also makes it interesting, if also somewhat unusual. It obligates us to treat equally seriously the obvious pleasures of the body, the subtle enjoyments of that special part of the body the brain, and the closely related senses that bring us the arts.

Not only that; we may find it useful, indeed necessary, to treat both mental and physical kinds of pleasure as rather more similar to each other than is usually the case. They enjoy a common origin in evolutionary history. The famous mind/body problem is a dull fake and a misleading one at that. Sensuality and the arts as we experience them today both reflect in real ways our history as a species. We are unitary.

The Pleasurable Is Political

Here is the underlying point of the chapter that follows: *Pleasure is a guide to what worked for us in the past*. By contrast, pain is a sharp advisory to avoid or confront its cause. It reveals our evolutionary history in contemporary bodily experience. Similarly, the behavior that yielded survival advantages in the past was translated into forms of pleasure — from sex, food, warmth, comfortable sleep, conviviality, and so on.

Both pain and pleasure encapsulate our history. They unfold our evolutionary nature to the present. In general, pain is taken quite fully into account when we organize the present and plan for the future. There is a vast and well-supported system called medicine that specializes in pain. There is hardly any doubt that it is self-evidently valuable to reduce pain as much as possible for as many people as possible.

But there is no such certainty about pleasure. It is not self-evidently necessary or even valuable to maintain a supporting system for pleasure. Pleasure is in a significant way seen as a luxurious, lucky, inessential addition to the serious and even glum coerciveness of life. There is always a minister of health but virtually never of pleasure.

However, pleasure is an entitlement. *An evolutionary entitlement*. Human beings need it the way they need vitamins, conviviality, carbohydrates, surgery, political representation, water, warmth. It should be treated with full seriousness in political and economic as well as psychological terms. But it isn't.

GNP: Gross National Product, Not Gross National Pleasure

Perhaps because good news is no news, the subject of pleasure has been substantially undervalued as a matter for study and a feature of political analysis and action. Certainly in the industrial world, and since industrialization everywhere else too, there has been overwhelming emphasis on productivity, efficiency, labor discipline, and the relationship between time and wealth. This has yielded far greater attention to the role and organization of work and wealth than to leisure and pleasure. Two major ideological forces, communism and capitalism, have dominated the world's political and military attention. The controversy between them has centered mainly on how wealth is produced and distributed and how political power should be deployed to facilitate economic life. They have focused far less on the public and private amusements that wealth and power may yield. The priority has been clear. Journalists and scholars concerned with the world's basic processes have centered principally on the avoidance of pain — hunger, disease, homelessness, unemployment — rather than on the pursuit of pleasure. Good news is banal news and bad news is better news or at least more interesting. As a result there has been a preponderance of serious attention to the serious issues.

This is wholly understandable and socially desirable. But there are consequences. One is the relative rarity of considerations of pleasure such as this one. Other far more significant implications have to do with both public and private priorities for investment, political emphases, and with how industrial communities define their goals, ethical purposes, and the essence of their communal nature. GNP refers to gross national product, not to gross national pleasure. It is of trophies of production that rich countries boast and to which poor ones aspire. (Of course, earnest high productivity is not always a pleasure. It appears that often people from rich countries visit poor ones precisely because the relative lack of economic intensity offers an agreeable and desirable change. This is called "being on vacation." There is a clear shift in the ratio of productivity to pleasure. Ironically, however, at the same moment that

Banker Number One is supine on the beach of Vacation Paradise, his colleague Banker Number Two in Washington or Tokyo or Geneva is negotiating with a representative of Paradise for aid or loans with which to establish more of the productive system that Banker One has traveled to avoid.)

And yet there may well be a simple and understandable reason for the inattention to pleasure. Consider the consequences of asking a centipede how it walks; too much self-consciousness could easily interfere with its successful movement. Self-consciousness can affect dancers' smoothness, the faith of priests, lovers' ardor, orators' connection to their audience. It is mainly gastronomically marginal restaurants that ask the preemptive question "Is everything all right?" Where there is robust enjoyment of decent food and drink, an unanswerable question is simply irrelevant. That is, if the pleasure process is not broken, why putter about trying to fix it?

Pleasure as Inheritance

This is a larger matter than it seems at first glance. Pleasure is the evolutionary legacy that suggests which behaviors, emotions, social patterns, and patterns of taste served us well during our evolutionary history. They were experienced as pleasures and encoded into our formative genetic codes. The decisive and major evolutionary changes producing these codes occurred deep in the past, from about 100,000 years ago and beyond. The modern period in which we live has had no significant and fundamental impact on what we are.

Of course there have been vast changes in the technological and organizational arrangements under which industrial people live. But our basic form as an animal species endures. We are hunter-gatherers adapted to living in social groups ranging normally from 25 to 200.

That is what we did for the longest portion of our history, perhaps 2 million to 4 million years. Only about 8,000 to 10,000 years ago did *Homo sapiens* begin serious agriculture and animal husbandry. Even so, at the time of Christ half the people in the world were still hunters, gatherers, and perhaps occasional scavengers. Only some ten generations ago, about 200 years, did any significant number of people turn to the industrial way, and what they accomplished was extraordinarily influential. They changed the world drastically and rapidly. Nevertheless, it remains probable that nearly all adults in the world are still within three generations of agricultural and pastoral life — great-grandmother was a country wife.

It also seems that agriculture has been a passing phase in our history and that basically humans beings don't like it. They leave it first chance they get. The movement of people from the country to the city is still one of most convulsive major social changes of the late twentieth century.

Whether these people are pushed or pulled is an interesting question. Let me note promptly that I think that one reason people move to the city is because it is more fun than farming. More readily than agriculture it represents the demands and rewards at which we excelled during our formative period of hunting and gathering. But even urbanity appears to be significantly transitional. As we shall see later, once people get jobs in the city and some money, they try if they can to acquire a country retreat or move to the suburbs. The underlying reason is that the country and even suburbs are closer to our evolutionary home as environments of pleasure, comfort, and a sense of safe control. The conclusion is inescapable that industrial life is still a widespread novelty for countless people even if still others begin to define their lives as postindustrial.

But, please, what does all this mean for our subject?

Here is the picture in broad strokes. Evolution is a kind of stimulus-response experiment over an immensity of time. Characteristics of individuals who produce successful solutions to life's challenges are rewarded reproductively while those who fail are not. Giraffes with long necks able to reach food high off the ground are more likely than short-neckers to be healthily fed, to survive to adulthood, to mate successfully, and to contribute effectively to the raising of young. They are likely in turn to inherit a tendency to the same long necks that favored their parents. And so it goes, and so it went for other obvious and more subtle elements of the repertoire of efforts that aided survival. The past is prologue, and also part of the script. As the Irish poet wrote, "To the blind, everything is sudden." But you are not blind when you understand the power and process of evolution. Then you comprehend and appreciate how failure and success in the past have yielded the lines of the map to the present.

When Survival Kills

Now let us jump to the human case and consider a basic pleasure — the sweet tooth. This echoes the giraffe's neck as an indication of evolutionary history. Almost universally, human beings are equipped with taste buds that respond very positively to sweetness. Children barely days old will choose to suckle from nipples that yield sweeter rather than blander liquid. Mother's milk is itself sweet in taste. In general, desserts tend to be sweet, as if only something as flashingly delicious as sugar can be consumed after the main, sustaining, useful part of the meal is done. The economic and political power of the taste buds for sugar has often been dramatically clear. For example, it was preeminently the taste for sugar, along with tobacco and cotton, that caused the convulsion of slavery. Once planters learned how and where to grow sugar cane, which had formerly been a rare plant, human beings were seized in their homes and transported halfway across the world to grow the crop as the market for it expanded explosively.[2]

But why this avidity for sweet taste? You have to remember that neat sugar as such did not exist as an available product until the late seventeenth century. Before then, it was rare, mainly used by the wealthy, mainly as medicine. Before then, sweet taste was associated with fruits and vegetables that were safe to eat and ready to eat. Unripe fruit is sour, ripe fruit is sweet. In order to secure any appreciable amount of sugar, a person must consume a fairly considerable amount of the foodstuff that carries it. This places some simple limit of volume on the amount that can be comfortably consumed. Acquiring the sugar means acquiring the bulk too. How many yams can a ten-year-old eat? And having a "sweet tooth" also enabled hunter-gatherers to refrain from consuming unripe foods that might be dangerous, sometimes even fatal. Sugar was not only a rich source of calories but an irreplaceable diagnostic tool for choosing healthy food.

So the sweet tooth, like the giraffe's neck, served a useful function in survival. Contemporary *Homo sapiens* derives enormous pleasure from sugar because sensitivity to sweetness in the past was a vital characteristic of successful diners during our evolution. The taste remains because our apparatus of taste has not changed appreciably since the Upper Paleolithic. One consequence is that people consume enormous amounts of sugar in itself, as an addition to fruit, as the most characteristic ingredient of desserts, as flavoring for drinks, and as components of other foods, even seemingly unlikely ones such as ketchup and frozen manicotti. By 1970, about 9 percent of the calories that the world's people consumed derived from sugar. Even though almost everybody knows that sugar calories are "empty" and even though countless members of industrial cultures strive endlessly to lose weight, nevertheless the consumption of sugar is vast. Since 1965 annual US consumption of milk fell from 24 gallons per capita to 19.1 gallons, while sales of sugared soft drinks more than doubled from 17.8 gallons per capita to nearly 47 gallons in 1990.[3] On average, Americans each consume about 540 cans of soft drink a year!

As plain as day, this is because people derive enormous pleasure from tasting sugar.[4] However, this is hardly surprising in a biological context. Milk is the infant food par excellence, whereas sugar is more obviously an adult prize. A nutritious food once its butterfat is largely removed, milk is nonetheless something of an anomalous drink for adult mammals. That may explain why it is so often consumed along with a sweet confection such as cake or cookies, or heavily flavored with chocolate, coffee, or tea. As well, since their tolerance for lactose is limited, in an increasingly heterogeneous population such as that of the United States, increasing numbers of people of African and Asian origin digest milk and its products with relative difficulty. They will pass up milk in favor of sugared drinks — a second essentially biological reason for their choice.

What was adaptive in our evolutionary past — sugar lust — has now become a maladaptation directly related to the power of the body to seek and acquire pleasure. The sweet tooth is an evolutionary misfit with contemporary consequences. The health and weight statistics of industrial countries reveal this clearly. There are behavioral consequences too. When Yale University researchers William Tamborlane and Timothy Jones gave children the equivalent of two frosted cupcakes' worth of neat concentrated sugar — remember that neat sugar was never available in nature before — it appeared in some youngsters to drive adrenaline levels up an astonishing tenfold.[5] Sugar can stimulate hyperactivity, irritability, or aggression and other assertive behavior. This response did not occur with adults. Perhaps the most apt comparison is with alcohol — never before available neat in nature either — to which children are far more susceptible than adults. But alcohol is usually kept from children. Sugar rarely is. The opposite is true. Sugar is the currency of choice for intergenerational bribery.

And of course sugar is also combined with other substances in a highly attractive way — such as with flour and fat to produce cakes and cookies. Perhaps chocolate is sugar's most popular confectionery mate. Many of its ardent, often even obsessive consumers (including me) are helplessly subject to the lure of chocolate. First, it has neurochemical properties linked to pleasure receptors in the brain — part of the same system with which the coca derivatives form such a complex and inviting connection. Second, when it is combined with sugar, which itself so vivaciously pleases the taste buds, the mind-altering confection made from ground-up cocoa beans is a decisively attractive luxury product.

Luxury? No, necessity. It can turn otherwise capable and prudent people into neo-babies in thrall to a dark, mysterious lure. In Great Britain one-third more money is spent on chocolate each year than on bread![6]

Dying Off the Fat of the Land

There is a more morbid example of this same phenomenon — of the contemporary impact of a taste once highly useful and still experienced as a pleasure. Once upon a time it motivated human beings to undertake actions useful for their survival. Now the same motivation for the same pleasure can cause death. I refer to the taste for animal fat.

Compared with the other primates, who almost exclusively dine on fruits and vegetables, human beings are avid pursuers and consumers of animal and marine protein. Like other carnivores, we take advantage of other beings' work of finding, consuming, and digesting foodstuffs. We eat much or all of their bodies and so inherit their digestive effort. Tippy-top of the food chain. Much of this is protein and fat. Protein is very luxurious because it delivers a high ratio of food value to volume. Fat in particular also yields bountiful calories — as any dieter knows. But through nearly all of history, and in much of the world still, calories were and are scarce. This is directly reflected in the taste for fat. From the Inuit (Eskimos) for whom neat blubber is a highly desirable arctic food to the American plutocrat for whom prime sirloin (about 30 percent fat) is preferable to choice-grade sirloin (about 18 percent), there is a general association between richly fat food and prosperity.

A central reason for this is that fat tastes good, like sugar. Cooked fat as in barbecues and roasts or as bacon or hamburgers is sensually attractive. It causes a brisk response of pleasure in the apparatus of taste. Until about ten thousand years ago, if we wanted animal protein we had to hunt it. The creatures we caught were lean because they were athletic — runners or fliers or swimmers. We were lean too because we had to run after them. For example, venison meat is about 2 to 4 percent fat; rabbit is about the same, as are quail, pheasant, and the like.

When we turned to agriculture and to animal husbandry, however, suddenly we could grow our own animal fat in the form of sheep, goats, pigs, and cattle — the original fatted calves. They had nowhere to jog and hence burn their body fat because we fenced them in or trained dogs and shepherds to keep them in line. Various species also produced milk, which we consumed as well. Here was another tasty and bountiful source of fat in the form of cheese, butter, or milk itself. One indication of how recently we developed dairy food is that many ethnic groups, particularly those from Asia and Africa, are unable to digest dairy products easily. With its typical bias, Western medicine calls them "lacto-intolerant" even though they may well be the human majority. It's the minority Roquefort lovers, mainly deriving from Europe, who evolved the ability to secrete the gut enzymes that digest milk products. Those who don't produce it often can consume yogurt, in which chemical changes have already taken place through the added cultures that compensate for the first stages of digestion.

Not only dairy products raised the cholesterol stakes. When cows, for example, ate grass, they yielded meat of about 18 percent fat content. But when we discovered they could be fed the grains we grew — principally corn — they produced even fatter, more succulent meat: prime, up to 36 percent fat. Some Japanese producers feed their "Kobe beef" beer, which is, of course, concentrated grain, and then massage their bodies to disperse the fat evenly through the tissue. The result (on sale in New York City at the end of 1990 for $150 a pound at a Greenwich Village food shop) is a product highly prized in traditionally beef-poor Japan. (No longer so beef-poor, though; when McDonald's opened its first store in Tokyo, the new outlet sold the most burgers in the company's history and the cash registers burned out.) Consumers enjoy the animal fat — even the French fried potatoes that often accompany the meat are preferred when they are fried in animal lard rather than vegetable oil. (Several fast-food chains have changed to vegetable frying oils exclusively, while McDonald's now mixes vegetable into what was formerly wholly animal fat for their deep fryers. The same highly influential company — and others will presumably follow — has been successful in developing hamburger meat that has considerably less fat but evidently retains the usual taste. Water, binding gums, seaweed, and some other substances are added to beef that is very lean to begin with.[7]) The international growth of hamburger sellers — and also of sellers of pizza, which is, of course, baked fat in the form of cheese, sausage, meatballs, and the like — has been nothing short of phenomenal. In part this is because the entrepreneurs supplying the food are adept and vigilant about the quality of their products. But the central fact is that *people want to eat what these skilled purveyors sell.*

The perilous taste is there. But it was developed during a time when there was no butter, no cream or creamy cheeses, not even plentifully produced eggs (with their high cholesterol) from caged chickens, and when meat contained only a few percent of animal fat.

Once upon a time, during a nutritional golden age, our cardiovascular system, our taste buds, and our food supply were in harmony. This aided our remarkable success as a species able to live healthily in a rich array of different habitats and to take advantage of myriad flora and fauna. We adapted felicitously to the generous natural cafeteria we found. What we enjoyed was good for us. For example, perhaps one reason we still enjoy hot foods in preference to cold or tepid ones is that before cooking and refrigeration it was safest to eat freshly killed and hence unspoiled animals at body temperature. And we still enjoy the association of warmth with food. Hot dinners! Hot dinners!

The Extermination Model of Food

These old preferences and pleasures produce new problems. Now heart disease is the major cause of premature death among inhabitants of the rich countries. The main reason is that high and chronic doses of animal fat are readily and tastily available. But our arteries and lipid-management systems are wholly unequal to the task of digesting the unprecedented amount of animal and other fat we consume. Smooth cheesecake turns into clogged arteries. The effect of shortcake is long. Heavily buttered staff of life — bread — is a question mark. What gives us pleasure is killing us. Ancient pleasures generate modern mortality.[8] Food that was once upon a time unquestionably desirable and valuable has become ambiguous. A straight pleasure has become a complex test of knowledge and character. At once it sustains and destroys. A delicious steak *au poivre* thickly painted with a cognac-cream sauce and crackling with pepper and luxury is a clause of a death sentence. Confront your Maker three times a day.

An extermination model governs thoughts of food and drink.

A graphic indication on a large scale of the relationship between diet, food, and the pleasurable satisfaction it provides emerged from an unprecedented strike by coal miners in the rich but distant coalfields of Prokopyevsk in Siberia, in 1989. Among other shortages of goods against which the miners protested — including soap, which was in tight supply even though it is necessary for the miners to wash off after work — were particular foodstuffs they demanded from a suddenly compliant government. As the *New York Times* reported, "they were not bought off with a bit of sausage; there was none on the list. But there were 5000 tons of canned milk, 10,000 tons of sugar for stores long devoid of candy, and 5000 tons of animal fat, all guaranteed by the Kremlin to the strikers of Siberia."[9] In a somewhat comparable American situation, a similar dietary enthusiasm is manifested among workers installing oil production equipment on the North Slope of Alaska. Unduly high fat, cholesterol, and calorie intake results because employers provide rich food, which becomes a source of comfort for employees enduring bleak and unpleasant circumstances. The abundant food generates necessary warmth for outdoor workers. But for most employees, the *8,000* calories a day they consume yields implacable weight gain.[10] Meanwhile, back at the "climate-controlled" shopping mall, under far less environmental duress, contemporary mainland Americans spend $3.6 billion on potato chips each year — about six pounds per person — and also consume nearly as much of tortilla and corn chips. These fried carbohydrates — laced with salt (potato chips have 250 times as much sodium as potatoes) — are clearly addictively attractive to consumers, who must surely be at least faintly aware of their dietary consequences.

The issue is not only what food is taken in but what behavior is put out. The sedentary ways of industrial life are very different from the energetic food-gathering of our Upper Paleolithic ancestors. It has been recently learned that one consequence of vigorous exercise is the secretion of high-density lipids in the blood, the "good cholesterol." In what is almost a morality playlet, this substance attacks the "bad cholesterol" — low-density lipids, which contribute to clogged arteries. The exercise required to catch our paleo-dinner made the cholesterol content of that dinner relatively unimportant because the exercise itself controlled levels of cholesterol. Now, this exercise must be carefully secured, often artificially and at cost of convenience, funds, and, of course, time. Instead of running for our dinner, we jog before we have dinner. Vigorous exercise has also been identified as an antidote to depression. Brain chemistry is changed. Damn right, because strenuous activity was always associated with securing dinner. Now it means we can enjoy dinner. Virtue rewarded. Tummy toughened. Calories at bay.

Salt of the Earth

A similar problem involves the recent ready availability of salt. Our sense organs respond very directly to sugar and salt, both of which were difficult to acquire during our evolutionary history. Salt has been particularly prized in warm countries — those in which people liberally sweat, which in turn obligates them to seek salt. Salt is essential for retaining the high level of bodily water necessary for survival (this is a legacy of our original aquatic origin). The word "salary" derives from the Latin *salarium*, the money paid to Roman troops to buy salt. As well, salt in various forms — slabs, bars, wrapped in leaves — was widely used in Africa as a form of currency. But in modern times both sugar and salt are among the cheapest and most readily available of foods. Big, thick sacks for next to nothing. Virtually at will, nearly everyone can overdose on sugar and become fat. And virtually everybody can overdose on salt, which raises the blood pressure in the body — another contributor to dangerous heart disease.

I have already described the sudden luxury of animal fat in the recent years of our dietary history. Now let's haplessly mix all the tasty-bad commodities together. Generous and tasty helpings of sugar and fat and salt (and, magically, add some flour and heat and you get shortbread) are examples of new dilemmas that arise from the profile of pleasures that define our species.

Are there other pleasures that are similarly dangerous?

Of course. I have described three that are obvious and ambient and that have a clear, direct impact on the human body. Other pleasures, such as exercise and sexual activity, also have a bodily impact. Still others, such as songs and rituals, produce an effect that may be more subtle or evanescent but is nevertheless real. Almost invariably, surrounding every major kind of pleasure there is a social procedure about its enjoyment. A code of behavior governs its existence and its cost. Pleasure does not stand alone. It is part of something embedded somewhere. This is why the question of who gets pleasure and controls it is always salient. The supply of pleasure is fundamental. Pleasure is about behavioral bedrock.

The philosopher George Santayana famously said: "Those who cannot remember the past are condemned to repeat it." We can expand on this to say that *those who do not learn from prehistory are condemned to repeat its successes.*

Sufferers to the Head of the Line, Please

There has always been a tension in human societies between production and consumption — another form of the classic Greek distinction between hedonism and asceticism. As Joseph and his biblical brothers knew, it was best, or at least most prudent, to boogie only after the granaries were bulging. This was obviously a central and pressing concern earlier too, when people lived from hand to mouth, from day to day, from hunt to hunt, from forage to forage, and where there was no refrigeration, no granaries, no serious cushion against hunger tonight other than today's effort. Except for the very poor, most industrial people don't experience the problem directly or have to endure the tension very dramatically. There is a lot of food. We can freeze it, can it, irradiate it, smoke it, pickle it, or just eat it. But the emotional turbulence produced by scarcity of food is always close to the surface.

Lean Gene in a Fat Machine

Why? If, as Bertolt Brecht announced, "a man is just the food he eats," perhaps also a species is the food it eats. A species is decisively influenced by the way it acquires its food — with what emotions, skills, and uncertainties, and what kind of social and economic arrangements. It will also be affected by how it uses its food — with what form of sharing, what tastes, what schedule, what mythology. The history and prehistory of how we acquired and consumed food were certain to have been inescapably significant in the formative evolution of basic human characteristics. This must be why the dialogue between cooking/hedonism and dieting/asceticism remains such a potent preoccupation to this day. Why the war between the cookbooks and diet books continues unabated, with fresh reinforcements every week. Why everybody's body is not just a functioning entity but a symptom of moral discipline and the quality of personal care.

There are two sides to the matter. How much time and work are needed to acquire food? And how much of this food should be consumed? On one level these are straightforward questions of caloric accountancy. How much time and energy does it take to accumulate how much energy? How much food should be eaten rather than stored, if storage is possible? Every human society develops ways of answering these questions.

But the questions are also symbolic. They stand for a host of attitudes and practices that surround the relationship between pleasure and practicality. Several factors come into play directly. The first is that, as I have noted, people clearly crave the tastes of fat, sugar, and salt. But a diet balanced in all the nutrients must involve an array of foods. These foods have to be made tasty, interesting, and varied. Hence, the remarkable range of items that people find, grow, prepare, and eat.

Second, our obviously imperfect mechanism for controlling or shutting down our appetite was formed during a prehistorical period when there was no good way of storing food except in the body as fat. There was also chronic uncertainty about the next meal. Therefore, there was likely to be a pronounced and useful impulse to indulge fully during the meal currently on the table. So stopping eating requires a kind of decision, if the matter is not decided by sleep or nausea. In a wonderful irony, it is even possible that since we appear to have a rather poor natural mechanism to curtail our eating, perhaps dessert functions in its stead! Dessert is so sweet that after eating it we find it virtually impossible to consume anything more. As often happens, here a social ritual compensates for a biological deficiency.

The lion consuming his kill eats till he sleeps and then hunts again when he is hungry. He is such a master of the food chain he can afford to be imperially confident. By contrast, squirrels "squirrel away" their nuts first in their balloon cheeks and then in their hideout when they sense that winter will soon curtail the generosity of their cafeteria. People appear to fall in between these two extremes, capturing as we do both the gluttonous enthusiasm of the lion while we're eating as well as the nervous, skeptical worry of the squirrel when we're not.

In a very direct and personal way, this underscores the general challenge of adjusting present resources to future needs. The result is a chronic problem for people in rich societies — endless provocation by the lure of overeating. Countless people are on diets. The bathroom scale is a virtually ubiquitous rebuking presence in most homes, a negative physical analogue to the crucifix or Star of David or Buddha. It is an almost invariably successful compliment to say to someone, "Oh, you've lost weight." At virtually no other period of history would this be a positive statement rather than a remark of foreboding concern about health, or poverty, or depression. But given the bounties of nature, the skill of cooks, the cunning of the food industry, and our frailty at table, losing weight represents something of a triumph — a triumph over nature's failure to provide us with an effective mechanism to govern how much food we consume. After all, we don't breathe too much air and hardly ever drink too much water. But food is different, because it provides pleasure.

Not only that. I have already noted that once upon a time eating food was the principal way of preserving it, as body fat. To this day, body fat is still a factor in prosperity. For example, women who become very skinny may cease their regular menstrual cycles. The onset of the female cycle at adolescence depends on the ratio of fat to overall body weight. In effect, a young woman will become physiologically ready for childbearing only when she carries enough body fat to sustain a pregnancy. Similarly, female athletes whose bodies are lean and relatively fat-free are also likely to experience irregular or very infrequent menstrual cycles. Among men, severe diets lead to loss of libido and then to decline in the vigor and amount of the spermatozoa they produce. Obviously, the body is a symptom, as well as a sack of skin, bones, and behavior.

Breasts

During the lean times of our evolutionary history, fat served a significant, even decisive function in regulating sexual cycling and fertility. It still does. An internal bodily mechanism appears to determine whether a woman's body can sustain the additional burden of childbearing and nursing.[11] There may also be a social mechanism as well, one that has to do with the characteristics men find attractive in women. As Nancy Friday has observed, the contemporary female obsession with decisive thinness is chiefly of female motivation. She asks rhetorically but practically: When has anyone seen a group of lascivious men on a street corner comment about a passing woman, "Look how thin she is!"[12]

The bounteous body seems more desirable to men, and not only in industrial societies, either. David Buss of the University of Michigan has shown the pervasive influence in a wide array of cultures of physical attractiveness in how men choose women.[13] With enthusiastic, controversial, and remarkably adroit scholarship, Camille Paglia has provided a version of the looming influence of fleshy physical reality over even literary fantasies about behavior, to say nothing of behavior itself.[14] While the subject seems surprisingly underdiscussed, perhaps *because* of its emotional impact, the female chest is of enormous and endless interest to men. The coverage and display of women's breasts animate much of the complex passions surrounding fashion. Breasts are of course also of deep concern to women and wield much influence over the systems of sexual status that arise among them.

For much of the life cycle, female breasts are mainly fatty tissue with little practical function. For women who have no children or do not breast-feed those they have, they are as functionless as men's breasts. But women's breasts generate social power. The relationship is not accidental. It likely reflects ancient understanding about the conditions of successful sexual and reproductive episodes. This is hardly surprising insofar as producing a viable infant requires from 50,000 to 80,000 extra calories, while breast-feeding requires from 500 to 1,000 per day — as much as some particularly demonic dieters may consume altogether. For this reason, female bodies are roughly 25 percent fat, while males' are 12 to 14 percent.[15] There is a direct connection between fat, sex, reproduction, and prosperity. There is also a modern tension between pleasurably eating a lot and becoming fat and potentially sexy, and eating austerely, remaining healthy, and advertising a good level of self-discipline. So even the length of the string that encircles your waist offers an insight into both the prehistory that formed us and the up-to-the-minute circumstances of daily life.

Caught by the Food Chain

I will come back to discuss food more in chapter 5. For two reasons. More important and generally, it provides one of the most interesting, recurrent, and colorful forms of human pleasure. Much less important and personally, I hereby confess to a hectic, intense interest in the subject. I teach a university course on the topic and have written academic articles on the social uses of food and the relationship between diet and evolution, and also a general book on China's food. One of the great triumphs of my life was to have been asked to become a secret inspector for the *Good Food Guide* in England. I have traveled profligate distances to try a particular dish or provocative or perfect restaurant. I select meals the way more serious people select investments. I vouch that it is possible to experience a full aerobic episode striding from menu to menu posted outside the restaurants of a midsize ambitious dining town such as Avignon or Bordeaux or Siena or Groningen.

Not too many years ago I could have not written this belligerent confession. I would have been embarrassed to admit that I truly enjoyed something, particularly something as ordinary as food. In this I think I am not alone. My personal reluctance to celebrate frankly the pleasure in a simple aspect of life is common among professional and academic commentators on the culture. Doing so is seen as simpleminded, trivial, and, worst of all, "unsound."

It's Acanemic

This reluctance is an aspect of the distancing technique of professional life. It is also of central relevance to this book, because it suggests an important reason for the professional and scientific inattention to pleasure. In turn, this has helped shape more general public reluctance to acknowledge the significance of the enjoyment of fun in its various forms. The control of wealth and legislation are treated by scholars far more seriously than the control of pleasure. Paradoxically, even scholars of pleasures such as in popular culture and various forms of sexuality often try to relate such subjects to existing economic and political systems — for example, in Marxist and feminist literary criticism. The result is that the matter of pleasure becomes ghettoized, associated with vacations not with work, with sports not with politics, with nights on the town not days with the kids. Duty and duress are more acceptable sources of animation than is delight. New parents are often astonished to discover how much fun their child provides.

In one realm of life, sexuality, there has, of course, been considerable attention paid to its pleasurability, its consequences, its meaning. In the second volume *(The Use of Pleasure)* of his *History of Sexuality*, Michel Foucault defines the question that guided his grimly influential if relentlessly fuzzy inquiry: "How, why, and in what forms was sexuality constituted as a moral domain? Why this ethical concern that was so persistent despite its varying forms and intensity? Why this 'problematization'?"[16] Foucault's focus on sexuality is appropriately concurrent with the Freudian program. They both tie a wide array of behaviors to expressions or repressions of sexual energy.

But there is a wider issue. Sexuality is only part of a fundamental and implacable concern with the nature and functions of pleasure. Behavior involving the mouth has plain sexual meanings. The language, both formal and slang, of food and sex are closely connected (such as the slang term "eating" for oral sex). The neurophysiology governing the behavior is interconnected for both. Mythological association shows this interrelationship too — for example, the link between eating the forbidden apple of Eden, nudity, sexuality, and the concept of sin.

There have always been decisively practical reasons for attention to sex. Throughout history the existence of venereal diseases was as well known as the fact that they were difficult to treat. More important, there was an ever-constant possibility of pregnancy.

This was in itself so consequential for people's lives and for their families that admonitions about sexuality would never go entirely unheeded. These could also be buttressed by substantial and effective rules to which the priesthood, when it emerged, was able to pay great and often dramatic attention. Censorship of sexual images and behavior has been a consistent favorite of those who want to control the behavior of others. It could be argued that the existence of clothing itself, except where it is necessary for health and comfort, has centrally to do with efforts to curb the emotional impact of gazing at the sexual organs and to discipline how, when, and to whom they are revealed.

In short, it is easy to be falsely persuaded as Freud was that the pleasures surrounding sexuality are the most important and that the arrangements governing all other pleasures are outgrowths of this central theme.

The Struggle of the Pleasure Classes

I want to go beyond this position, however, to broaden the case and to place sexuality in a wider context. What happens when you begin with the most general concept of pleasure and then narrow it down into its more specific versions? This becomes especially pertinent when sex becomes less drastic — when the sexual odds become more comfortable to play. When venereal disease is relatively controllable. When safe and reliable contraception permits sexual activity with sharply reduced fear of unwanted consequences. Does this change the moral calculus? Would sexuality have loomed less formidably in the minds of the biblical architects of the structures of sin had there been condoms, antibiotics, and hence fewer potentially severe results? "No" appears to be the answer, to judge from the many contemporary communities such as China and even the United States in which strong sexual controls endure, or at least controversies about such issues as abortion and contraception for minors. Between 1900 and 1915 a similar concern about the consequences of pleasurable indulgence animated the movement throughout the industrial countries to restrict the use of alcohol — a movement that yielded Prohibition in America. The phenomenon appears to have resulted from a mixture of higher incomes and lower relative prices, an economic circumstance that stimulated broad societal concern about the dangers of alcoholism among working-class people.

Herewith a vital question. Does this suggest there are some "natural limits" to pleasures beyond which communities are reluctant to go once they know what is going on? Or are there unlimited options for cultural variety in the enjoyment of pleasure and the amount of it people can sustain? With pain, it is well known among hospital staffs that there are perceptible differences between different ethnic groups in how noisily they respond to childbirth. Can it be that Tribe Stiff-upper-lip suffers less physical pain than Tribe Scream-a-lot? Physiologically, this seems unlikely. So the question becomes, do different cultures *encourage* the experience of pain by permitting expression of it?

By the same token, can different cultures *encourage* the experience of pleasure by permitting expression of it, not to mention by creating conditions under which it can easily occur? That would seem to be so, if only because it is clear that different individual people and different families appear to have varyingly active capacities for pleasure. Some bounce and shine and appear to be on a near-permanent rampage of enjoyment. Others shuffle with heavy heart and are reamed with trouble. Biological systems are all about variation, and there may well be variation in this too — not only in height, weight, foot speed, and the like, but in capacity for pleasure. If there is such a sorting, is it permanent? Can pleasure-loving be learned? Be taught? Be graded?

Yet another problem. Here is a possible inequality. Does this mean governments should strive for equality in income of pleasure just as some have tried or want to try to give all citizens equal income of resources? There is, after all, the endlessly influential American dictum that "life, liberty, and the pursuit of happiness" are the birthrights of all. Is this a reflection of natural law — a biological claim on the political system? Does "happiness" here include pleasure too? Is this another way of defining what I have suggested is an evolutionary entitlement?

Even though this was evidently not the intent of the framers of the Constitution, it nonetheless appears that one reason for the impact of the phrase is its radical and surprising inclusion of the domestic, almost intimate right — happiness — along with two major public, classically political themes.

And this is not as innocent or purely juridical a question as it may seem. In its way it is inextricably linked to political rights as well as economic and social options. Coping with the socioeconomic prosperity of successful members of the industrial world may directly *require* some hard public definitions of pleasure and the rights of citizens to it. A politics of pleasure may need to emerge. The control of time and energy may become as politically interesting as the control of wealth and legislation. One sign is the Green movement, which is nothing less than a claim by people that they want to have pristine primordial pleasure when they are in nature, not ugliness, bad odor, and disillusion with the impact of human action. One cigarette butt can defile a majestic canyon.

Take It Easy? Take It Hard?

As a first step, the discussion of pleasure can focus on the concept of leisure. This is an understandable beginning. At minimum it encompasses the notion of voluntary activity as its own reward. Particularly in Europe, the issue of pleasure becomes the problem of leisure insofar as workweeks have been steadily reduced. By 1992 the German workweek is expected to be 32 hours with some 30 vacation days to brighten the routine. Should European economic integration occur as planned, these numbers may become more typical of currently harder-working communities as well. (A 1988 survey by the Union Bank of Switzerland indicated that the world average was 42.3 hours of work per week, with 21 holidays. The hard toilers of Hong Kong supplied 52 hours a week and indulged in only 7.5 days of holiday. Americans averaged about 40 hours per week with about 14 days off. The Dutch enjoyed 35 days off amidst workweeks of 39.5 hours, while residents of Brussels enjoyed the Belgian capital 24.3 days a year while working 37.3 hours per week.)

There is compelling evidence that the usual incentives to extract more labor from people — more money, more seniority, even satisfying work — are proving inadequate. At a 1989 conference on the subject in Zurich, even the less affluent economies of Eastern Europe sent representatives eager to learn how to anticipate what was defined as an oncoming shift in personal budgets of time and priority.[17] There is a broad, ineluctable move from work to leisure. This creates very direct practical problems, such as how and where people will actually spend the hours and days newly available for an array of activities other than work.

The emergent situation may also compel governments to acknowledge that prosperity poses new challenges. Perhaps new notions of political responsibility will emerge — Orwellian ministers of pleasure? — from new psychological realities associated with deep reduction in the importance of work for millions of people. This will require an appropriate scientific perspective within which practical action can occur. Economist John Kenneth Galbraith has said of economists that "the final requirement of modern development planning is that they have a theory of consumption."[18] In essence, the developed communities will also require such a theory of consumption. But it will have to include resources now treated as luxuries, such as travel, cultural participation, art purchases, exercises to Brazilian music, intriguing architecture, and so on.

Dutch Treat

The problem is not new. It appears that each human community must find some solution to a relatively rapid onrush of resources if it becomes prosperous. In his extraordinarily generous study, Simon Schama has portrayed the efforts of the Dutch of the seventeenth century to achieve a measured response to the enormous wealth provided by their sea trade, their control through their ports of grain movements, their ownership of foreign grainfields, and their generally industrious internal economy. One response was to decide that their wealth was their "godly allowance." A Calvinist belief in providential favor offered them a basis for trying to "create a moral order *within* a terrestrial paradise." As anyone knows who has seen paintings of this period, the Dutch were vividly fond of food and drink, which they consumed in enormous measure, particularly at banquets. But, as Schama notes, there was "a self-adjusting gastric equilibrium built into the pre-Reformation festive and religious calendar in which the excesses of carnival feasting were offset by the austere regime of Lent." There were also efforts to control consumption through sumptuary laws, such as attempts to limit weddings to fifty guests, whose gifts could total no more than 5 percent of the dowry involved. Both the Calvinist clergymen as well as the secular magistrates agreed that divine precepts had to be obeyed. This included modesty in consumption. Otherwise, it was feared, the wondrous, unprecedented prosperity would be mocked and could disappear.[19]

There was a clear sense of the absolute requirement for a measure of control in both the public and private spheres. Calvinism offered an extraordinarily helpful, effective, and convenient explanatory scheme. It congenially accommodated both wealth *and* austerity. Boisterous, luxurious bonhomie and restrained, reflective piety coexisted with little sense of farce or inconsistency.

Schama persuasively argues that this resulted in part from the peculiar situation of Holland. Remember that its very soil was the hard-wrested product of dikes, which were all that stood between the people and the Flood. Earnest enjoyment of the pleasures of daily life had to be placed within the perilous context of the realistic possibility of massive disaster. An angry God could easily and instantaneously summon up such retribution. This provided an unusual incentive for turning survival into a moral issue. Now it depended on self-conscious piety and on pleasing God, rather than on random luck or aggressive competition with less adept European neighbors.

Another response to sudden wealth is that of modern Libya, which has had chosen for it a sharply different path by its leader, Colonel Muammar Qaddafi. Radical Muslim fundamentalism is combined with seemingly belligerent austerity in the midst of considerable public wealth raked in from selling a million barrels of oil a day. As the journalist T. D. Allman has written: "Thanks to oil, the average Libyan has an annual income of more than $7,000, about half that of the average American. But in neighboring Tunisia, where the average income is $1,100, people are better-dressed, and the markets are full of low-cost high-quality goods difficult to find in Libya at any price." The four million Libyans have housing, free medical care, and no material poverty. At the same time, "everyone has a car, but there is nowhere, really, to go. . . . Though Libyans are crazy about soccer, The Leader deplores spectator events. What makes the sensory deprivation complete is that there is also almost nothing to do during working hours." Even though some individuals are able to amass large sums of money through various overt and covert means, it is difficult to spend it within Libya. But if they flee the country to use their wealth, there is evidently a practical likelihood they will be added to the list of those slated for assassination by hirelings of the leadership.[20]

As is so often the case, this is justified by moral dogma. The possibility for personal pleasure has been sharply curtailed by pious political fiat and for seemingly political reasons. Contrast the Libyan regime with other governments that also adhere to a revolutionary intent but are eager to increase discretionary income for their populations in order to ease pressure on their political systems. The societies of Eastern Europe come rapidly to mind. Public pressure there has forced a shift in emphasis from production for the sake of production — more steel — to production for the sake of consumers — more sausages.

To Hell on Wheels through Heaven on Earth?

What causes such changes? Is there a self-conscious effort to increase the happiness of people? Or rather a pragmatic, perhaps cynical decision to improve the standing of politicians by advancing the interests of their constituents? Presumably both elements are involved, and a variety of others too. But it becomes fascinating to consider if and how the pleasures of people become a factor in the calculations of those in power.

Nevertheless, there is no precise formula that can assess "people-pleasure." No measure of gross national pleasure, no rate of pleasure-growth, no index of pleasure-employment, no reckoning in the millions of the balance of pleasure-payments. There is in American political accounting the "misery index," which is an amalgam of the numbers revealing inflation, unemployment, and availability of housing. It is fairly generally conceded that some such composite number does point with fair political realism to the dissatisfaction a population will feel about its circumstances. There is no comparable index of public satisfaction, even though during the 1970s in the United States an effort was made to create a "happiness index," through the Bureau of the Census. Several variants were produced and tried with enthusiasm. But according to the director of the bureau at the time — who had considered this a promising venture — the effort was abandoned because it was too imprecise, there was broad disagreement about what to measure, and the level of controversy seemed to far outweigh the gain of insight.[21]

This is not altogether surprising given the general view I have been sketching here, which is that pleasure is defined as an addition to life, a form of luxury, a fortunate afterthought — the cake — rather than a centrally motivating and defining feature of social action. Compare even the theological equivalents. Where is there a concept as amusing and hopeful as Original Sin is depressed and mean-spirited? Does anything in either Testament to the will of God — New or Old — compare with the awfulness and gravity of the story of Job? What is on a par with Abraham's near-murder of his son at God's demand?

These are efforts to cope with the classic and poignant problem of celebrating the existence of an all-powerful God who is nonetheless willing and able to permit — perhaps even encourage, if only as a test — the most desperate and bewildering suffering by the faithful. Human beings are intelligent enough to perceive suffering and anticipate death. At the same time, we generally insist that there may be more to life than this — actually, that there *must* be more. Therefore preoccupation with what provokes pain is fully understandable. But let's not forget the great escape, heaven, and the great rebuke, hell. We can learn a lot about how people experience their lives from how they foresee what happens when they die. The stories are chillingly insightful.

The Architecture Is Heavenly

The brain accepts and analyzes pain. It accepts and analyzes pleasure. Therefore it is consistent and hardly a surprise that it has contrived symbolic descriptions of these. The most obvious are heaven, hell, paradise, purgatory, utopia, the happy hunting ground. This is not an invariably ethereal pattern. For example, Islamic beliefs, which are often regarded as somewhat more effectively influential over behavior and more complex than the Christian ones about the afterlife, emphasize frank enjoyment and describe basic forms of physical consumption. Aquinas and others of his time were appalled by the Islamic idea of heaven because it permitted sexual pleasure. It was also so physical that precise notions about excrement were necessary to round out a realistic heavenly ambiance.[22]

In general, people seem to have a persistent, even affectionate, commitment to some concept of interesting and significant life after death. Obviously, the notion of final nonexistence is neither attractive nor reassuring. The dream of heaven is an understandable antidote. More simply, notwithstanding Job, Jeremiah, and others of like disposition, perhaps life is so much fun that its absence is altogether unacceptable. Hence heaven.

Even if the concept may be peculiarly formulated, it exerts its hold. A 1982 Gallup poll found that 71 percent of Americans answered yes to the question "Do you think there is a heaven where people who have led good lives are eternally rewarded?" This was a decline of one percentage point since 1952 and a small gain over 1965.[23] Notwithstanding its strong popular appeal, the idea can provide a feast for skeptics and critics. Alfred North Whitehead commented: "Can you imagine anything more idiotic than the Christian idea of heaven? What kind of deity is that who would be capable of creating angels and men to sing his praises day and night to all eternity?"[24]

Nevertheless, there is a recurrent if banal hope among people questioned about heaven that they will be reunited with family and friends.[25] This is a reverie concretely reflected in the ubiquity of gravestone inscriptions and depictions about families who resume in heaven their domestic lives on earth. There's a rather direct and more localized version of this in West Africa, where it is thought that ancestors somehow reside in the earth. Consequently, before a significant celebration or similar event begins, there is a ritual pouring of liquor, usually gin or palm wine, into the ground. This satisfies the ancestors and in effect invites them to join the party in the proper spirit.

Don Juan in Heaven

The place of pleasure and the role of the body in heaven are intriguing and highly various. Heavenly conceptions reflect the earthly practice. For example, Saint Augustine began his life as an apparently sensual individual who enjoyed a concubine and fathered a son. His subsequent (conveniently timed) embrace of Platonic Greek philosophy led him to celebrate celibacy, which prefigured the heavenly existence he describes in *The City of God:* ". . . eternal bliss consisted of the supreme enjoyment of 'seeing God.'" Like a bossy schoolchild playing house, he later expanded this vision to include contacts with family (though not friends). Men and women would be beautiful, and their sex organs would be solely beautiful, not functional or erotic. Heaven was the scene of *caritas* — love — not *cupiditas* — lust.[26]

Later on, perhaps because he was trying to reduce the confusions created by the complex delta of human emotions on the move but also contained by heaven, Thomas Aquinas was crisper on the matter. He foresaw no activity at all except for contemplation. Still later, during the Renaissance, the good times on earth appeared to generate confident expectations of continuity in heaven. Lo and happy to behold, there were more gardens, more love, more nudity, more music, more general elegance. There was a sense that death/life in heaven was a glad opportunity.

But this notion of permanent amusement in heaven was not to last. Turbulence in the world of churches between the sixteenth and eighteenth centuries yielded a more restricted and cautious reemphasis on service to God in heaven. The Calvinist scheme offered permanent religious reward in the hereafter for firm material diligence on earth.[27] An American poet, Richard Steere, who lived between 1643 and 1721 was moved to remark conclusively that "all temporary honors, riches, pleasures are vain, uncertain, short, and transitory, and in comparison of heavenly joys they are not worthy of the least esteem, but rather to be scornfully despised."[28]

Unless we take rather literally the heavenly recipes of one or another religious enthusiasm, it seems reasonable to conclude that the texture of earthly life affects if not determines the dream of the nature of life eternal. The chaplain to the English duke of Ormonde unsurprisingly decided that heaven boasted a rigid social hierarchy. Jean-Jacques Rousseau in *Confessions* and *Julie* envisaged heaven as an occasion for revisiting with a favorite lady friend. The grandly assured mining engineer Swedenborg (1688–1772) at the age of fifty-nine claimed to receive special "messages" from heaven. He was able to enjoy the unusual fortune of not being required to die before actually visiting heaven. This he described as a version of the luxurious, subtly sybaritic baroque Swedish nobility to which he aspired and which he was eventually invited to join. His sense of heavenly arrangements was reassuringly and almost lyrically precise. For example, if a woman had somehow managed to have seven husbands in life and encountered them all in heaven, her ultimate marriage there would be to the one to whom she had been most fully wed. Their sexual intercourse would literally be a divine pleasure.[29]

Other strategists of heaven had similarly punctilious anticipations of its rewards. For example, Charles Kingsley (1819–1875) was the chaplain to Queen Victoria. An avid supporter and practitioner of erotic pleasure within marriage, he was convinced marriages were utterly permanent. Accordingly, he foresaw sexual continuity in heaven. Presumably, it was this belief of her chaplain that prompted Queen Victoria to be buried wearing her bridal veil.[30] In evident preparation to meet both her Maker and her husband, she chose this highly symbolic, rather haunting costume.

And then, during the late-nineteenth-century period of confidence in the permanent progress of the world in all things — at least in England — heaven became a location for self-improvement and public service. In his book on the subject *Out of the Body*, John Oxenham (1852–1941) decided that among other remarkable things in heaven even civil servants could at long last become "whole men." There would be an inclusive work-based society. While there would be no spectator sports, there would certainly be tennis, boating, and soccer, as well as dancing. And, of course, pets.[31] More voluptuous, and less English, is the promise contained in the Koran that men who are acceptably religious will secure roosts in heaven where they will be attended by houris — desirable dark-eyed women — who will not only create and satisfy wonderful sensual needs but who will themselves be made wholly of sandalwood and hence offer the sublime pleasure of pure scent.[32] Whether sweet-smelling wooden men will be available to reward pious Muslim women is unclear from this account.

What's a Heaven For?

It is not necessary to believe in the existence of heaven to appreciate that the form it takes on earth suggests those pleasures and assurances that the imaginers of heaven have enjoyed on earth, or wanted to. For example, Stanley Tigerman has very evocatively described the relation between notions of paradise, architectural plans, and buildings.[33] However, this kind of analogy — of heaven as a kind of projective test — can be carried only so far. After all, heaven involves an obligation to serve God that is presumably implicit in the deal, in return for achieving heaven. Whether this service takes the form of singing endless songs of praise in the manner Whitehead objected to so bitingly, or contemplating the nature of existence and goodness as Augustine foresaw, the playing field of heaven is decisively supervised by the presence of God the Rule Maker. Perhaps this is why heaven is so constrained a place — no *grands bouffes*, no sweet sex orgies, no nonstop comedy or Puccini shows, no Milanese couture, no champagne kirs on the Riviera beach. It is not a boisterous, luxuriant reward. Heaven seems instead to be the decorous and sanitary accomplishment of decent-living folk who were as duly and dully attentive to the concerns of God in life as they will be in God's presence after death.

And politics need not be very far from cosmology. A wry economist from Hungary told me his local version of a classic joke: The East German leader Walter Ulbricht died and of course, according to the Hungarian, was assigned to hell, where he saw among other spectacles the former Soviet leader Leonid Brezhnev kissing passionately an attractive maiden seated on his lap. When Ulbricht raised with the devil his surprise that Brezhnev would be permitted such an amusement even in hell, the devil replied: "But you do not understand. That is *her* punishment." Here heaven and hell serve a directly secular purpose. It reveals political disillusionment, and it is appropriate that the availability of pleasure in heaven is the focus of the story.

The impulse to control pleasure is so persistent that it is carefully meted out even in heaven. It does not swell in a royal flush, an endless cavalcade, a gorgeous triumph of enjoyment. There seems instead to be some sense of restraint and limit. Again, nothing in the pleasure line compares with the sufferings of Job, which are so relentless, so astonishing and extreme. An implication is that pleasure is *always* constrained. Why? Because it becomes too uninteresting if it is untrammeled and constant? Because it produces perilous effects on individuals and on the community? Because it is disruptive to existing power holders? Because permanent pleasure is physiologically unsustainable? Or because of all of the above, and more?

Whatever the reason or reasons, heavenly pleasure as it is generally imagined seems far less extravagant than even a modest vacation on earth. Presumably, one reason for this is that it has been principally the work of church officials to establish what heaven is all about. Not entertainers or cooks or race car drivers. That's why there has been a bias toward heavenly restraint that reflects the largely restrictive functions priests perform on earth.

Voilà. With surprising convenience and symmetry, heaven matches the earthly prudence churches generally want their members to display. This is revealing, because it suggests what people might do if they had the free opportunity. It hints at what the moral leaders of the community would decide it is appropriate for them to do.

Even when dreaming of heaven, the managers of pleasure are ever so cautious.

Perhaps navigators can steer by the stars. But a student of pleasure trying to describe and understand it cannot be guided by heaven, or by hell for that matter. There are more factual directions to take. If pleasure is an evolutionary entitlement, as I have claimed, then what in evolutionary history would justify which contemporary pleasure? To try to answer this question, we have to turn back, to look back, to our prehistory.

What is there to learn about the period that formed us? At this point I want to take a tour of the available information.

And a look in the mirror will help too, because we are the best available evidence now of what happened then.

TWO

Let's Spend a Quiet Evening in the Cave

IF THE HUMAN SPECIES is not the result of divine creation, then we are the result of a real process. Knowledge about that process will help us understand the conditions that formed us and those that we created. But there are no living witnesses to that history and prehistory. Hence, we must rely on the archaeological record that has been uncovered. Genetics and physiology can also tell us something about the story of our evolution.

The most interesting, most complicated, most available, and most provocative piece of evidence is — us. So I will treat contemporary people as a major part of the evidence that will help solve the puzzle. I want to describe how elements of our lives in the past might be the basis for the pleasures we seek and enjoy in the present. My reasoning is simple. In part I have already described it. The basic point is that evolution works as a reward system over many generations. Particular physical, social, emotional, and cognitive characteristics of our species helped to reproduce offspring and ensure safety. These were likely to become significant elements of our genetics and hence of our nature. My proposal is that an important clue to those successful kinds of sensation and behavior is whether or not their descendant sensations and behaviors are pleasurable today.

I have already introduced an analogy, with nutrition. Because hunting seemed to give us some useful advantage over other primates, who had different capacities going for them, we appear to require and to enjoy the kind of food that animal protein provides. We ate many fruits and vegetables and we need those also. Nutritionists can describe a rather good profile of a suitable diet because our bodies prosper when they have access to the foodstuffs that kept us healthy and effective in the past. As a case in point, without fruit we develop scurvy. But the past is not an infallible guide to good eating habits in the present; for example, the ancient taste for animal food draws us to a radically and hazardously fatty kind of animal protein such as prime beef.

The past is a fact. Therefore it's a potential clue with which to assess the hypothesis that our pleasures are not simply arbitrary, whimsical, or the fruit of fashion and conspiracy. No: they reflect central and indeed vital human capacities and needs. That is why I have claimed that pleasure is an evolutionary entitlement.

I want to reemphasize George Santayana's aphorism that those who do not know history are condemned to repeat its failures. It delivers a critically important message for this book, even though it's an unduly one-sided interpretation — again, it is as important to understand successes. I have already asserted a vital evolutionary extension of this: those who do not know prehistory may fail to benefit from its successes. A valuable clue to what these successes may be are the pleasures that continue to lure behavior and define effective communities. Now I want to define these pleasures in a systematic way.

Four Easy Pleasures: Inventing an Inventory

Physio-P

Pleasure comes in various shapes and sizes. A rough set of categories may be useful. Of course, categories are ideas. In the real life they refer to they shade over from one category to the other.

Let me delineate four general basic kinds of pleasure. The most obvious has to do with the body. Call these *physiopleasures*. They include the sensory experiences involving the sexual organs, and the sensations of taste and smell that derive from foods, drinks, and perfumes both natural and man-made. There are also more general physical impressions that occur as a result of massages, exercise, plunging into hot or cold water, lying in the sun, stretching, and the like.

As with all the categories I will outline, even this relatively simple one is confusingly interconnected with the others. Is the adolescent boy kissing the prom queen experiencing only tactile contact with a woman's lips and tongue, or is there not a substantial impact here involving his fantasies, the meaning of the touch, and so on? But at least there is a physical sensation — one that would be much clearer and more dramatic were the act they shared sexual intercourse itself, in which case there would be undeniable sensations describable as pleasure. So physiopleasure is an imperfect but plausible and useful category.

Socio-P

Let's call the next most literal category *sociopleasure*. I refer to the fun people have when they are with other people — for example, at a party, or when they are singing in a group, or making a "wave" at a football game, or simply having conversation. The extreme negative of this pleasure is solitary confinement, which, significantly, is the most feared penal punishment after torture and execution.

When we consider the evolution of pleasures, we will see how closely linked sociopleasure is to survival itself. In a gregarious and cooperative food-gatherer such as *Homo sapiens*, exile to loneliness usually meant nothing less than a death sentence.

Sociopleasure is almost as general as air. It is why there are so few hermits and so many willing members of vast cities, so many concerts, displays of fireworks, and such a swirl of people in the piazza. It is almost wholly taken for granted that people generally enjoy some company of other people. There appear to be far fewer people and certainly fewer religious, political, and similar groups who believe in absolute aloneness than who accept severe embargoes on physiopleasure. That is to say, on the evidence it appears people are far more willing to give up physical pleasure than the pleasure of the company of others. For example, in Roman Catholic monasticism, all nuns and priests vow to remain celibate but in only a few orders is even silence an obligation, let alone relatively severe solitude.

For the reason that it is so common, and because loneliness may have been rare in history compared with the present day, the importance of sociopleasure is underestimated in people's lives. Even though countless North Americans will live substantial periods of their lives alone, how seriously is loneliness treated as a theme in the high schools and colleges supposed to prepare people not only for work but for afterhours too? My point, repeated, is that sociopleasure is so much taken for granted that little notice is taken of the fact that legions of contemporary people receive it in tiny pittances by historical standards. It is scarcely seen as an entitlement, though there are some interesting innovations under way, such as providing pets for elderly people and prisoners who are otherwise alone. Symptoms of irritation as different as elevated blood pressure and aggressive behavior decline in such people once a dog or cat is on the scene and interacting with the human. Simple. But a sign of something.

An important kind of human sociopleasure involves morality. We are a species so committed to the social group that evading its rules is unsettling and even physiologically disturbing. For example, while it seems quite likely that the lie detector test can for some people evaluate anxiety as much as honesty, the galvanic skin response it monitors is nevertheless an utterly basic biological measure of an inner state of fear and vulnerability that is difficult to fake. I think it is associated quite directly with a prehistoric fear of ostracism as the most drastic of punishments. It is like the fear of the dark felt by children suddenly alone at night.

The sociopleasure of morality is one reason why the good guys usually win and why morality plays, from Chaucer's tales to today's television network serials, have always gained a serious and appreciative audience. Justice done is to sociopleasure as sexual love accomplished is to physiopleasure — a consummation. And in a community such as the USA with variable and changing definitions of law and normativeness, the citizenry is so committed to obtaining the satisfactions of apparent morality that it keeps in employment a huge army of lawyers through which it simply tries to purchase justice.

Psycho-P

The third category is *psychopleasure*. This derives principally from activities initiated and carried forward by individual people. Someone who accomplishes even a mundane task, such as mowing a lawn or preparing egg whites for a soufflé or sorting some clothes to distribute to homeless people, is finding satisfaction in the act and in using the skill, energy, and resources to complete it. Psychopleasure depends on the existence of other people and on the real world. But more than the two preceding categories, it is independently motivated and enjoyed. It does not require someone else's body to touch or someone else's conversation to share. From a historical point of view, it appears that this is the most recently emergent pleasure because it is so focused on the individual person — a figure relatively unusual in human society. The ancient Greeks had no word for "person." While it has been asserted that the rise of the individual as a historical figure began as early as the eleventh century,[1] lonely experience is nevertheless a relatively unusual factor in human social life.

A West African example is suggestive. Anthropologist Ronald Cohen, now at the University of Florida, told me this story when he taught at McGill University in Montreal. He had been involved in a long-term field research project among the Kanuri people of northern Nigeria and had been living in a village with them for some time. One day he wanted to be off by himself, to sort out his experiences and simply have a break. He walked to the edge of the community's land (to go beyond the boundary would have been a kind of diplomatic incident) and sat down on a fallen log. Within twenty minutes a member of the tribe arrived and sat down quietly at the other end of the log. Cohen asked: "Why are you here?"

"The Chief sent me."

"Why did the Chief send you?"

"Because he said you were alone and therefore you must be ill."

The anecdote dramatizes an interesting cultural difference between the Kanuri society and that of the Euro-American industrial nations, where private experience is seen as a value ("I vant to be alone"). Take the seemingly simple issue of where babies sleep. The middle-class Western ideal is that children should have their own rooms and should sleep alone. From a cross-cultural point of view, this is sharply exotic. A comparative survey of 183 traditional societies studied by anthropologists revealed that the number of them in which babies slept alone was exactly zero. In at least 44 percent of them the mother and infant shared a bed.[2] The notion broadly held among such societies is that babies cry because they want closeness — an obvious and understandable demand for a helpless organism. When they are older, they will adapt to and want greater independence.

Good evidence exists that such initial closeness is likely to be the result of a kind of biological predisposition to intense bonding. Nevertheless, in some circles of Euro-American society, responding to an infant's demands is widely thought to "spoil" it. This was certainly the lesson of the early version of Benjamin Spock's manual on child care (which remains one of the most widely distributed books in American publishing history), although Spock himself has recanted his position on this.

There have been suggestions that SIDS — sudden infant death syndrome, or crib death — may result from the simple but significant fact that infants have been left alone. In the United States about 1 in 500 infants die each year in this puzzling manner — a huge number. One explanation — among others — is that the very young infant is still too immature, between two to four months of age, to perform adequately the otherwise automatic process of breathing without the presence of another person.[3] Researchers at the Presbyterian Hospital in New York City have found that babies carried in soft carriers enjoy better social development: ". . . carried babies developed a more secure attachment relationship with their mothers at 1 year. We also found that the mothers became more sensitive to their babies' signals."[4] Consider the different experiences of the infant held gently to an adult's body and the privileged English baby installed in a large pram with a hood that cuts visual contact between adult and child and isolates the latter physically as well as socially. Is the stiff upper lip formed here, in uncomprehending resentment?

The cultural and attitudinal response to bodily contact between adults and children has also had more general results. For example, fears about sexual molestation and the lawsuits that can result in school systems around this subject have inhibited school personnel in some jurisdictions from any physical contact with youngsters. Even parents may be criticized for touching their children's bodies.[5] Students of mine who work in the social welfare system in New Jersey have described cases in which children in families in difficulty are able to control their parents — fathers, in particular —by threatening to claim sexual abuse to caseworkers monitoring the situation. Of course, there is sufficient evidence of child abuse, particularly by stepparents, for this to raise a justifiable alert. However, it also seems to be true that it is precisely in troubled families, where the expression of legitimate affection may serve as a restorative step along a path to healthy family life, that physical expression of such affection becomes controversial and even dangerous to innocent adults who are just normally and expressively fond of their dependent children.

It has been proposed that maternal touch — or the touch of any concerned person — helps promote protein synthesis and weight gain in infants. This finding in studies of rats was echoed in subsequent studies of human infants at the University of Miami. Touched premature babies gained 50 percent more weight and showed enhanced neurological development over a twelve-day period as compared with infants left untouched. Even after eight months, and after the infants were living at home, the touched babies retained their advantage.[6]

What is astonishing to anybody who knows even rudimentary evolutionary biology is the great surprise of the medical profession and psychologists at the power of touch and their belated understanding of its relationship both to health and to evolution.[7] Touch is the first general connection newborns have with the wider world. The skin is the body's largest organ. How could touch *not* have a major role in development? Like the feral children of legend to whom no human speaks (with predictably bizarre consequences), children whom no one touches appear to endure damaging deficits. For example, essayist Diane Ackerman recalls the plight of Canada's Dionne quintuplets, who were installed by the government in sterile zoolike cells until their mother sued in the courts to retrieve them. Notwithstanding their homecoming, "none of them grew up normally."[8]

Despite the evidence, the force of law may threaten child-care workers and even parents (especially stepfathers of girls) with retribution if they touch as well as look. The skin is not only an envelope containing a person; it is also a means of communication. No body is an island. Yet there is an obvious danger that a carapace of legality will cover over this ancient mode of human connection. Where is the proper balance here?

Ideo-P

The last of our loose categories is *ideopleasure*. When you are standing in line to enter a movie theater perhaps you experience, as I do, a philosophically peculiar situation: you peer at the people filing out who have just seen the same film you are going to see. What is the essence of the difference between you? The difference is that they have had the ideopleasure of seeing the movie. In a sense, the ideopleasure has been inserted in their brain. The mental microchip recording it is the difference between you and them.

One kind of ideopleasure is what people receive from experiencing or creating theoretical entities such as movies, buildings, plays, music, art objects, books. Or when they do crossword puzzles, or create scientific problems and excitedly try to solve them. Ideopleasure is mental, aesthetic, often intensely private. An observer might never know that the person experiencing ideopleasure is experiencing anything at all. Indeed, it is often obligatory to say and do precisely nothing — as in a concert hall or library or theater in which silence and appropriate physical stillness are mandatory characteristics of the acceptable audience.

Another kind of ideopleasure involves more activity, is far older in evolutionary time, and is probably far more difficult to define and understand. I refer to the pleasure found in nature — in landscape, the look and smell of animals, the general impact of natural circumstances. Despite its possible subtlety, there are strong everyday clues to signal the importance of such ideopleasure. For example, enormous numbers of people in seemingly inappropriate urban industrial settings insist on housing and caring for domestic pets. There are some 118 million dogs and cats in the United States, nearly one for every two people. And there are about 500 million pet creatures in all — two for every one person. Numberless people import plants and other forms of natural growth into their dwelling and working places — in fact, nearly everyone does. How many people have not one plant? Countless other people also try to surround their homes with as much vegetation as they can sustain and afford. As we will see later, they even move to otherwise inconvenient suburbs to accomplish this easily and luxuriously.

Why? Because nature gives us ideopleasure. Even in towns, we want that pleasure so much we undertake elaborate schemes in order to enjoy it in our households through pets and plants. In suburbs, we try to balance the aesthetic pleasure of natural landscape with the economic action of cities. To an extent, social status may be an issue in choosing prestigious and unusual breeds of dog and in planting rare and showy shrubbery. But the basic animating factor is that people *enjoy* these often costly and usually demanding additions to their urban or near-urban lives. Flora and fauna are fun.

Look Back in Pleasure

I have suggested some very simple and straightforward categories of pleasure. They go from the most physical to the most ideal. This is to help establish some analytical ground rules for trying to assess which evolutionary features of our species might have been associated with which pleasures and with which consequences. Now I want to take a series of snapshots of our general evolutionary history in order to try to understand the specific evolution of pleasure.

People familiar with the general story of modern anthropology will know that this is very controversial. There is always some colorful conflict under way between people who have different interpretations of the same findings.[9] At one point humans are defined as the toolmaking animal. At another we are hunters-gatherers. At still another time we are thought to be primarily scavengers. One day we are described as deeply warlike, while five years later "deeply cooperative" is the trade name. Popular figures such as Louis, Mary, and Richard Leakey, Jane Goodall, Robert Ardrey, Konrad Lorenz, Desmond Morris, Steven Gould, and a host of other commentators have all said their boisterous and noisy piece.

The controversy is understandable. Compared with the immensity of time and the enormous number of variables involved in the story of our evolution, the available firm facts are relatively scarce. Whole industries of speculation have sometimes rested on the fragile shape of one piece of one skull that purports to prove that the owner had been bopped over the head by a man-made weapon and hence was a member of a violent species — our ancestors. A piece of a hipbone will be identified as proving that a particular ancestor was walking upright; hence this predecessor must have split off from the other apes at a certain time. Another find is treated with a new style of carbon dating and with chemical analysis that reveals traces of human blood on what seems to be a weapon — and quickly we are back to Mayhem Man the Murderer as the general model.

Then another school of thought argues that most of the food early humans ate was fruit and vegetables, which females chiefly gathered. Therefore the male hunters who introduced aggression to the picture were irksome but really rather unimportant to the general scheme of things. Surely this must mean that if society this very day seems highly bellicose and dangerous, it is because our species has fallen — usually because of capitalism or some variant — into a state of male-dominated dis-grace from an earlier egalitarian condition of female-dominated grace.

Such argumentation is legitimate, important, worthwhile — in fact, vital. It is an aspect of the controversy about nature and nurture. It is the tree considering its roots. These fossils are our ancestors and the stories told about them will have an effect on how we see ourselves. After all, even the idea that humans are evolved is relatively new. Just over a hundred years have passed since Darwin's original publications on human origins. Not only has the dust not settled but new storms are created all the time. Vast religious groups such as Catholics and Muslims dispute the very idea of natural human creation and claim the direct intervention of God. Elsewhere, for example in India, there is belief not in evolution but in reincarnation. Even in communities of relatively easygoing secularism such as North America, militant fundamentalism challenges the very basis of the idea and meaning of evolution. And we have already seen that large numbers of people soberly hanker after heaven.

The struggle continues within the secular camp itself, with deep divisions of opinion over whether or not our genetic nature firmly coerces our behavior. Or is it determined by the social and economic circumstances called society that we create? Have we been created or do we create ourselves?[10] My own noncontroversial but defensible conclusion is that we are obviously the result of both processes. Otherwise we would exist as genetically determined bodies without societies, or, by contrast, as social groups inhabited by no bodies. Both extremes are absurd in practice and unnecessary in theory. What I want to do here is simplify — and also improve — the argument by discussing the possible role of the four categories of pleasure in affecting particular evolutionary behavior. How in turn would this result in particular genetic outcomes that in the long run resulted in — us?

What follows is an educated guess. Re-creating a sense of our evolutionary past involves a pastiche of data about contemporary primates, about cultures simpler and usually far smaller than ours. It is difficult and controversial to reconstruct early human life from the relatively few generally credible fossils that have survived from our early past.[11] Nevertheless, we did have a history and it had impact. We cannot ignore it.

We are not new, astonishing flowers, sprung full-blown from nowhere. We are immigrants from the past. Therefore we have to look back in wonder. If we understand what we did capably and successfully in the past, this offers a clue to what we may enjoy doing in the present. Remember: today's pleasures are likely to reflect the accomplishments of the yesterday of evolution.

Our cabinet of pleasures are family heirlooms, of the human family.

A Nosy Small-Town Primate

Perhaps only one thing is not controversial: that our forebears lived in small communities. It appears our typical social unit ranged from perhaps twenty-five souls up to two hundred. This has a host of implications, ranging from the fact that everyone was "familiar," very possibly related by blood, to the likelihood that everyone ate more or less the same food, which in turn meant that body scents were also likely to be rather the same and hence familiar.

Cooking and general smells from previous tenants are always unsettling to new occupants of residential hotels, furnished apartments, and the like, which is surely a reason for their relatively déclassé role in the housing industry. One innkeeping solution has been to douse everything with a strong, neutral chemical smell so that all human trace is masked and the environment is freshly available for the scent-marking of the new occupants. The writer Mary Cantwell has commented in the *New York Times* on how significant it was to her daughters and herself to take possession of a new apartment by creating cooking smells in it. This is an excellent and easy way to mark personal territory. Smell is not simply an indicator of what is pleasing or not but also of what or who is familiar. Parents become nearly immune to the smell of their infant's excrement, a substance usually radically irritating to strangers. Of course, other animals are more sensitive to scent and use it more elaborately than people do. Nevertheless, contemporary humans probably underestimate the impact of smell — we even disguise it with deodorant — and consequently lose access to cues that revealed kith and kin in earlier days, when there was no constabulary and when self-protection required personal judgment. Sniffing out the potential enemy, perhaps?

This becomes a plainer issue when we remember that early humans lived in close quarters, possibly in caves or similar enclosures that may have been poorly ventilated, if only to retain heat. The communicative impact of smell was firm, omnipresent, and real. A consequence of evolution in small groups was sensitivity to the smell of familiar people, a smell that was reassuring and pleasurable.

I stress the relationship between group size, pleasure, and smell to try to illuminate the fact that the power of olfaction as a mode of communication has been underestimated by industrial people. In fact, the smells of the body and of such odors as cooking food appear to be so troubling that fans, vents, and deodorants are used to mask them.[12]

There may be an important practical explanation for this other than undue fastidiousness. The reason may not be aesthetic but rather have to do with reducing aggression. Perhaps the industrial enthusiasm for hiding smells results from a simple reality of contemporary urban life: people have to encounter many strangers many times a day. Proximity to these strangers could be very unsettling were their bodily and living odors intense. So all parties tacitly agree to modulate their behavior so that their personal smells do not threaten the olfactory blandness of the group — not too much strong perfume, no garlic for lunch, vodka rather than gin, bathe frequently — a workable nasal truce.

There may also be a sex difference in perceptions of smell; a teacher of nursing told me it was common medical lore that female nurses and doctors were better able than male doctors to diagnose the welfare of patients by their odor.[13] Certainly females are far more likely than males to employ scent in their personal grooming and in marking that most significant territory — themselves. Perhaps greater female interest in scent and skill in its use was associated with specialization in gathering fruits and vegetables; smell may be a useful aid in determining ripeness and safety. In contrast, human male hunters suggest their possible relative inadequacy by the fact that when dogs were domesticated a significant part of their job description was smelling on our behalf.

Nevertheless, both men and women appear to enjoy the smells of nature. "Country air" is preferable to the urban variety. People derive pleasure from the scents of flowers, trees, grasses, water — a clue to the environment in which we evolved.

But back to the small group. Among such ungulates as deer, sheep, and goats, the mother of a newborn must fixate or "imprint" on the individual smell of her offspring right after birth. Otherwise the necessary pattern of bonding that is the basis of suckling and other maternal care does not occur and the young animal is endangered. Is there a comparable physiopleasure among human newborns and their mothers? Certainly there has been much support for the trend toward childbirth without anesthetizing medical intervention. One result is that mothers and newborns can not only see and feel but also smell each other. Whether or not it is decisive in bonding them to their babies, mothers comment frequently on the attractiveness of the scents that babies produce. In the soft, warm cocoon of physical interaction with infants, smell is clearly a factor, surely a pleasure.

Even pets can provide a similar sense of comforting familiarity. For example, puppies emanate a characteristic odor. My own adult dog yields an appealing nutlike smell when he wakes up. Something about the quiet and closeness of his sleeping position produces a scent that emerges at no other time. I find myself strangely reassured and pleased by it.

Nasal Sex

What about grown-up sex? A quick survey of perfume and cologne ads suggests that the buyers of these products broadly expect them to enhance sexual attractiveness or boldness, not improve their statistical ability as investors or originality as engineers. The general promise is for a varying mixture of passion, youth, status, exoticism, and wordless allure. The appeal of the scents is to enhance intimate behavior. There is no perfume designed for giving speeches or speaking over the telephone. Indeed, personal-decor counselors to men and, particularly, women in business often advise against using any intrusive scent during the workday.

This is hardly difficult to understand. It underlines the fact that the physiopleasure of bodily scent is highly associated with personal intimacy. An intriguing finding of French researchers on receptivity to odor was that women who are ovulating are some *ten thousand times* more sensitive to smell than they are during their menstrual period. When I told this to a female colleague, she said, "So that's why I use so much perfume during my period." This makes biosocial sense, since if women are alert to the sexual state of men through odor — and we know that women are — then it would be advantageous to be most skillful and sensitive at that time in the cycle when conception is possible.

It is not wholly clear what male clue would suffice to "turn on" a female interested in intercourse that possibly could lead to reproduction. However, there are indications that elements of male underarm odor can be attractive to females. This may reflect the general function of pheromones — messenger smells between bodies — in facilitating sexual behavior.

At the same time, I have been told by a highly successful French creator of perfumes, Guy Robert, president of Quintessence in Paris, that there are no specifically male or female scents. But certainly among the other primates there is clear indication of the role of pheromones in affecting sexual behavior. For example, with some colleagues at Rutgers University I did a study of the impact of Depo-Provera, used as a three-month contraceptive given subcutaneously to female monkeys living in a community with a sexually active male consort. Invariably, those females who received the drug were not approached sexually by the male, even if they had been among his favorites when they were not medicated.[14]

The evidence was decisive. The implication in broad terms is that since the contraceptive drug works by simulating pregnancy chemically, the female monkey ceases producing the pheromonal smells that are otherwise very much connected to male response. It is difficult to extrapolate directly to humans. Nevertheless, it is provocative that the same medication is used rather widely for human contraception, though not legally in the United States, where regulations prevent its use for this purpose (because it may cause cancer). It is a perverse irony that the contraceptive inhibits not only conception but possibly also the behavior that can produce it!

The broader implication is even more interesting to us here. The sense of smell can be active and consequential even when the producers and receivers are unaware of its role. Sensory modalities and sense experiences direct us to act in ways that yield pleasure even though we do not know we are seeking it.

This is a kind of "sensory unconscious," elements of which have been elegantly described by Diane Ackerman, and earlier by Lorus and Margery Milne.[15] I use olfaction with all its subtleties as the example of a pleasure system that guides behavior significantly but surreptitiously. Recent research by specialists at Columbia University even suggests that the olfactory system "knows" what it is smelling without necessarily involving the brain; there are an unexpectedly large number of genes associated with nasal tissue sensitive to odor.[16] The "familiar smells of home" loom large, with profound meaning for our formative history. In terms of daily food-gathering as well as maintaining group security, they underline the importance of intimate cooperation for survival.

Both physiopleasure and sociopleasure are directly involved here. Bodily smell is clear social communication as well as plainly physiological, even when — perhaps particularly when — the communicators are unaware of what they are exchanging. We know that the taste of food is decisively affected by its smell. The bouquet of wine decisively affects its attractiveness. Other phenomena may be similarly influenced by their olfactory impact. For example, oral sex may achieve the intimate impact it does in part because of the complex and rare exchange of bodily smell it compels. And I have already alluded to the appeal of "country air" as opposed to the contaminated urban variety — an appeal that must surely derive from the fact that country air is our natural air while the industrial variety is not.

Of artificial smells defined as desirable, even commercial fragrances essentially mimic the natural environment that produced us. The most desirable perfumes are the result of intense reduction of the scents of flowers combined with alcohol and other substances that carry and magnify them to re-create the pleasurable environments in which the flowers originally grew. A sweet physiopleasure with ancient roots. Perhaps when our first family spent its quiet evening in the cave, it brought some flowers inside — though we have good evidence only of flowers associated with cave-dweller burials. Flowers are still useless. But florists still prosper.

One Rm/WBF

Perhaps the most pervasive scent of the quiet evening at home in the cave was the mixed aroma of people, cooking food, and woodsmoke — still the keenly sought country-cabin ideal. Despite the fact that securing and handling logs is cumbersome and that fireplaces are inefficient as sources of heat, millions of humans nonetheless enjoy fireplaces in semihypnotic general contentment. Primordial though it is, a fireplace is a major selling attraction in real estate. In regions such as mountainous Colorado where thin air compounds the problems of pollution, fireplace users are willing to subject themselves to a quota of a few wood-burning hours per day lest their paradise mountain valleys become unhealthy. In New York City and other urban centers, shops sell bundles of a half-dozen short logs for the price of T-bone; the buyers are acquiring entertainment, as with a movie on cassette. Richard Nixon had the Oval Office fireplace vigorously stoked, then turned up the air-conditioning to make his working climate tolerable. A "roaring fire" in a generous hearth is an invariably evocative feature of advertisements. Fireplaces please. Please, a fireplace.

This is hardly surprising in view of the importance of fire in our history as a species. The conquest of fire was a clear human breakthrough. In one swift, concise innovation, it provided warmth and the ability to cook food. It lit a comfortable haven in the endless pool of nighttime darkness. It was an effective warning to predators — both flickering light and smoke were security weapons. Even in warm climates, nights may be cool, especially in mountainous areas, and so a fire was associated with comfort (particularly during the ice ages), with safety, and, no doubt, with families. It is no wild speculation to claim that — like their contemporary descendants — our ancestors found comforting pleasure in nothing more complex than sitting by a fire and watching its ever-varied motion.

Perhaps one reason for the appeal of tobacco smoking despite its clearly dreadful consequences for health is that it provides a portable fireplace — a signal of our control of fire and a hint of the pleasures of the hearth. The ritual of lighting up is comforting and interesting on its own, and the smell of the smoke is domestic. While the smoke smell of a cigarette becomes increasingly acrid as it burns, the initial puffs are often pleasingly sweet in odor. Certainly pipe smoke from the blends of aromatic tobacco, frequently with added perfume, produces an often agreeable smell. So do cigars, to connoisseurs and enthusiasts. Combine these sensual pleasures with the weakness of the human body to nicotine addiction and, voilà, a major, costly, tax-rich, and endlessly dangerous industry emerges. Yet it is interesting — indeed, striking — that few people become addicted to nicotine itself, without the intervening experience of smoking.

That is, unlike heroin or cocaine, for example, consuming the raw narcotic itself is insufficiently appealing. Alone, it is not pleasurable enough to induce addicts to support the expense and hazard of using it. But they are willing and even eager to use the substance when the nicotine is embellished by the control of fire and the smell of smoke. Aesthetics and not only chemistry appears to be the source of the social and medical problem of nicotine addiction. Once more, back to the quiet evening in the fire-lit cave.

Smoke Gets in Your Mouth

Another index of the power of the sensory experience created by that comforting evening around the fireplace is the widespread human affection for charred — barbecued — food, meat in particular. In communities that can afford to consume large chunks of animal protein, such as suburban America, the barbecue is a standard source of pleasure. It is also an assertion of prosperous status. Restaurants even attract clients by the smell of the smoking wood with which they cook some of their food. Mesquite, applewood, hickory, cherry, olive — these have become flavors, rather like herbs or spices. And certainly there is an extensive and complex culinary tradition surrounding other smoked foods as well. Smoked salmon is but one example of the luxurious products yielded by the contact of smoke with edibles.

Like the sight of fireplaces that produce smoke, the taste of smoke on food is generally attractive. Usually, spices and sugar are added to the sauce that frequently bastes the food. Though there are regional variations, it appears that the overwhelming number of widely distributed barbecue sauces contain rather high levels of sugar. Evidently smoke and sweetness combine to make the food nearly irresistible. Steaks, ribs, chicken, pork, lamb, fish, and vegetables appear to be attractive throughout the world when they are prepared in this relatively unsubtle way. The manner in which many French people order steak — "*bleu*," or "black and blue" in America — involves a fierce broiling of meat on the outside to provide the smoky taste while the inside remains rare and tender: two tastes at once.

We can be certain that smoking food or cooking it over an open fire was a bedrock experience of evolving human beings during the first quarter of a million years in which we had some control over the use of fire. It takes no gymnastics of the imagination to decide that contemporary affection for smoky tastes recalls Sunday dinner at the hearth of the first family's cave.

Who's for Dinner? Cannibals and Kings

We've been on the subject of food. Let's stay there, to discuss another pleasure that appears to be closely linked to evolutionarily successful behavior and also continues to have elaborate implications for contemporary life. I refer to communal eating. Here two major themes are united: the necessity of securing nourishing food that tastes good and looks interesting, and the sharing of it in the community of others.

Mammals are creatures who feed their young from the mother's body. It is scarcely a surprise that with whom one eats is an important issue from the very beginning. The Chinese ideogram for home combines the symbols of mother and child. But there are many other species of mammal. None has the kind of formidable apparatus of hospitality that people do. There is obviously something characteristically complicated and special involved in our need for food. On the sensible principle of producing virtue from necessity, human communities have combined the requirements of nutrition and the human need for society into a remarkably bountiful and interesting source of recurrent pleasure and reassurance.

A central experience of camping is the evening fire used to cook food hunted or fished or trapped or carried along. Even youngsters accustomed to the easy fast-food grazing of urban environments adapt easily and with seeming enjoyment to a mode of eating far more troublesome and demanding than normal. The aesthetics and social symbolism of the setting overwhelm the inconvenient logistics.

Camping is a version of hunting, a pastime that not only retains its hold on urban people but is growing. The US Fish and Wildlife Service estimates that the number of Americans hunting big game has doubled in twenty years, to nearly thirteen million. A costly primordial sport maintains and increases its "emotional market share" in a wholly urban society. For whatever reason, people enjoy it. Despite inconvenience, people seek it. Campfire dining is part of the syndrome.

While ordinary dining is not the same, it contains many similar elements, enough to reveal a plausible connection between Upper Paleolithic dinner parties, contemporary hunting, and dinner for four at Le Bistro Provençal. What connections? For one, the more luxurious the spot, generally the less light, the more candles — and candles, after all, are only miniature fireplaces. Candlelit dinners in quiet rooms with small booths, corners, niches, are more "romantic" than identical meals eaten in half-acre cafeterias lit by fluorescent glare. Carefully engineered restaurants will lower the light levels as the evening proceeds. Of course, domestic meals will not share these characteristics, though there may well be somewhat reduced lighting, with dinner served in a pool of relatively murky candlelight.

What homes and restaurants do share is the conviviality and the food. Eating with other people is one of the animating organizing principles of human existence. It is almost astonishing how much time, energy, and resources go into this. "Let's have lunch" — and people do. It is even this way in that new genre, contemporary industrial life, in which individuals must carry on their work lives while adhering to demanding schedules and operating in wide-ranging territories.

As a matter of fact, many of the busiest people are busy *because* they rarely eat at home. Instead, they convert feeding into social structure. They may dine away from home for days on end as they weave their world out of food and its convivial consumption. Particularly busy people will have three meals a day established around a social connection; their lunch dates may be booked weeks in advance. Particular restaurants become prosperous when they can become arenas in which people display their commercial or political status through the people with whom they share food and time. A favorite restaurant of mine is Galatoire's in New Orleans, which serves appealing food, is delightful-looking, maintains relatively moderate prices, and has a policy of not accepting reservations even though it is a choice destination. This often obligates people to line up for a place, and the consequent egalitarian conviviality of the restaurant repays the affectionate favor.

Who looks happier — people eating alone or those with people? Human beings generate endless opportunities for social dining, which they do not do for toilet functions or filing tax forms. One role of restaurants is to provide neutral, professionally crafted ground for the enjoyment of sociopleasure. The issue of physiopleasure — will the food taste good? — becomes another occasion for the demonstration of shared social taste and for making social alliances. Just as the cost of a restaurant meal may run at least three or four times the cost of the food itself, so the social effort is similarly far greater than the nutritional value of the dinner. The difference in the cost of restaurant food compared with homemade is a kind of self-imposed tax on consumers; they are purchasing an opportunity for certified conviviality.

Eating together is disproportionately more important than what is eaten. Eating alone is disproportionately more dispiriting than what is actually happening. And eating in public, particularly in the "hot" restaurants of the moment, those to which people of similar assertive status flock, offers both simple nutrition and complex reassurance about social acceptance.

If you wonder why, imagine eating alone in the cave, away from the other diners, or in a separate cave. What kind of complex antagonisms could this represent? Exile? Arrogance? Disfavor? A malefaction or malady? Perchance the solitary person didn't cooperate in getting the dinner and therefore can't share it.

Once, when I lived in London, I was with a party of people who had had a leisurely Sunday lunch together and were then invited along for further talk and drinks at the home of one of the guests, an heiress of an overwhelmingly wealthy family. She graciously offered us all a choice of liqueur. When we had been served, as inconspicuously as possible (but not quite enough) she reached into a separate cabinet to pour herself some brandy, which from the glance I had at the bottle seemed to be rare and valuable in the categorical way the possessions of extremely wealthy people can be. She did share her brandy with us — the brandy she owned, but not the brandy she drank.

Nights at the Round Table

From then on, in my opinion, the heiress was eating alone in the cave. In contrast, among the Chinese, the most honorable guest is he who eats least of the food he most enjoys. This is how he displays his commitment to the group whose society he shares, however temporarily. The host must dispense and never reserve the choicest items for himself. In fact, a generous host may be called a "big spoon" in appreciation of the utensil with which he distributes the food from the hefty platters on the table. Since all the food is available to all the diners, the issue of equity is much more pertinent than in Euro-American restaurants that serve each diner an individual ration, usually separately ordered and individualistically allocated — a nutritional analogue of the Protestant Revolution.

My suspicion is that beyond the tastiness, economy, and interest of the food itself, Chinese cooking has been so phenomenally successful throughout the world because it permits and even compels what appears to be the enjoyment of sharing. And it is a favorite of children too, because they needn't suffer the ignominy of "children's portions." They can eat just what the adults eat if they want. Since the food is already largely cut into small bits, they needn't endure the dependent inferiority of having adults visibly and condescendingly clip their food at the table. They can share in every way. For a while they are like everyone else.

The pleasure of sharing food is the other side of the necessity to share work in order to acquire food. Humans evolved as cooperative food gatherers. We try to remain cooperative food consumers, even if we rarely join together to acquire directly the materials for our dinner. And when the food *has* been acquired by the group, as hunters, gatherers, shoppers, farmers, fishermen, then the campfire dinner, or the restaurant dinner, or wherever it is held, gains some added luster of pleasure.

Way Beyond the Pleasure Principle, Quickly

Physiopleasure, sociopleasure, psychopleasure, ideopleasure. These are the terms I've been using to identify different forms of human satisfaction. I've tried to show how they are linked to what is known about our evolution as a species, and how they are also rather consistently associated with the behavior of people in families. I've also tried to connect some very ordinary contemporary pleasures, such as smelling fragrant perfumes or sitting in front of a fireplace after dinner, with experiences of prehistory involved with successful reproduction, food gathering, and social behavior. These have been broad assertions. This expansiveness is necessary because of the vast time scale involved. Also, I want to highlight brightly the outline of the story to be told, so that the specific details discussed later on are in appropriate perspective.

My most general point is that our pleasures are as much related to our history as a species and products of it as they are products of our invention. This is a useful point of departure. It raises a variety of interesting related questions, such as these: If certain pleasures are characteristically human because of our evolutionary history — for example, the vigorous use of large muscles in play — does this mean that a "new, improved" view of human rights will include the right to exercise? If sensual pleasure has been central to human experience and continuity, should advocates of celibacy be held to a higher standard of public accountability than they currently are?

Should managers of groups of zealots be obligated to offer their followers the right to enjoy ideopleasures that challenge the worldview of the cult in question? That is, is private censorship even in voluntary groups as inhuman as the governmental kind? Is solitary confinement a "cruel and unusual punishment" (to say nothing of its questionable rehabilitative value) and hence subject to the same kind of legal restriction as the death penalty?

Let us assume for the moment — and it's not an eccentric

assumption — that cooperative contribution to the group's food supply or some other significant social function is an ancient pleasure and part of the daily life of any dignified adult. Does this then mean that people without jobs should be offered "employment insurance" so that they can be certain of working and contributing? In effect, is workfare a more sophisticated and vivacious policy than welfare, which is a first step and not a solution?

I don't know. However, these may be legitimate versions of the "evolutionary entitlements" to which I referred before. Notice that I have relied rather heavily on observations about ancient families and on the conservative social tradition on which kinship depends. For reasons that are elaborate and often overwhelming, industrial people are living in a period that neither makes family life easy nor dignifies it with the automatic value it was seen to have in the past.[17] In Manhattan, 50 percent of people living in rental accommodations live alone, while 70 percent of Oslo's inhabitants are single (a figure that has risen by 1 percent each year since 1968).[18] There has been a similar consistent increase in the number of single-person households in the United States.

If our capacity and need for pleasure have been prehistorically and historically linked to family life, then our chance to achieve real pleasures becomes diminished. The broad reason is that social arrangements inhibit how people can enjoy family life or those other social arrangements that yield pleasures like those that families provide.

In an unexpected and curious way, it appears to have become historically and increasingly difficult or undesirable to undertake child rearing, an aspect of life that has been necessarily central to human evolutionary success.

Of course, this reflects people's choices. It may indicate nothing more than that human beings are no longer subject to an inevitable lifelong process. Certainly such freedom of choice is a source of satisfaction and pleasure in itself. Certainly the burgeoning press of people on natural resources and the fragile planet that contains these basic necessities obligates every person to consider what existence itself means to the equipoise of life.

Nevertheless, only the Chinese have limited directly the opportunity of their population to bear children. They maintain a complex policy not widely loved if perhaps reluctantly accepted. It is also fairly skillfully evaded by many. There may be no choice to that policy. But it is a limitation on the pleasure that adults may draw from having children. In China the law restricts parents to one child. In the industrial world not law but formidable circumstances appear to make two or more children increasingly unusual.

But a family policy is also a pleasure policy. A biologist could argue that having no children is a version of having no sex. They are, after all, part of the same urgent process and reflect the same profound motivations. Are societies entitled to restrict such enthusiasms by design or inadvertence? Who says?

Now we must explore the sources and expressions of these and other motivations. What makes people tick, sing, sigh, grunt, bellow, clam up, hum?

THREE

Guess Why?

THE GENERAL ASSUMPTION about people is that there is always a reason and a motive for what they do.

Motive can be a matter of life or death. In a criminal trial the motivation of the accused determines whether the crime is manslaughter or first, second, or third degree murder. Strikingly, the most severe punishment is given to the killer who was most thoughtful, most sensible, most rational, most deliberate in his action — though these are qualities that are otherwise highly prized. If financial gain is involved, even in jurisdictions that are reluctant to apply the death penalty, such as California, the penalty may be execution nonetheless. In other jurisdictions, a particular event such as finding a spouse in sexual activity with someone else and flying into a murderous rage will be regarded as somewhat excusable if deeply unfortunate. Not only are specific actions judged by the law and by society in general, but so are their causes. Cause cannot be separated from effect. Motivation matters.

In this chapter I want to explore why people do various things that yield them pleasure. I will discuss food a little, sex more, alcohol even more, and other drugs a lot. Throughout, the body obviously looms large, in particular its complicated managerial organ, the brain. Throughout, I begin with the assumption that what people *do* do reflects in important measure what they *want* to do — that human action is not primarily the outcome of compulsion and that human choice is not a lottery. It follows a pattern. That pattern is a revelation of our nature — may *be* our nature.

Also, I make the naturalist's assumption that our first task is simply to describe and the second, to analyze. Only then, if we want the job, may we make judgments about the behavior we see. Actually, I do have some judgments to make — for example, about the hazards of legalizing drugs that are currently illicit, and also about the possible social value of other substances about which there is moral controversy, such as alcohol. But this is secondary to the more intriguing matter of exploring which pleasures people import into their lives, take into their bodies, share with their chums, and why they do this.

Fat Pacific Oysters

What causes pleasure? Why do people seek it and how do they know what they are going to enjoy? Are there rules of pleasure-seeking that apply across cultural boundaries? Can you fool a lot of the people a lot of the time? Can you induce them to purchase pleasures that a moment's cold inspection would reveal as worthless? I found it extraordinary when I first perceived that my infant child preferred bean mush to potato mush. It seemed he had been born with taste preferences. He preferred some foods over others though the adults around him neither offered him particular guidance about one baby food versus another nor consciously influenced him by example — after all, no adult ate any of his charmless menu. Whence did that preference arise? Was it a defined feature of the nature of his mouth just as that mouth had a distinct physical shape?

What is the source of taste? I hereby confess, or at least record, that for no discernible reason there will be weeks on end when I sustain a clear-as-a-bell hankering for oysters, particularly the luxuriously fat and companionable Pacific ones I grew to know when I lived in Vancouver, British Columbia. Source, please. An industry the size of the economy of a small country produces "snacks" that people eat because they like them. Why do they like them?

Certain human beings called actors or artists or writers or singers or dancers behave in such a way that causes countless other people to admire them. Audiences may be deeply affected by their work and become involved with their careers and perceptions. These civilians find their own lives enriched by the work of these specialists in artistic communication. Creative people provide elegant, churning, and surprising varieties of pleasure. Some of them are among the most complexly influential and plainly persuasive humans on the planet — Chaplin, Goethe, Sinatra, Brontë. On what do they base their successful claim for attention. What wins them affection? What replenishes their fund of music, poetry, taste, phrases?

What motivates them? What motivates their audience? What keeps the show going?

Pleasure Central

I first want to approach this complicated question very simply and basically. A practical and realistic point of departure is the body itself. Finally, this is the instrument of pleasure. The body is a genuine fact. It also is a library where experience is recorded, both as memory and as habit.

We can begin with physiopleasure because it is primary and relatively clear-cut. But there are still complexities here. Consider the implacable impact of the life cycle on the experience of the body. For example: a ten-year-old boy sees a mature female naked. This may be interesting or confusing or irrelevant at ten. But it has a very different meaning for the same person when he is eighteen. Now the body responds differently and more urgently. An erection may anatomically — and quite autonomically — certify the impact of this nudity on the viewer. Also, the conceptual role of the naked body is drastically different from before. The brain and the sex organs respond in a new way. This is extraordinary. The unfolding mind and maturing body are tightly linked. Something palpable has happened to the body over the eight intervening years. The brain and perceptual functions have changed too. They affect psychophysiological process in a different way from before.

Nevertheless, the body remains at the center of the matter. It possesses sensory systems that alert it to undue cold, heat, moisture, dryness. Ancient parts of the brain constantly monitor the comfort of the body and obviously seek to reject pain and seek pleasure.

This may be conscious, but it needn't be. Like the exemplary moth drawn to the dancing flame, people may also find themselves pulled rather inexplicably by a song, a carousel, an inviting plaza, a raconteur with a gift for subclauses, or an oasis of luxury such as the Schoenbrun in Vienna or the gold museum in Bogotá. Certainly there is nothing mysterious about the appeal of pastry shops anywhere, stores that sell woolens in cold countries, cool fruit drinks in the tropics, or a congenial inn that welcomes a pair of desperate travelers who show up without reservations as dusk falls. Such pleasures are clear-cut. A generous corps of society's members, sometimes called "the service industries," actively seek to provide these pleasures and also add new ones to the menu of options.

But there is an order, a hierarchy, to these obvious pleasures too. We can begin with a fairly narrow calculus of pleasures. Which foods do people like and dislike, why, and what mechanisms are at play to produce the preferences we discern? As Ralph Norgren of the Hershey Medical Center at Penn State has said, taste is "an obvious and perhaps unique probe for examining the neural mechanisms of pleasure."[1] He notes that despite twenty-five years of research, the neurophysical basis of pleasure has not been identified, that both pain and pleasure cause still-unspecified neural activity, and that since pleasure itself cannot be traced, it is most efficient to trace taste preferences in order to try to determine their source.

It is helpful in this enterprise that out of a considerable array of taste qualities, animals, including humans, are able to distinguish at least four: salty, bitter, sweet, and sour. Studies of taste depend on manipulation of these in experimental and natural settings to determine what preferences are. Researchers have proposed an evolutionary reason for the existence of this taste quartet.[2] The work of the system of taste is principally to assess the value or danger of foods and liquids. The molecules scanned by taste and olfactory systems produce relatively consistent and clear-cut responses in humans and other species too. Sodium is always salty and is vital for human life; we come from the ocean and need the water and salt in which we were once housed. The other primates who groom each other will eat specks of salt they pluck from other bodies. This is highly direct recycling — from sweat to salt. Sugars taste sweet and contain rich supplies of calories. Alkaloids are unpleasantly bitter and are also found in poisonous substances. Acids are somewhat ambiguous in taste, though when they are assessed together with sugar content, they help reveal the ripeness of fruit; this may account for their persistence. In any event, they contribute to a popular "taste treat" — sweet-and-sour food, which is found in many cuisines.

In the simplest possible system, we can see that taste and the pleasure and pain it delivers have been directly related to our success as an evolved species. This is our starting point.

It Was Such a Sweet Revolution

The most obvious human enthusiasm of taste is for sweetness. Nursing babies prefer sweet milk hours after birth — again, mother's milk is sweetish — and this preference appears independently of other taste preferences in the wider adult culture. Not only is mother's milk rather sweet, but it is also not rich — certainly not as rich as the milk formulas that replace it in the diet of infants not being breast-fed. This has suggested to Nicholas Blurton-Jones of the Neuropsychiatric Institute of UCLA that human babies are adapted to frequent feedings of lean milk. In turn, this implies that babies are "designed" to be carried by their mothers until they are weaned, or at least to remain in proximity to them. This is another element of the characteristic picture I drew earlier — which applied across cultures — of mothers and infants in close physical relationship, even during sleeping. And for a while, they are a single link in the food chain.

We must remember that the most likely source of sweet taste

after weaning was ripe fruit, until the easy cultivation of sugar became possible in the eighteenth century. Before then, sugar was precious, expensive, more a medicine than a food — sugar was the original sugar pill, as a matter of fact. When the process of growing neat sugar was perfected (it grows in very particular climates and must be handled with quite precise timing), it caused an enormous convulsion in the world. The main impetus came after Columbus brought it to the New World on his second voyage, in 1493. Thereafter, slaves were increasingly captured in one part of the world to work in fields and climates in another. The world growth of sugar consumption was explosive — nearly 500 percent between the years 1860 and 1890.[3]

The taste was attractive. The calories provided not only rich desserts for the rich but sustained the urban poor who had been driven off their lands into difficult cities. Sugared tea, sweet bread with treacle, or other "puddings," for example, provided calories and allayed hunger. But the sugar-based diet resulted in a general decline in the health and stature of poor citizens in the early days of the industrial revolution. There was too much of one good thing, not enough of others — such as complex carbohydrates, animal protein, and the like, to say nothing of fresh air and space in which to move around. And, of course, once gin was added to the English mix and widely distributed in the gin palaces, a broad and sustained disaster developed that eventually resulted in sharply restrictive alcohol licensing laws that are largely in effect to this day. But there were no licensing laws regulating sugar. The food value and pleasure it provided were central to survival among the urban poor.

There are individual differences in how intensely people desire and enjoy sugar. But it also appears to be an overwhelmingly general preference. Presumably it evolved because everyone needed to consume fresh fruits — recall that scurvy is decisively caused by their absence — and the sugar they contained was a good inducement to seek them out. Once neat sugar became available and relatively cheap, the kinds of sweetness that could be created and enjoyed expanded enormously.[4] The activity of responsibly and energetically looking for sugar in order to expand its intake — through healthy fruit, which was also rather filling anyway and could quickly spoil — was ultimately replaced by the modern problem of *reducing* its consumption in the form of confections and drinks. Here we can see the relationship between innate taste preferences for sugar, which nearly everyone has, and what happens when the community produces a wealth of new forms and uses. Suddenly, the nature of motivation changes from positive (get sugar in fruit and vegetables) to negative (try to avoid refined sugar because it will make you pudgy, rot your teeth, and even reflect badly on your character).

This spotlights a fundamental aspect of the problem. Our evolution and hence our nature motivates us to a certain course of action. But now social and technological conditions of life have changed, in some ways immeasurably. A once-desirable pattern of motivation/action/satisfaction can become quickly hazardous to your health. Too much becomes as important a moral and political issue as not enough. The politics of pollution and crowding emerge alongside the politics of scarcity and equity. Resonating in the center of all this is the individual person trying to navigate between the obligations of a healthy life and the temptations of pleasurable experience. Restrained by priests, lured by advertisers, calibrated by physicians, goaded by poets, and taunted by the example of hectic celebrities, what is a lad or lass to do?

A first step is understanding the problem. In the instant case, the problem is that for several million years it was good to seek out sugar, but then, some two hundred years ago, the situation abruptly changed. The motivation, originally, was rather simple. Some things tasted sweet, hence good. They were often available in the environment, so people acquired them. Since these sweets usually didn't have to be shared, there wasn't even much social negotiation involved in completing the circle. Motivation. Satisfaction. Good health. Simple.

Then the world changed. Not so simple.

Seduced by Sex

Now let's consider sex, which is also not so simple. Here is another motivation that has been central and essential for the survival of the species. Certainly it is far stronger and more persistent than the search for sugar, though not, of course, for food itself, which takes priority. While it is possible to engage in sex alone, more often than not, and probably as the preference of most people, it involves another person. So while choosing to consume sugar in whatever form may involve a self-justifying monologue with the self, enjoying sex needs at least a dialogue. Someone else has to be taken into account. Most people treat sexual behavior as serious and consequential. There is usually rather a lot to consider.

Where does private motivation fit into this social complexity? Immediately, we can see that a sexual interaction is not governed solely or even principally by the search for physiopleasure, even though this continues to be an urgent and central goal of the interaction. (Psychiatrist Michael McGuire of the UCLA Medical School calculates that a male having intercourse twice a week between ages eighteen and seventy-two will experience the peak of orgasmic pleasure for 9.3 hours during his lifetime.) There are other considerations. Let's assume a couple is heterosexual and unmarried. They have ascertained that they are both healthy, so the fear of disease is not an issue. Let us also assume they are broadly interested in securing a durable relationship, possibly marital. However, they are also playful and enjoy the sexual experience whether or not it leads to what they regard as durable commitment.

If we look at what they do through the lens of contemporary behavioral biology, several levels of motivation become evident. First and most simply, local and immediate issues may affect whether or not they decide to spend the night together and perhaps have sexual relations. Are they comfortable where they are and is it late and are they tired? Is it raining or snowing fiercely outside or is there bad traffic or delayed planes or trains or buses because of an accident or a holiday?

But there are subtler issues, involving what have been called "ultimate causes" of behavior. These are distinct from those "proximate causes" that are usually at work in the obvious here and now. As an example of this, it has been widely asserted that men and women in general employ different strategies when they conduct their sexual lives, whether they are aware of it or not.[5]

The Classical Cad: *La Différence Vive*

Men are in general more inclined to seek sexual relationships with a wide array of women — the behavior of the classical cad. The ultimate effect of this is to maximize their opportunity for successful reproduction. Since their commitment can endure for less than an evening or an hour, this is a plausible plan for males if the underlying point of sex — its design goal — is for each individual to produce as many viable offspring as possible, who will themselves reproduce.

But the situation for women is sharply different, because their level of commitment is incomparably higher. If they become pregnant, then they gestate the fetus for nine months. If they seek an abortion, that involves some disruption, some danger, some cost, and possibly much moral and emotional trauma. If they bear the child and release it for adoption, we know that this can be an agony for some women and at least a potential problem for nearly all concerned. If a woman elects to raise the child, then that is what she has to do. She may have to do it alone.

Unless, that is, she is very careful in her choice of bed partners and hence potential fathers of her possible children. Other things being equal, she should have sex only with a man she believes will want to share child rearing, whom she would be happy and rewarded to spend time with, and who would be an appropriate father of the child she might bear. Given her ultimate sexual strategy, she should employ coy behavior in contrast to the man's cad behavior.

A raft of evidence indicates that this distinction applies rather generally and consistently across cultures. Even in homosexual communities, we see that women are far more discriminating in their choice of partners. The average lesbian will have four partners in a lifetime, perhaps with a maximum of twelve or so, whereas many gay men will enjoy sex with dozens of partners, in some cases with many hundreds. There are no female equivalents of the pre-AIDS bathhouses in which men could take part in a number of often anonymous, literally hole-in-the-wall sexual episodes. Thus, even when there is no issue of reproduction at all, men and women homosexuals will nonetheless act as if they are participants in the kind of ultimate-cause reproductive program I have described.

Why Liberal Legislation about Abortion Followed the Pill

An indication of what happens when the strategy is misdirected is the large number of women who either out of a lack of concern or misjudgment give birth to children with fathers who then abandon or ignore them. These women may decide to seek abortions if they expect undue difficulty as single mothers. Related to this critical choice-point is a seeming paradox: pressure for liberal abortion legislation and passage of such laws followed quickly on the availability of contraceptives controlled by women, principally the IUD and the pill. There is good evidence that when contraception was a male matter — the condom was the principal contraceptive until the 1960s — or a somewhat mutual issue, as with the diaphragm, there was some reliable amount of joint responsibility. Many men and women married during a pregnancy — and in some communities newlyweds who were not pregnant were regarded with quizzical concern.[6] This was a rather abrupt form of mate selection, though not an altogether unreasonable one, since both sex and reproduction were clearly within the couple's competence. But once women had new forms of reproductive control, men assumed males were largely liberated from responsibility. The apparent consequences of this change are, of course, enormous. They range from a continued decline in birthrates, to increasingly unstable marriages, to a dramatic rise in the number of single mothers and, perhaps, a corresponding emergence of males who have become what I have elsewhere called "alienated from the means of reproduction" — men engaged in what, from a very different point of view, Barbara Ehrenreich has called a "flight from commitment."[7] Perhaps in no other human arena has there been more decisive technology-driven change than in the consequences of the pursuit of pleasure.

If we take seriously the distinction between ultimate and proximate causes, we can see that the pleasure that results from each is also predictably different. We have learned from various sources, including the work of Heather Remoff and of David Buss, that men tend to choose women who are young, defined as attractive, and seen as fertile. Women choose men who are older than they and who are defined as likely to provide secure and resourceful companionship.[8]

Once, I was at a dinner table at which a powerful member of the fashion business was advertising the virtues of his unmarried son to a young woman who is a highly successful publicist. Her first and only question about the young man was "Does he date models?" The father's reluctant admission that yes, this had been known to occur occasionally, was enough to end the negotiation. Not a serious prospect, in the shorthand inquisition by the to-the-point lady. Her instant prediction was that this was a man devoted to the proximate causality of glamorous sex, not the ultimate goal of well-husbanded parenthood. I do not mean this woman had self-consciously decided to have a baby and that she would admit no man into her life who did not join in her ultimate plan. Perhaps she did want to have a child, perhaps she didn't, perhaps she didn't think about the matter at all. Nevertheless, it is plausible to say she revealed — even somewhat ingenuously — that she preferred to have pleasure, of various kinds, with a man whose broad agenda was in general accord with her own. It was more fun, she was saying, when ultimate and proximate motivations were both satisfied. Both participants would produce their own brand of pleasure. If Mr. Right for the long run could be the same person as Mr. Suddensurge, or even Mr. Goodbar, this was good.

What of the male? If we go by the book, we can infer he will have a direct interest in the actual physiopleasure of intercourse and orgasm and may even press his case severely, against the clear wishes of his partner. One grim indication of this is the vastly greater incidence of rape of women by men than of men by women, and the less dramatic but equally indicative matter of "date rape" or "acquaintance rape." The statement of a Rutgers student is suggestive here: "I met a guy at his fraternity and when he went to drive me home he decided to kidnap me to his apartment in Woodbridge (at the time I had no idea where I was). I was scared but ever DRUNK and after an hour he still wouldn't take me home, so I slept with him to get out of there, and got back at 4:30 A.M. It could have been a very bad experience. I was lucky."[9] Camille Paglia has in fact defined rape as "a bigger danger than feminists know" and regrets the tendency among college students, in particular, to see rape as a matter of consciousness and theoretical equality rather than one of aggression and violent power.[10]

Revealed! Sex Secrets of Female Rabbits!

Scientifically, from the Kinsey reports onward — and from folklore forever — we know that women are more concerned with, and more sensitive to, the "romantic" (psychopleasure) aspects of sexual behavior than men are. Men are far more likely to respond sexually to straightforward impersonal depictions of female bodies, such as in magazines. Men in vast disproportion call "phone sex" businesses, which hire employees to converse lasciviously and intimately with callers, who usually pay for the service by the minute. It is overwhelmingly men who attend shows in which women or men strip off their clothes, as well as shows in which various sex acts take place. Visual inspection of women's bodies in virtually any medium excites men; perhaps it is a form of symbolic control. And perhaps that is why nude photos of famous women occasionally featured in magazines such as *Playboy* are so disproportionately interesting to men — in some minor way, they can experience a celebrated woman. It is men who also in great disproportion patronize prostitutes or massage parlors in which the social interaction is minimal and even the physical contact is fleetingly brief.

Equivalent facilities for women are incomparably fewer. While it is true that significant kinds of social prejudice, stigma, danger, and convention may inhibit women who want to do just what men do in these sexual areas, my opinion is that the simpler reason is that women do not nearly as much care to participate in those experiences. Their agendas are different. Their pleasures derive more directly from personal elements of the sexual encounter. These are related to broader reproductive issues, even if they are symbolic and metaphorical, rather than to the specific sex acts involved. Of course, men are not simply "interested in just one thing," either. As Wade Mackey, among others, has shown, fatherhood can be vitally important to men, as is shown by male behavior that ranges from jealousy over other possible mates of the women they cherish to what is often an adult lifetime of work for money to share with families.[11] It is also telling that men with children live longer than those without.

The historical and ethnographic facts about the behavior of men and women suggest that while they share many pleasures, particularly when they share each other too, they nonetheless also engage in discernibly different ones. This is very subtle indeed. The point is that the individual person may act because of a motivational system he or she is not aware of — call the person unconscious of it. But the pattern is knowable to informed outsiders — it is an ancient reproductive strategy. This is certainly the case with animals. Obviously, they cannot conceptualize their reproductive strategies. But scientists know they have them. However, the contemporary person implicitly acting out a strategy may be explicitly concerned with a wholly different set of issues. Am I handsome enough for her? Can I dance well enough? Does he approve of my views on politics and movies? Does she enjoy oral sex? He or she may be seeking a different array of pleasures from those that the sexual clasp may ultimately yield — parenthood, say, rather than the immediate thrill of making a splash at a desirable party or making love to a desirable member of the popular crowd.

It is tempting to say that people who understand both their ultimate causation and their proximate one and are best able to align them will have the fullest and most enjoyable time. They can best unite the survival necessities of the past with the opportunities of the present. I acknowledge that this view is a prejudice fermented from the juices of my trade, which is the business of restoring a sensitive link between the biology of the past and the anthropology of the present. I suspect, however, it is correct nonetheless.

There are intriguing data on the experience of the body — yes, back to the body. The claim is that the body knows. Like many others, I have heard the tales of people who say they prefer to make love without contraception, when there is a real chance they will also make a baby. Proximate and ultimate — together at last. I have heard and we have all heard from people who say they knew during a particular sex act, or just after, that it would lead to a baby. There seem to be people who are metaphorically like the female rabbit. They share her great sex secret, which it is time to reveal: she ovulates when she copulates.

Perhaps the rich in pleasure are different from you and me. Ultimate and proximate processes fuse in total identity. Like the ability to jump high or bow a violin or chair a meeting or carve a side table, some people have a better talent for pleasure and can always ovulate when they copulate, in whatever sphere. Why does it seem at once a whimsy and a necessity? Why do people have to take holidays to try to achieve it? Has anyone seen on sale a *Guide Michelin* to ultimate causes and proximate solutions? Perhaps that famous book title is correct and "living well *is* the best revenge." But what is the revenge against?

This is a chapter about the motivation of pleasure. The female rabbit enjoys a pleasure that accompanies an action that leads directly to the result the entire episode is directed toward. The rabbit is rather exceptional in this talent, if its sexual reputation and its fertility are any indication. Nevertheless, in the example of people eating sweets, enjoying a pleasurable taste and ingesting useful calories happen at the same time too. The only problem is that too much pleasure from sweetness is available too easily, because our circumstances of life have changed. Be that as it may, with sex and sugar (and notice how often the imagery of sweetness is used in the language and song of romance, to say nothing of gifts of bonbons), the physiology of the process is quite clear. Therefore, so is the motivation.

Addicted

Sexual congress offers pleasures to people at the same time that it may produce certain empirical consequences, such as babies and marriages. It is a bonding mechanism that can bring and keep people together. While frowned upon under certain circumstances, it is frequently socially acceptable, and it is unusual for it to be explicitly illegal when consenting adults are involved.

Now I want to turn to some other pleasures — ones that may produce no practical results, involve no necessary social bonding, and are often against the law. I refer to the addictions. Their importance varies in time and space. But there is clearly a chronic human vulnerability to various substances that when taken into the body produce states of experience often seen as desirable. For some people they may well become physiologically necessary.

From the addictions of individuals often flow medical and judicial consequences of no small compass. Why do people take the substances in the first place? What do they get out of them? Can pleasure centers really end up producing such personal and social turmoil? Have analysts of this problem been missing something?

Just Say Hello

A proposal: one function of mind-altering substances is to replace in people's lives the kind of social and psychological experience an Upper Paleolithic hunter-gatherer evolved to enjoy and probably to need.

The chemical and associated substances we have found and created compensate for the Paleolithic social pleasures and certainties we have lost.

That is probably why the maturing of the industrial revolution led to widespread alcoholism and multinational efforts at prohibition. Perhaps it is also why the drug crisis of the twentieth century falls disproportionately on industrial communities.

As with virtually any human activity, sustaining an addiction becomes a social matter. People develop habits, affections, patterns, cliques, loyalties. They generate ways of feeding whatever habit they have within a social context. Sometimes this milieu will initiate the addiction — for example, by peer pressure among teenagers. Or it may merely facilitate it — for instance, when alcoholics who may uneasily and secretly drink alone are also offered legitimate occasions, such as parties and other celebrations, where they can indulge their habit. Almost invariably, it seems that at least the initial stages of addiction are characterized by a mixture of chemical and social pleasure. Whatever substance is involved first smoothes the path between the user and other people. The nervous smoker receives stimulus from nicotine, and a sense of social assertiveness from smoking is also reinforced by skillful advertisements in the mind's eye when he or she confronts other people. The shy youth drinks a substantial dose of alcohol, which "breaks the ice" at a party and gives him a sudden sense of social confidence — now everyone is his friend.

In its first stages addiction is likely to be socially responsive — prosocial, not pathological. To "just say no" may require a person to reject a social group that provides crucial human contact. In effect, for souls with thin social lives, just saying no may result in self-exile. The major drugs that induce addiction generally first make social interactions seem less threatening. Think of that first glow of self-assurance after your first drink at an otherwise stiff party populated by looming strangers.

Why do drugs have this social effect?

Because human beings evolved in small-scale communities, we are generally uneasy with people we don't know.[12] The substances that can become addictive initially help create a sense of familiarity and well-being among relative strangers. Particularly in industrial societies, people have to be able to have successful interactions with strangers in commercial situations that are mandatory and social ones that are usually optional but nonetheless vital to a sense of well-being. Whatever stress this induces may seem to be reduced by ingesting substances that provide a sense of comfort and familiarity.

Climatic factors may be involved too. My friend Joseph Slater has noted a relationship between northern climate and alcoholism.[13] For example, there is a problem with heavy drinking in the northern Scandinavian countries and particularly in the Soviet Union, where winters may offer just a few hours of light a day. Does alcohol provide a rumor of the comfort, clarity, and warmth of sunlight? It is easy to underestimate the importance of light, for which an addictive substance may be a substitute, though some societies explicitly recognize its value. For example, disturbing someone's natural light is actionable in Japan, while in some Scandinavian jurisdictions it is illegal to build office structures that do not provide all employees with access to natural light. In North America, corner offices are valued not only because of who gets them but because of what they offer, which is mainly light and perhaps interesting things to see from two angles.

Even in the tropics, a significant ritual drink, maybe the first of the day, is the "sundowner." When "the sun is over the yardarm," when dusk is falling, it becomes permissible to drink. This is also the time North American bars hold happy hours, during which an effort is presumably under way to compensate both for the demands of the workday and the emergence of the night. Also, the ritual success and enduring popularity in the Judeo-Christian tradition of Christmas and Chanukah owe much to their spirited usage of festive lights and to their often alcohol-touched celebrations. It is central to their appeal that in many locales they occur in the gloomy context of deep winter and long nights. These events have religious roots. But their translation into ongoing activity depends on social acceptance and communal energy, and on the fulfillment of real needs for convivial pleasure.

Would Christmas work in July? Doubtful.

The Two-Martini Breakfast

Here is an interesting practical issue. People who drink in the morning seem doomed to serious alcohol problems. Even drinking at lunch may have a disproportionate impact on an afternoon's activity. This more pronounced susceptibility to the effects of alcohol consumed in the early part of the day presumably has to do with the fact that bodily metabolism speeds up as the day progresses. The impact of the alcohol is mitigated more rapidly.

There is a legendary tale about what happened after the advertising industry's fashionable shift from the traditional gin martini at lunch to one made with vodka.[14] An important reason for the switch was that vodka ostensibly leaves no telltale impact on the drinker's breath, so no one need suspect the nature of the individual's lunchtime beverage. But the head of one agency convened all his staff and recommended they return to the gin martini. "When you deal with our clients in the afternoon," he explained, "I prefer that they think you are drunk, not stupid."

A common misconception is that Prohibition was an American specialty. But I have already noted that in the first quarter of the twentieth century — when the industrial system was most fully establishing itself in Europe and America — there was a cascade of efforts at prohibition.[15] There was legislation in Austria, Belgium, England, Finland, Iceland, Norway, and Russia (where in the summer of 1923 half the prisoners in Moscow's jails were there for illegal alcohol trade). The barrage reflected widespread concerns that drinking reduced industrial efficiency, was of no nutritional value, and was a general depressant. This outlook was shared by very different societies, which all seem to have acted in the same way, in a new context. Alcohol could now be produced more efficiently because of industry. It could be purchased with wages earned from less labor time. And it had potentially dangerous impact on work performance, particularly when machinery was involved. The main common denominator of this was the universal response of the human body — and human consciousness — to the chemical. Countless consumers relished that response. They sought it out and purchased it — they purchased a physiological state.

How? Why? We must separate casual, occasional users of psychoactive substances from those who become committed to them in a desperate and potentially ruinous manner. A definite physiology is involved. Animals experience many of the responses to drugs that humans do. The literature of pharmacology contains many discussions of how animals ingest substances and display interesting behavior as a result.[16] Humans appear to follow suit.[17] There are also apocryphal tales such as the rumored discovery of coffee by an Abyssinian goatherd who observed the unusual friskiness of his animals after they ate certain bright red beans later found to be coffee.[18] Certainly, pigeons enjoy and seek out hemp seeds, which contain small hits of cannabinoids and have been called "pigeon candy."[19]

If animals are given access to cocaine, other psychostimulants, and the opioid drugs for only a few hours, they will self-administer the substances: ". . . drugs can elicit their characteristic patterns of behavior on a normal biological substrate and . . . no preexisting psychopathology or addictive vulnerability is required for initiation of drug self-administration."[20] Having one hit of a drug does not produce irrevocable results. Other animals and presumably humans are able at least for a short while — perhaps a very short while — to sample drugs in a relatively recreational manner. Extensive evidence indicates that "captive primates will show a remarkable drive to intoxicate themselves" and that humans and apes will "share a pursuit of the exact same drugs."[21]

There may even be an evolutionary basis for this, given the close interdependence of animals and plants throughout time. It has been argued that the origin of the substances that become used as mind-altering drugs was no more recent than 135 million years ago, when plants began producing various toxins as a defense against herbivores. By and large nature is a miser, a keeper. These toxic weapons of flower wars have endured. Isolated, refined, and spotlit, they are the basis of many psychoactive drugs.

Prison Cells and Brain Cells

So addiction is in some deep sense "natural." It is lodged in basic cellular processes of not only human brains but other animals' too. This raises dramatically difficult questions. Is it ethical to interfere with a "natural" process? If it is, who should have the license to do so — medical, legal, moral authorities? Or is the fact that addiction has animal roots reason enough to assume that it is therefore primordial and *should* be under strict control?

And what are the consequences of such interference? Could some inner ecology be disturbed? For example, we know that people deprived of REM sleep (rapid eye movement is a sign of dreaming) often show deterioration in social function. If everyone is naturally addictive in some sense, what does this mean for the validity of the concept of the so-called addictive personality? Is everyone an addictive personality?

But of course there is natural variation too. For example, though the matter is controversial, there are indications that vulnerability to alcohol may be linked in some degree to genetics. Among humans, "children of alcoholic biological parents are more likely than other children to misuse alcohol, even when they are separated from their biological parents in infancy and placed in stable adoptive homes."[22] Rats have been bred for alcohol preference.[23] Serious suggestions propose that ethnic differences in enzyme response may produce different kinds of social patterns of alcohol use — for example, a contrast between Amerindians and people of Mediterranean origin.[24]

There is also a different genetic predisposition to seek alcohol than there is to lose control after drinking it. This is a fascinating and medically important finding because though the huge majority of Americans take alcohol, only some 10 percent of them consume 50 percent of it.[25] Does a similar pattern apply to use of, say, crack or cocaine? If it does, this could significantly alter how societies at large respond to drug use. It could also calm any public fear stimulated by statistics about rising consumption; perhaps the same people are consuming more each, just as wine drinkers are consuming more premium bottles. This is an obvious oversimplification, of course, because the culture surrounding drug use has clearly expanded its influence, particularly among very poor citizens.

The relationship between potentially addictive substances and social behavior can be seen in the case of alcohol. Initially, it is a weak stimulus. But it follows rules similar to other addictive substances once a particular threshold is crossed. This varies for each individual. On the other side of an individual's threshold, dependency begins.

But there is a significant difference between alcohol and some other major mind-altering drugs. Alcohol acts on considerably more sites in the brain than either the coca or opioid derivatives. More of the brain is involved. This suggests that alcohol is linked to a broad set of social and communicative responses associated with particular bits of the brain. Alcohol possesses more keys that turn on more parts of the brain. Here is a potentially revealing neurophysiological clue to the social impact of alcohol: it blankets the brain with effective stimulus. This may also underlie the widespread association throughout our species between alcohol and social occasions.

A striking indication of this relationship is the growing alcoholism among young women, who increasingly drink like men. This behavior is linked to new pressures faced by women who have entered the labor force. They are affected by the social patterns connected with work that center around drinking.[26] The problem is exacerbated for women who match men drink for drink: "since women typically weigh less and have less muscle tissue, they can expect to have more unpleasant side effects, like vomiting, slurred speech, mood swings, hangovers and depression, than men."[27] There are also enzymatic digestive responses that cause a relatively sharper and quicker impact of alcohol on women than on men; almost twice as much alcohol is not absorbed by the female body before it goes to the bloodstream and then the brain.[28]

Here is a graphic case in which an addiction may result from a single pattern of socializing, even if there are two rather different groups operating by the same rules. These rules of convivial conformity appear quite robust — for example, in the Canadian army there is a process that has been called "drinking level": everyone consumes equivalent amounts. This both exerts group control on consumption and shares out fairly the cost of successive rounds of drink, since in groups of drinkers each individual buys in turn. This is similar to the traditional Japanese way of drinking sake: people do not pour their own drink but instead pour that of their partner, who in turn pours theirs.

Like many others who regularly drink among familiar people, the Canadian soldiers in this process are not feckless and undisciplined. They are people whose skills at work and self-control have permitted them to acquire and hold desirable jobs that are intensely cooperative and rule-oriented. This sharply focuses the basic issue here: the addictive process, which can become antisocial and pathological, begins with intensely social, normal, pleasurable behavior.

This is obviously central to our problem in this book. It appears to depend on the underlying fact that the human brain is richly equipped with receptors for pleasure-giving substances. In nature, and presumably during our evolution, these substances were produced through social interaction itself. Now, with the aid of vintners, distillers, and chemists, they can flow from the mouth of a glass. Or you can get to heaven through the tip of a needle. This poses for society and its members a remarkably vexing problem. Or is it a colorful opportunity?

Guided Tour

How precise a problem? How manageable an opportunity? Dr. Larry Stein chairs the Department of Pharmacology at the University of California at Irvine. With his colleague James Belluzi he has been able to train single brain cells to respond to a rewarding dosage of cocaine. To a journalist he said:

> The fact that *cells* respond to a reward shows just how deeply embedded in the design of the brain this reinforcement mechanism is. . . . The purpose of life is to activate our reward systems. . . . Dopamine and the opioid peptides are transmitters in very powerful control systems based on a certain chemistry. . . . Along come poppy seeds and coca leaves that have chemicals very similar to . . . these central systems. They go right in, do not pass Go. . . . To say that cocaine or amphetamines — or heroin or morphine — should be highly appealing is an understatement."[29]

Stein and Belluzi show that these responsive cells are dispersed in various parts of the brain. Their great sensitivity to addictive substances suggests that addicts suffer from a biomedical brain disease or flaw, not a character flaw. A healthy brain is like a healthy animal, evolutionarily designed to respond positively to what has supplied pleasures to those receptors in the brain for thousands of generations.

The pleasure centers function as a bureau of physical and behavioral quality control. They "advise" — even individual cells can — the organism whether or not what it is doing is consistent with the good and successful things its ancestors did before it. Is the fruit sweet and healthy or sour and poisonous? Does a particular behavior feel pleasurable and secure or does it produce anxiety? Does the environment seem controllable and prosperous or is it replete with random menace and intimidating, abrasive foreign forces? And if at the end of the day the bottom-line balance of neurotransmitters lurches heavily in the direction of anxiety, well then let's have another drink. And let's call it the "happy hour" or the "attitude adjustment hour" that marks the transition from the apparent stress of the impersonal workplace to the generalized comfort of private life.[30]

This is hardly complex. At the level of a whole society, however, something fascinatingly consequential is involved. Suddenly, here is an intensely political question every society faces: what should we do about private pleasure? Can we let people have unlimited amounts of it? What happens to communal activity when private experience is overwhelmingly interesting — when private enjoyment is more compelling than public service? What does a sensible community do when surprising private pleasure can be derived from substances that are generally available?

This is what Prohibition was about, and the war on drugs, and the perceived restorative virtue of martial law. It is at the heart of the distinction between the etched certainties of discipline and the colorful turbulence of experiment. It underlies the persistent seesaw between the austere decisiveness of Apollo and the flowing fun of Dionysus. It is the main flavor of one of the most enduring human dialogues. A hot question versus a chilling threat.

Finally, all of this is experienced, integrated, summarized, and evaluated in brain cells.

Brain cells. Meat.

The Waterloo of Addicts

Essentially, it is with their brain cells, not their politics, that many people yield up their grip on freedom. They become addicts. To the imperatives of breathing, drinking, eating, and eliminating, they add an obligation to find and consume a particular substance. Whichever one they choose will give them a rush of pleasure. It will sweep away the grave anxiety and generalized physical anguish the deprived addict invariably feels. While the physiological process of becoming addicted is complicated, the essential first step is the use of some substance such as alcohol or nicotine or cocaine to which receptor sites in the brain will respond.

This is the cortical equivalent of the sweet tooth. It is also the bitter danger. The process of evolution has for whatever reason resulted in a human neurophysiology that responds vividly and avidly to some quite common substances. The addictions are a considerable and chronic problem for societies mainly because they depend on very common mechanisms.

Everybody's brain has them. Everyone is a potential beneficiary of their pleasure and a potential victim of their depredations. Jesuits claim they will own a person's spirit if they can secure their being to the age of seven. But infants are born with addicted bodies because their mothers are addicts. They can receive a fix with mother's milk. When I was in high school, perky pretty girls in cheerleaderette costumes would stand near schools and hand out free samples of cigarettes in packs of five to older students. Around the turn of the century, Brazil, experiencing a coffee surplus, sent a year's supply, free, to Japan, which had no tradition of coffee drinking. Since then it does — it's hooked. A whole country. Similarly, modern crack dealers give a few free hits to youngsters, some of whom become addicted. Since they have no money, they must either engage in crime to acquire some or recruit new addicts, to whom they then become suppliers. If they are female, they may turn to prostitution. Especially desperate women haunt crack houses where the price of a sexual episode is the price of a fix of crack — in 1991, about five dollars.

This is all grimly predictable. It is a far cry from the occasional romantic memoir about the liberating and artistic effects of various potentially addictive substances and their importance to the creative process. Without question, there is a relationship between the various addictions and the arts. It appears, however, that creative people use such substances in a kind of self-defense — because artistry is difficult and lonely rather than because they make artistry easier. Psychoactive substances may facilitate the work of some creative people. For others they may offer the illusion of competence but yield quite a different reality. For still others the effect may be broadly negative, causing either avoidance of work or outright physical deterioration, or both. In any event, notwithstanding enthusiasts such as Samuel Coleridge and William Burroughs and the narco-redemptionists of the 1960s, the negative relationship remains.

I want to take a deliberately simple and straightforward approach to addictive behavior based on several general biological principles. One is that since there are pleasure centers in the body that respond to materials brought into the body, we assume in practice that the pleasure the substances deliver is indisputably "natural." But at the same time, we see that a particular substance may produce physiological effects such as lung cancer and death, or psychological effects such as extreme paranoia and reckless aggression. These are plainly harmful to the user. Therefore, we cannot assume that the dose or use level is "natural" in the benign sense.

Some threshold has been crossed. The tickle has become a scratch. The scratch becomes a gash. A difference in degree becomes a menace of danger.

The question changes rather suddenly. Are we also entitled to conclude that if a lot of the substance produces danger to the individual and is therefore not "natural," even a little is aberrant too?

This has been firmly believed by many moralists and governments. There are people who think a little beer is okay but insist that a little heroin isn't. There can be, and are, a variety of positions on this matter. They all have to come to terms with the relationship between pleasure, nature, and social control. The availability of pleasure-giving substances dramatizes this relationship in ways that can become convulsive both politically and economically.

With alcohol in the early part of the twentieth century and cocaine toward its end, the control of access to the pleasure centers of the brain became a central feature of political action and moral dialogue. The Opium Wars of the nineteenth century were about the freedom of the British to continue to supply narcotics to China, in effect to legalize their distribution and use: free trade for British pushers and Chinese addicts. This was 180 degrees different from modern events such as the US invasion of Panama to capture Manuel Noriega or threats to blockade producing countries such as Colombia with warships. These are about the opposite impulse, to control drug use. But whatever happens in its neighborhood, the complex thriving brain remains ever vulnerable and ever experimental, always at the core of the array of intoxicating possibilities that man and nature proffer.

A Reader's Advisory

A brief note in review. I am trying to re-view the matter of addiction by stressing the demand of the body for pleasure and identifying some of the natural mechanisms humans have for receiving such pleasure. Brain secretions and receptors, which evolved usefully in response to social stimuli, may now be affected by either natural or chemical substances that people can acquire or make. This changes quite decisively the importance of "yes" and "no" in the chain of events that leads from abstinence to moderation to addiction. The question is, are individuals *capable* of saying no? If so, how difficult is it? What responsibility, if any, does a community have to help their decision?

Please note this is not, at least so far, a discussion about morality or right and wrong. It is about mechanisms, chemistry, about the physiology of Nirvana, about the struggles of reason. This approach is technical but still very consequential.

One for the Road

There are at least two important differences between the pleasure yielded by certain significant addictive substances and the pleasure derived from other, more social enjoyments, such as conversation, sport, gardening, and sexual congress. These are specifically social pleasures and involve other people. By definition, there is some limit on them. Sex involves partners and so do conversation and sport. Physical limits of endurance and patience clearly define these activities. Gardening involves natural reality, such as earth, seeds, light, and the seasons that affect implacably the extent and kind of pleasure a person can have.

But there needn't be any social or natural control of addictive drugs. A person can dose himself up to the earlobes with cocaine or cognac or heroin without intervention from anyone else and without looking at the calendar or the clock. The potential protectiveness of other people is not necessarily available. In fact, as with drug users and their suppliers, the people involved with the addict's habit may exacerbate it, not control it. In the case of alcohol and cigarettes, glamorous advertising campaigns legitimize and support the addiction. For example, beer producers advertise heavily during televised sports events or sponsor teams and events themselves to try to create a robust association between the use of beer and the healthy competence of athletes, an association particularly influential among the young.[31]

There is yet another broad biosocial principle involved. Not only may there be no social control on the addict, there may be relatively poor physiological control too. The physical deterioration that results from drug use takes far longer to emerge than the addiction that causes it. By the time the addict can be fully aware of the impact of the drug on the body, it may be too late to recover from the addiction without extraordinarily demanding measures of detoxification, therapy, and life changes, to say nothing of coping with economic, personal, and legal consequences that may be massive and even overwhelming.

It appears that certain professional athletes have been able to use drugs for fairly prolonged periods before their exacting performances have been noticeably affected. Obviously, there is a fair amount of self-delusion too — the individuals believe that they can control their use of the drug just as they can handle various other physical requirements of a highly demanding athletic career.

The use of illicit drugs by celebrated athletes is quite remarkable in fact. The extent to which highly rewarded players jeopardize their careers reveals the power of the substances they abuse. It also may suggest the social pressures that drive them to use drugs. For example, in 1989, before what was likely to be the most important football game of his career — one that would earn him tens of thousands of dollars if his team won and that would be watched eagerly by hundreds of millions of people — a player on the Cincinnati Bengals was suddenly suspended for using cocaine *the night before* the Super Bowl.

It's dramatic and revealing that players of a difficult and dangerous game, at the peak of their careers and with full knowledge of both the peril of the drug and implications of discovery, would still consider the use of controversial and illegal substances. It is also quite striking that many other outstanding athletes — football players Dexter Manley of the Washington Redskins and Lawrence Taylor of the New York Giants, the masterful Naples soccer player Diego Maradona, pitcher Dwight Gooden of the New York Mets, and boxer Sugar Ray Leonard, among numerous others — were at some point in their careers sufficiently committed to the pleasure of drugs that they missed action and required extensive therapeutic treatment. If such extraordinarily well rewarded and adulated individuals succumb to the lure of brain cells distorted by chemical desire, it is small wonder that people with lives of far smaller dimension yield to the blandishments of brief moments of chemical grandeur.

Drummers' High

But there is another way of looking at this too. Perhaps the lives of athletes, popular musicians, and other celebrated entertainers are so intense, experienced at such a "high," that only powerful drugs can match the experience of performance. Perhaps rock concerts are phenomenal experiences for talented performers, or maybe games are for athletes. Such activities may occupy relatively few hours of the week, however, and hardly any over a year. What happens in between?

One possible solution is to import the dazzlingly high experience chemically. But the essential problem and the basis of addictive tragedies is that in a substantial group of people there seem to be relatively poor natural controls over using the addictive substance. Even with food, the overeater becomes literally stuffed and may be unable to hold down what is consumed. (The Romans famously attached "vomitoriums" to their dining rooms so that indulgent gluttons could easily repair to these facilities, relieve themselves quickly of their feasts, and return and start eating anew.) The avid drinker discovers he has consumed too much long after he has actually passed the point of competence. The smoker may never know she has smoked too much until the cancer is diagnosed. The crackhead may lurch from obligatory high to obligatory high without understanding the nature and meaning of what happens to him in between, let alone what's going on during the magnetic event itself.

One possible reason for the popularity and general acceptability of alcohol is that the overdrinker has a survival advantage: he may harmlessly pass out or will act so incompetently that others may quarantine him from trying any activity at all. Obviously, however, such protectiveness is frequently absent. Particularly when the drinker is also a driver, accidents can occur. Stricter enforcement of traffic laws that prohibit drunk driving can have a positive impact, as was first seen in Scandinavia.

But what happens to the drug user depends on the specific drug. The addict may be energized by crack, dazzled into hostile action by amphetamines, or lured into gentle false security and a sense of quiet omnipotence by tranquilizers. He can remain active nonetheless, destructive to himself and to others. The problem is compounded by the variety of drugs that are currently available, the wide assortment that are likely to emerge, and the complexity of understanding individual (or even general) responses to them. Given the spirited inventiveness of amateur botanists and skilled chemists, there is little doubt that promises of novel thrills through new products — which are often relatively inexpensive and easy to produce — will continue to tempt the market. It seems clear that the rapid spread of crack, for example, had to do not only with its impact on the user; significantly, it is uncomplicated to produce and handle, and even more important, the per-dose cost is low enough to attract almost everyone. Certainly the relatively low cost of alcohol is also a factor in alcoholism. In the United States in 1990, there were some 17.7 million adults with apparent alcohol problems; slightly more than half that number — 9.5 million — were chronic users of illicit drugs.[32] In the Soviet Union, alcohol consumption rose 250 percent between 1955 and 1984. It is estimated that some 20 million Russians are dependent on alcohol, which is, of course, a legal drug.[33]

In this context it is necessary to wonder about the consequences of legalizing drugs. Doing so could have the effect of making them widely available under benign public scrutiny. As well, perhaps they could be salable at reduced prices, since the cost of illegality — of maintaining criminal conspiracies to import, produce, and distribute — would be removed from the final charge (though one estimate is that the "cost of illegality" is less than 10 percent of the street price, because the cut taken by smugglers is but a small percentage of the final price).[34] My view is that the legalization argument is wrong and dangerous, and I will return to the fray of that discussion later. But for the moment, it is enough to note that many of the liberal commentators favoring legalization of drug distribution are also skeptical critics of the free market. It is difficult to discover why psychoactive substances should be exempt from their general suspicion about unregulated trade.

The Lean Gene Revisited: Man Is a Foul-Weather Species

Here is a proposal that I have to admit I think is bold: *The fact that we have so few reliable natural controls on the addictions suggests that we evolved to live in environments in which scarcity was more common than overabundance.* We are not designed to cope automatically with whiskey, heroin, and Valium in the way we are able instantly to reject putrid meat, too-sour fruit, and air that smells of death. It appears that our natural systems are not adapted (or "preadapted," in biological terminology) to cope with the buffet of potentially perilous options spread before us.

Presumably, this is why in countries with an abundance of food, overeating is a serious health problem. It is as influential in its impact on health as undereating is in poor countries. Cardiovascular disease remains the most serious killer in North America. It results mainly from eating too much of the wrong kind of food. The principal control over this misconsumption is the good sense of individual people. Of course, this can be abetted by the efforts of responsible cooks and other producers to create foodstuffs that minimize sclerotic impact on the consumer — for example, replacing butter with olive oil and other minimally hazardous fats. But finally will, or conscience, or intelligence, or sense of responsibility, or effective caloric accountancy must be the mechanism in place. For countless people — future victims — this conscience or censor appears unequal to the task and then years later the ambulances scream in the night.

Nature endowed us with enormous inventiveness, curiosity, and capacity. In the case of food, this virtuosity has resulted in our omnivorous ability to acquire and consume an elaborate array of different foods, differently prepared, varyingly presented. Humans create and enjoy a remarkable range of foods and occasions on which to consume them. In the long run, however, some of these appear to be deleterious. Nature did not provide us with quick and infallible ways of sensing the danger before it is too late. It is certainly difficult for many people to appreciate the cumulative effect of their dining choices over what must seem an incomprehensibly long time. It is difficult for a hungry teenager with three bucks in her pocket to comprehend with conviction that an inexpensive, satisfying, and tasty bacon cheeseburger savored at eighteen will have a discernible impact on longevity at sixty-eight — even though there is graphic evidence that dangerous fatty arterial deposits form as early as three years of age.

But, hey, if evolution is the mighty force I have claimed it to be, why didn't *Homo sapiens* evolve a physiology friendly to greasy hamburgers? The answer is, time, in two senses. The most direct is that the preponderance of diet-related disease, such as heart attacks, occurs late in life, once the reproductive phase of life is over or nearly so. The deleterious effects of dietary choice will not reflect themselves in the changing genetics of the species. Unless eating hamburgers directly affects the hormonal or associated systems of reproducing couples — for example, by rendering cholesterol consumers less fertile than connoisseurs of broccoli — the impact of diet will be felt too late for there to be any difference.

The same consideration, time, is likely to apply to the astute question asked by writer Jeffrey Steingarten, who wonders how at least fifty thousand years of human cooking could not have had a discernible impact on human genetics.[35] It is certainly possible there is some such consequence, perhaps equivalent to the development of the enzymatic capacity to digest dairy products, which northern Europeans acquired after they took up pastoralism. But this involved a relatively modest change in the balance of digestive secretions. Altering the manner in which the cardiovascular system copes with unprecedented amounts of cholesterol would require substantial genetic variation. But the historical time period of high-fat meat is far too brief to encompass it, and the number of cholesterol consumers worldwide is relatively small. Here is another example of the potential dangers in the volatile interaction of attractive substances from outside the body and the very conservative processes inside it.

The Right to Life, the Right to Death

Genetic change may be very slow or nonexistent. But social change can occur rapidly and with great consequence. As far as diet is concerned, informed individual decision-making broadly works. There have been substantial changes. People in the industrial communities eat less fat red meat and butterfat products and this has resulted in clear improvements in mortality. There has also been some reduction in consumption of hard liquor and inexpensive wine.

Of course, the stimulus for much of this is related to reasons of personal health care, vanity about the body, and the like. Also, some of the decline has been caused by legal changes, such as the driving-while-intoxicated laws I've already mentioned.

Nevertheless, while the casual use of alcohol and of some drugs has stabilized or been in mild decline in various social groups, the overall problem of addiction, both to alcohol and to other drugs, appears to have increased in severity in many communities. Certainly the international scene in drugs is one of unprecedentedly large increases in demand and hence supply — the cocaine trade has expanded at least two-hundred-fold in ten years. Newly afflicted countries such as China and Yemen are beginning to feel the presence of growing numbers of addicts.

This raises quite striking issues about the significance of freedom and restriction. Do we need society's control because we can't depend on nature's? Like Larry Stein and James Belluzi's addiction-prone single cell, are we all readily open to a fix, and a fall? What does it mean that of the estimated 27.2 million alcoholics and other drug abusers in America, only some 615,000 are in publicly supported treatment, with 70,000 on waiting lists?[36] (Private centers average occupancy rates of only 55 percent.[37]) Obviously, there is a discernible shortage of public treatment facilities, a circumstance that cannot help but discourage already fragile and disturbed potential recoverees. Nevertheless, the persistence of the problem and the broad passivity of individuals in thrall to their central nervous system appears to indicate the depth of the problem. The situation is sharply exacerbated by the fact that only half of cocaine addicts remain drug-free for more than two years after treatment, while crack users appear to have an even more difficult time achieving full recovery.[38]

Note again that I do not raise this issue in a theological context. There is no suggestion here that the power of the addictions and their danger justifies the pageant of moralities based on God that celebrate the various famous "thou-shalt-nots" of religious theory. My point of departure is altogether secular. In a nutshell: is it the role of the government to protect people against the consequences of pleasures they freely choose for themselves?

This remains a central question of politics, religion, and morality. Many government activities are clearly disadvantageous to particular citizens — for example, the widespread promotion of lotteries, which beguile impressionable and largely foolish players with the dramatic lure of large winnings. The citizen-suckers are allotted disproportionately poor odds, and governments then employ the profits from misleading some of the people some of the time to support state activities that would presumably otherwise require tax monies from all of the people all of the time.[39]

Governments also obviously benefit from taxes levied on such addictive and dangerous substances as nicotine. But in only a few jurisdictions and only long after the scientific facts were made abundantly clear was there any serious effort made to inform users of the known health risks of their habit. As the century ends, more governments are adopting medically acceptable policies in regard to nicotine — for example, US and Canadian regulations that limit smoking on aircraft; Norway's control of public smoking; and France's restriction of tobacco advertising. On the other hand, the US government still supports export of cigarettes, the Soviet government still permits their import, the Japanese government offers only the most desultory admonitions to its population of heavy smokers, and the Chinese government appears to ignore the issue altogether while tens of millions of its people huff and puff despite potentially fatal consequences.

Government, Heal Thyself

Governments can be callous about exploiting the vulnerabilities of smokers and lottery players, among others. So how do they justify attacking other pleasures, such as using cocaine? And attack they do. In 1971 President Richard Nixon said in a Rochester, New York, speech: "Drug traffic is public enemy number one domestically in the United States and we must wage a total offensive, worldwide, nationwide, government-wide, and if I might say so, media-wide." Twenty years later, his successor George Bush sent troops into Panama, helped overthrow its military government, captured its leader, Manuel Noriega, and flew him to the United States to stand trial on charges related to drug trafficking. Between these two administrations, a parade of "wars on drugs" continued a long-standing crusade that had begun much earlier. As described by Edward Jay Epstein, it was sparked by Captain Richmond Pearson, who translated a celebrity fraudulently earned from his activity during the Spanish-American War into a highly public battle against alcohol. He became the highest-paid speaker on the lecture circuit and was an organizer and supporter of the temperance groups that proposed and achieved Prohibition.[40]

After 1921, when the new law was in place, Pearson was discouraged to notice that the various social ills such as crime and premature death that he had so convincingly linked to alcohol did not in fact decline. After a brief withdrawal from public life, he returned with a new and yet more villainous cause, heroin. This evil possessed the additional and attractive quality that it came from abroad. It was even, possibly, a substance wielded by foreign governments, particularly Germany, to deprave and weaken the American social system. (The drug was trade named by the Bayer Pharmaceutical Company, which had tested it on its German employees and found that it made them feel "*heroisch*." Thus the name.)[41] By 1928 Pearson was able to announce to the American people that "most of the daylight robberies, daring holdups, cruel murders, and similar crimes of violence are now known to be committed chiefly by drug addicts who constitute the primary cause of our alarming crime wave."[42] Sounds familiar.

Heroin is a depressant. In the first scientific studies undertaken of it, it was described as unlikely to lead to assaultive crime. Nevertheless, it generated a popular "enslavement theory" that "most crime was not the work of hardened criminals but of innocent individuals afflicted with an unquenchable addiction."[43] The perception was widely employed to justify more stringent police activity against the drug and its users. From 1930 until 1962, Harry Anslinger, who was director of the federal Bureau of Narcotics, expanded the prohibitory mandate by colorfully including marijuana; he stimulated Congress to pass the Marijuana Tax Act of 1937, all the while also stimulating the delivery of increased funding to his department. In a historical reversal from the earlier Opium Wars, there was even a charge that Chinese communists armed with opium were taking over the task begun by the heroin-wielding Germans of assaulting American civic integrity.

Epstein paints a remarkable, detailed, and wholly plausible picture of the function of the war on drugs in various questionable initiatives of the US federal government. It reached a culmination of some kind in the Nixon regime's Watergate scandal. An array of the personnel involved were officers in the drug war, such as Gordon Liddy, who as a prosecutor in upstate New York raided LSD advocate Timothy Leary's rented estate in Millbrook, and Egil Krogh, who convinced John Ehrlichman that yet another war on drugs could be an effective centerpiece of Nixon's 1972 presidential election campaign. In addition, various politically sensitive and practically difficult tasks could be accomplished in a seemingly trouble-free manner: "the Liddy plan . . . was that the White House agents would now act under the cloak of combating the drug menace"[44] — as the Office of Drug Abuse Law Enforcement.

I've no intent here to chronicle the mean-spirited near-buffoonery of political pawns elevated by unworthy leaders to positions beyond their moral and civic competence. But it is significant that the menace of drugs was seen — and remains relevant — as a morally acceptable and politically salable source of administrative action and bureaucratic ambition.[45] Nearly a generation later, a similar charge has been brought by Franklin Zimring and Gordon Hawkins of the Earl Warren Legal Center at the University of California, Berkeley, against a similar crusading enthusiasm of the

Bush administration antidrug leader, William Bennett; Zimring and Hawkins have asserted that by statistical malefaction an actual decline in drug use has been turned into an alarming increase, all to bolster the latest model drug war, the National Drug Control Strategy. Because fewer people are using cocaine, the proportion of people who use it frequently has necessarily increased — this is just baby statistics. Nevertheless, the actual number of real people involved has decreased. The issue is mathematical: "a man's arms will constitute a greater proportion of his total body if you cut off his legs, but that doesn't mean his arms have grown."[46]

In the Nixon era the drug vendetta was, in clear retrospect, a shabby affair of political opportunism. In the 1990s there may be a different, higher level of desperation among addicts and a somewhat greater public disruption because far greater amounts of drugs are being imported, grown locally, and sold. When does the celebrated difference in degree become the celebrated difference in kind?

Chemical Scapegoats

One constant steadfastly endures: the enthusiasm for drug bashing. Perhaps this is only as a convenient political tool. But with drugs is there something more, too? Is there an acknowledgment here of human tissue-frailty and a recognition that there but for the grace of . . . what? . . . go we all? Is governmental harshness against drugs a generous act?

The final point of any discussion of this issue has to be the question, Should drugs be legalized? Here is a colorful and controversial choice. Should we uphold private pursuit of private pleasure? Or should we continue to support the state's historic claim to define, regulate, and possibly tax acceptable pleasures?

Images affect the choice. On one hand, ultimately there seems no major difference between the stumbling addicts who scrounge for handouts near crack houses and the lines of registered English heroin users who would wait at the all-night pharmacy at Piccadilly Circus to get their next day's legal dose as soon as possible after the stroke of midnight (this system was abandoned in 1967 in favor of a clinic system rather like the American one). On the other, the phenomenal funds generated by drug dealers and the violence they commit to protect their interests, to say nothing of their corruption of the agencies of government, are hard evidence of the political and economic impact of the trade in its illegitimate form. Could anything be worse? It is small wonder that the grim consequences of drug illegality periodically stimulate a cadre of informed and responsible persons who push for a decisive shift in public response to the private demand for drug-driven experience.[47]

Does caveat emptor apply to such intensely private matters as sniffing a powder or smoking a particular compound? One of the most common analogies to illegal street drugs is with alcohol, and particularly with the Prohibition experiment in the United States that eventually resulted in repeal. It also left a legacy of criminal organizations that had been created or expanded to respond to a whole new opportunity to gain profits from widely used beverages. Instead of liquor taxes, which existed before and after Prohibition and went to the government, the markup went to a miscellany of adventurers, including organized criminals, Canadian and Mexican producers and smugglers, suborned officers of the law, and an extensive apparatus of people illegally performing services that had formerly been part of the essence of normal American life.

Certainly, a number of the practical goals of the protagonists of Prohibition were met. Consumption declined. Liver cirrhosis became a diminished medical problem. Fewer people landed in psychiatric wards because of alcoholism. Whether the moral character of the population was improved, and whether the quality of private life improved — presumably these questions remain a matter of opinion, most likely tied to the commentator's point of departure. But Prohibition undeniably remains a vital factor in the argument over legal drugs.

Just Add Water and Mix

Is the comparison of alcohol with other drugs fair?

No. The comparison is unacceptable. There are important differences, both practical and medical. (I leave tobacco out of this because it has a different, very long-range kind of impact and appears to produce no immediate, dramatic behavioral effects by comparison.)

One difference is of major importance. It is extraordinarily simple. It is also astonishing that it appears to be largely ignored.

The difference is water.

Distributing alcohol involves moving around a great deal of water. Alcohol is virtually always in liquid form. It requires containers, usually of breakable glass. It requires sturdy boxes to contain and cosset the glass. One result is that alcohol is heavy. Another is that its packaging is relatively fragile. Yet another is that it is cumbersome and relatively difficult to conceal, particularly at the production and wholesale levels. It requires substantial equipment for its transport. This is why in the USA during Prohibition organized crime developed a strong grip on the Teamsters Union, which was essential in illegal distribution. Because of its weight and bulk, it is advantageous to produce alcoholic drink near centers of consuming populations — no high Andes breweries for Chicago.

Because it is in containers, it is relatively easy to tax with excise stamps. It is also very visible when it is consumed. Bottles are left over. There are used glasses, cocktail shakers, and the like. Therefore taxing and police authorities can exercise scrutiny over where it is sold and, to some extent, to whom — for example, not (in theory) to underage patrons.

There are other aesthetic concerns that decisively affect how surreptiously alcohol can be dispensed compared with powder drugs. Consumers often prefer it cold, and frequently with ice. Hence, bulky, costly, and quite permanent facilities for controlling temperature are also part of the drinker's preferred package and the supplier's necessary installation. Since the psychological impact of alcohol may take some time to affect its users, usually seating must be provided too. Particularly for beer enthusiasts, relatively convenient toilets are essential. And since the majority of drinkers do so in company, it is usually good business to provide tables, booths, entertainment, a large bar, or some other comparable instrument of conviviality. (Remember, during Prohibition bars were called speakeasies, not drinkeasies.)

These are very different circumstances from those in which

illicit drugs are produced, distributed, and used. The most dramatic difference is in weight and volume. A large suitcase carried by air can travel from anywhere in the world to anywhere in the world. It can contain sufficient drug material to supply as many people with highs as would require truckloads of beer or wine. A retailer doesn't need a refrigerator and seating arrangements but can under a modest overcoat carry enough crack to satisfy a neighborhood. He or she is a walking bar. The wholesaler can make do with an ordinary automobile. Obviously, marijuana is far bulkier. But its storage and distribution are still far less trying than alcohol's. As well, like opium, it can be grown almost anywhere, even in underground bunkers; and it requires relatively little horticultural sophistication.[48]

Consequently, the movement of street drugs is incomparably less visible than that of alcohol. This implies that even were it a legal process, it would nevertheless be very difficult to monitor should it be necessary or desirable to do so. Inevitably, this means that restrictions — such as on consumption by the young, or at certain times of day or night, or on holidays, or in public places — would be more difficult to enforce than they are with alcohol, the supervision of which is clearly difficult enough as it is. For example, the use of drugs in pill form would be virtually impossible to regulate in public places such as schools, workplaces, and places of assembly.

Because of the physical character and highly portable and concealable nature of such drugs, they are relatively easy to consume quickly — and alone. This is very significant. It can underline and potentially exacerbate the alienating impact of drug use. It makes it easy for people to use drugs in isolation, without possible mitigating (or encouraging) influences such as "drinking level" and other forms of peer pressure.

The social element is, of course, central to my concern and my argument. Substances function as enhancers or replacements for satisfying conviviality. We know that "people who drink alone" are especially prone to alcoholism. Apart from the sharing of needles during the process of shooting up, which appears for some to offer elements of ritualistic, almost sacred conduct, there is no technical need — such as a bar, a cooler, storage — that compels users of illicit drugs to indulge themselves in the presence of others. Of course, "shooting galleries" and crack houses do exist, in many jurisdictions because acquiring needles and syringes requires a prescription and those who possess them rent them to those who don't. (Even where needles are distributed by government, usually relatively few are given out compared with demand, so those who do receive them can enjoy a ready source of rental income. Since AIDS is often transmitted through the sharing of needles, the human and medical consequences of such poorly executed and restrictive policies are clear.[49]) But such drug centers do not appear to be places where social control on consumption is effective. In fact, the anthropologist Phillipe Bourgeois of San Francisco State University, who is studying drug use in East Harlem in New York, described the situation in most houses as so morally structureless that on one occasion he violated his neutral status by interfering with a crack house manager who was about to sell drugs to a pregnant woman.

I am making a general point: the ability to purchase and use psychoactive drugs in a solitary manner reinforces and enhances a process of individual alienation that is a chronic and defining feature of the industrial form of society. Living in this system is sufficiently stressful that significant numbers of people will grasp opportunities to change or escape their experience of life by quietly and privately ingesting tiny amounts of substances that yield colorful psychological results.[50]

Does the widespread association of drug use with industrial society reflect the special stresses associated with it, as well as the wealth that members of rich societies are willing and able to spend on drugs? This raises a major question about the very nature of industrial social organization, and the more particular issue of the possible consequences of legalizing drugs within it.

First of all, there are very practical factors to consider. For instance, many members of industrial cultures operate large, heavy, frequently fast-moving machines ranging from aircraft to trains to electric generators to private cars, as well as installations in factories and workshops. It is significant that a study of transportation accidents revealed that no less than one-third of the people responsible had been under the influence of one psychoactive substance or another. There is no way of estimating how many other accidents are indirectly caused by drunk or otherwise drugged individuals. An obvious difference in the scale of consequences exists when an Andean coffee farmer receives a buzz from chewing coca leaves and an American boat captain drinks vodka close to the time he tries to guide a supertanker through a complex Arctic channel.

Presumably, legalizing an array of psychoactive substances in addition to alcohol, caffeine, and nicotine — all of which have some behavioral consequences — increases the likelihood that some proportion of people will use them in inappropriate circumstances, just as they now use the legal drugs.

Recall that I am now considering two strong forces: the lively motivation for pleasure, which depends on a central nervous system prepared for it by evolution, and a social system that does not readily provide sufficient pleasurable satisfaction of the kind with which we evolved. This same system also has the technical capacity to acquire or produce a considerable array of substances that affect consciousness in ways people find enjoyable. Yet these substances also degrade the body. And so the body is a danger zone.

Don't Motivate the Motivation

We have seen that people often want to change their psychological experience and can do so more or less easily and skillfully with the help of an array of available substances. The human brain has receptors for natural secretions that result from various natural activities important to our evolution, such as exercise, sexual congress, warmth, sociability, foods, security, and the like. But now people can induce such primordial satisfactions with a variety of substances that — to abuse an unduly graceless cliché — produce the gain without the pain.

Should the list of legal substances providing these satisfactions therefore be expanded? My own answer is that they should not. Not for a moral or legal reason, but principally because the human central pleasure system is too avid, too frail, and too addiction-prone. It doesn't make sense to subject it to any more perilous blandishments than it has already.

The medical implications of smoking are as plain as day and anyone who smokes must deny or obscure reasonable and simple facts in order to continue receiving physiopleasure. Yet hundreds of millions of people smoke and nicotine addiction is one of the most difficult to shake. If another substance like nicotine that provided a modest fix several dozen times a day were discovered, would it make sense to subject the population to the new provocation if it was also carcinogenic? No. Then why expand the floor area of the legal drugstore?

The matter is not altogether clear-cut. Though some people become addicts, most don't. We know from Phillipe Bourgeois that crack users will be more active on the weekends when they get paid than on Monday and Tuesday. We know that terminally ill patients permitted to choose their own dosage levels of coca-derived painkillers will usually choose the minimal amount to control their pain. We know that fashions in drugs wax and wane, that the dangers of one sink in and of another are forgotten. For example, crack use declines while heroin use — formerly disdained — begins to increase.

Many people can control their habit, whatever it is, and even if they approach the edge, they don't fall off. Nevertheless, there *is* a major drug problem in many communities. It is a problem more the result of the search for physiopleasure than of rejection by the legal system. It is historically true, if also an irony, that the most successful addiction entrepreneurs are those realists who disdain the substances that surround them and provide them their profit. In another context, distiller Samuel Bronfman, the Montreal patriarch of the house of Seagram, told his children: "Booze is to sell, not to drink."[51]

Legal but Not Tender

I underscore the power of "why" — the subject of this chapter. The motivation is there. It is strong. It is often surprisingly recalcitrant. Even a statistically compelling threat of early death is insufficient to budge battalions of smokers from their desired physio-

so pervasive, and so inexpensive. Can there be other sins — for example, sexual ones — as easy and convenient to commit and as cheap as buying a pound of butter and spreading it deliciously on fresh sourdough or whipping it into mousse or frying one soft-shell crab per generous tablespoon?

With so much tasty food available so easily, what is remarkable is not how many affluent people are overweight, but why there are aren't millions more. Why isn't a food-driven country such as France entirely populated by people the shape and size of its Michelin man, the jolly figure of the tire company whose annual restaurant and hotel guide is a vital icon of sublimated national gluttony? It is also interesting that France has a relatively low incidence of cardiovascular disease, though its diet is similar in cholesterol and other characteristics to that of Americans, who suffer far more from this affliction.[7] One serious explanation comes from R. Curtis Ellison, chief of the Section of Preventive Medicine and Epidemiology of the Boston University School of Medicine. The principal distinction, he suggests, is the greater consumption of wine in France. He relates the different health experience to the well-documented protective function of moderate amounts of wine, about two or three glasses per day, which reduces cardiovascular risk.[8] Consumption of large amounts of garlic may be involved as well — it appears to reduce cholesterol.

Surrounding food is an endless battle involving pleasure, calories, vanity, the fear of early death, lust for taste, and sociability. It has come to seem ever more theological, particularly in North America. The higher the death rate from food-induced diseases goes and the more rampant becomes the information about the extermination model of food, the more pervasive is the explicit conflict between meat and morality and between pleasure and prudence. Traditional supermarket products such as pastas irrelevantly boast that they are cholesterol- and sodium-free. Advertising copy about olive oil no longer rhapsodizes about the antique terraced groves of Liguria in which the fragrant source of the golden liquid is hand-picked. Instead, there is a grim medical report about saturated fats and the inner tubes of the buyer's arteries.

If in the name of science you eavesdrop on people talking in restaurants, you may hear them calculating which food is good or not for them, rationalizing the high-calorie animal-fat food because it's a celebration or a holiday. They decide, "Let's splurge on calories" — splurge, that is, on intake, not expenditure. Whatever their decision, it is clear they are wholly aware of the medical and moral meaning of the food they will consume. One person in the restaurant business told me that females frequently consult the dessert menu first and plan the rest of their careful binge accordingly. The writer and broadcaster Martin Goldensohn has commented that married men's eating of high-cholesterol food when they are away from their considerate and careful wives is a contemporary form of male infidelity. And even when fast-food outlets do offer low-fat, nutritious food, there is clear marketing evidence that customers continue to choose their traditional favorites.[9]

At the end of the twentieth century, the apple is widely regarded as a healthy food — vitamin-filled, fibrous, clear-cut, virtuous. But what if Adam had offered Eve an agonizingly rich apple *pie*, nearly hot, either with taut *crème fraîche* or sharp cheddar cheese?

In any event, even vaguely informed consumers contemplate the dilemma: should they sin by eating the hot apple pie with cream or cheese, die earlier, and probably go to hell? Or should they reject the dessert — any dessert — and linger firmly with a glass of spring water, extend their life, and get to heaven?

It is necessary to extend Bertolt Brecht's aphorism "a man is just the food he eats." Now, people's *souls* are the food they eat. It has gotten devilishly complicated.

Playing the China Card

If the mouth were a male sex organ, it would be erect all the time. It appears that people are in high and chronic readiness for the pleasures of food. This poses a particular problem for members of communities with ample food and no sense of oncoming scarcity. Is there a model to follow that will both yield pleasure and protect health? Or is the only plausible alternative to adopt stringent diets bursting with fiber, complex carbohydrates, just the odd morsels of meat, fish, and poultry, and microscopic traces of fat. One such diet, proposed by Dean Ornish when he was at the UCLA Medical

School, restricts animal and fish protein to 10 percent of daily intake — and there is some evidence it reverses cardiovascular damage suffered by heart-attack victims.

Possibly such a draconian diet is desirable for people already victimized by a lifetime of high-fat eating and in dire need of remedy and repair. However, there is some indication that whole cultures can develop patterns of diet that provide enjoyment and endurance at once. Two come to mind, the Italian and the Chinese. The Mediterranean diet of which the Italian is an exemplar uses much fresh fruit and lots of vegetables, little butterfat, much olive oil, and carbohydrates such as pasta, polenta, and risotto, fish when available, and relatively little meat. Because of strong local culinary traditions and regional pride, international fast-food restaurants have fared relatively poorly in Italy and the result of these and other factors is a health profile unusually positive in comparison with other industrial countries.

But perhaps the most interesting and significant healthy diet is the Chinese.[10] It confronts directly the desire for pleasure in food within the confines of economic constraint. First of all, it is an immensely successful cuisine, feeding as it does one quarter of the planet's population in Asia on a daily basis, and countless other people, too, who enjoy it virtually everywhere in the world. As well, because of historic famines and the pressure on arable land, food in China has unusual social importance. A common morning greeting is "Have you had rice yet?" or "Have you eaten?" And there is an extensive traditional lore that surrounds Chinese cooking — for example, about foods that are "hot" or "cold" — with implications for health and social solidarity.[11] Food has an importance equaled by the traditional skill of its chefs.

During my first meal in China, a central value of Chinese cuisine was clearly if simply revealed. This was at the Fragrant Hill Hotel on the outskirts of Beijing, near the Summer Palace. The menu handed us in the dining room was long and detailed, and the English translation was the second half of the document. The first entries were predictable and understandable enough. Appetizers, soups, beef, pork, seafood, fish, vegetables, and then — *Food.* Food was noodles and rice, the substantial carbohydrates. This was the essence of the meal and it was named for the generic substance. In common and traditional Chinese cuisine, all the other items — apart from the appetizers — were principally used as flavorings for whatever grain was being consumed. Unlike Euro-Americans, who will usually order Chinese food with one main protein item for each diner, Chinese people will extend the pleasure value of their rice or noodles by adding to them small portions of the special dishes. And this is why these preparations are usually so clearly and highly flavored — they have a lot of aesthetic work to do, much flavor to deliver. The sharp salt or sweet or spicy or otherwise highly sauced food rewards the diner with sufficient oral pleasure to make the bland rice or noodle staple tolerable. The chefs have responded at once to the need for pleasure and the constraints of China's economy by producing a vocabulary of dishes that ensures a lively dinner.

Because the food is usually chopped into small bits, it is quick to cook, retains its fresh food value, and is frugal with scarce cooking fuel. Because the small pieces each have a large surface area relative to their bulk, they can absorb and carry much more flavor than if they were in large portions such as steaks or filets or whole chicken breasts.

Several vital social features of this cuisine also help sustain its popularity. It is crucial that the food is shared. Rather than separate dishes arriving as the individualistic property of separate people, one per person, here there is a rush of different plates offering a variety of experiences. These are shared out either informally by the diners or by the host or hostess, who will wields that "big spoon" and urges guests to sample the array.

Another aspect of the social meaning of Chinese food is that because the food is shared, diners are obligated to attend to the intake of others and adjust their own choices accordingly. As I have noted, the most desirable and honorable guest at a Chinese dinner doesn't reveal his favorite food by eating much of it. He eats least of what he likes most. He must orient to the group. Also, the ethically ideal table shape is round, so that everyone is equidistant from the food, which is usually on a lazy Susan in the center. This emphasizes the democratic nature of the meal and the interdependence of the diners.

The net impact of the balance between carbohydrates and other foods, the negligible amount of dairy fat consumed, the colorful variety of choices, and the large component of freshly cooked vegetables result in a diet that delivers a large number of calories but by comparison with, say, the American or Belgian diet, leads neither to obesity nor cardiovascular damage. It is also possible that the ambiance of the Chinese meal makes what they eat particularly satisfying. People can eat less than they might on their own — no clean-plate club in China. Because the meal form is so satisfying, there is a relative lack of emphasis on desserts in Chinese cuisine. Traditionally, people would finish with soup or rice. This recalled deprivation and affirmed that during this meal they had eaten amply. The economic factor plays a role here. Nonetheless, fresh fruit is often the only dessert offered by even ambitious restaurants in China, and by overseas Chinese elsewhere who suffer no shortage of food whatsoever.

I Hereby Sentence You to Dinner in the Cafeteria

It is merely banal or redundant to announce that nutritious food should also be tasty and offered to diners under agreeable conditions. But this hasn't governed the catering for countless schools, prisons, hospitals, and even private kitchens in which convenience, habit, and sufficiency loom larger than pleasure and invention. I was once told by the Vancouver architect Arthur Erickson that he wanted very badly to design a hospital, along the lines defined by the classical Greeks. Sick people should have the most beautiful architecture, the best clothing, the most interesting artwork, and the most delicious food. After all, they are ill and need it most. An elegant idea, it took the industrial world's medical system many years to realize that a sense of treatment as punishment was not helpful to patient recovery. Meanness can cost more, too, because patients recover less quickly.

There is little reason why the same Greek principle should not extend to the healthy; pleasure is not only desirable but, as I have tried to define it, is also an evolutionary entitlement. Not only that. Where food is concerned and simple survival is not the issue, its taste and meaning, and its art, may loom far larger than nutrition. This can run easily to foolish extreme. The remarkable American gastronomic writer M. F. K. Fisher describes how during the fatal reign of Louis XVI of France, humble cow's milk became a fine delicacy when it was expressed and presented by aristocratic ladies. Evidently, the more adventurous not only offered the milk but provided their admirers with porcelain drinking cups made from impressions of their breasts.[12] The gruff Napoléon who followed later on and who had other priorities soon extinguished this folderol of food. But the principle of embellishing nutrients stands. Pleasure remains a principal goal.

Gone Fishin'

It has been wistfully observed that the heart is a lonely hunter. But human beings are not lonely hunters or lonely gatherers. While the move to agriculture some ten thousand years ago required our ancestors to complicate their social arrangements drastically, even hunters and gatherers lead strongly complex social lives and in general are intensely cooperative when they gather food. By contrast with the animals closest to us, the other primates, we are highly cooperative food gatherers. Once they are weaned, the other primates tend to acquire and consume their own food — though they will communicate with each other about fruiting trees[13] and will occasionally — among the baboons, for example — cooperate to catch and eat a small mammal such as an immature gazelle or other primate. Nevertheless, as adults they are principally independent operators who each eat what they can individually acquire.

Not so people. Not only do we cooperate but we enjoy it. In some contexts this we call work and in others recreation. For example, hunting and fishing remain the two most popular participant sports in North America despite the cost, inconvenience, and danger, as well as the legally restricted return even skillful predators may earn. (The Canadian government has estimated that the average sport fishing enthusiast spends about $350 to catch a single salmon.[14]) In an almost wholly industrial society in which 90 percent of all trout consumed in America are raised on farms, and despite ever-scarcer land and growing criticism of gun-using hunters, squads of eager men and, in some cases, women wake before the autumn dawn to squat in cold, damp blinds hoping to outwit ducks or to engage in spylike sorties in forests hiding leaping deer.

Such groups possess signal emotional meaning for their members. One hunter in British Columbia described the meaning: when he drank rye whiskey, he customarily purchased Seagram's VO; but when he went hunting with his chums, they drank only Crown Royal, the ranking premium brand. In American society, male hunting and fishing groups (as well as regular gambling cliques) offer one of the few examples of enduring groups that cut across the lines of social class. So a bank manager and a dentist and a mechanic and fireman may hunt together, though they will be far less likely to belong to the same golf or country club.[15]

My proposal is that the emotional satisfaction of cooperatively acquiring food, in nature, stimulates voluntary and often intense solidarity between men — the communal activity Wendell Berry refers to and calls a source of "pleasure . . . so to speak, affection in action."[16] They continue to enjoy this, however inconvenient the process and however costly per pound the ultimate yield of protein. It feels good to people when they do it now, when it's a luxury, because it felt good when people did it back then, when it was a necessity. Food gathering — what was acquired and how — was obviously critical to survival. The emotionality surrounding such cooperative gathering of food was part of the selective evolution of our species, like the emotionality surrounding courtship and sex. People who enjoyed each other and the process of cooperative food gathering were more successful than loners or noncooperators. This was part of the package of successful behavior and adequate nutrition transmitted to the next generation.

It is surely significant that people with all the money necessary to feed themselves and those they care about more than adequately nevertheless seek to reserve to themselves the privilege of the chase.[17] I have a cottage in New York State in an area rich with trout, deer, wildfowl, and rabbit. Hundreds of thousands of potentially valuable acres are kept pristine so that the members of dozens of hunting and fishing clubs can on a relatively few occasions during the year re-create the secretive strategies of the Upper Paleolithic less than two hours from Times Square. My outsider's sense is that the members think that what they are doing is close to the sacred, a luxury beyond dollar calculation. One legal deer per year, some trout, some noisy birds — worth it, worth it disproportionately for the *pleasure*.

There is controversy in anthropology about the status of the hypothesis that hunting had an overwhelmingly decisive physical and emotional impact on the evolutionary scheme. A strong and technically skilled group of scientists have asserted that early human beings secured most or much of their meat by scavenging — by taking or stealing the prey killed by master hunters such as lions. They base their interpretation of the archaeological record on detailed and exquisite study of, for example, the microscopic marks made on fossil bones found near human sites — marks that appear to suggest, among other things, that the teeth of other animals made the first or main impression on these remains.[18]

They have a point. There is evidence from various other fossil finds and from contemporary ethnography that reveals that people were and are opportunists.[19] They will take quick advantage of another species' kill if the killer is gone or can be driven off. Leopards and hyenas can be made to flee, though lions are reluctant and may become prey themselves if the human hunters are sufficiently numerous and confident.

Nevertheless, there are some problems, too, with this notion. One is, of course, that dead animals, particularly in the hot climate in which we evolved, would be dangerous to eat if not quickly consumed. Presumably for this reason, many animals, including domestic cats, will not eat a prey animal they have not themselves killed. This reflects an evolved inhibition, complex but understandable. As well, the existence of the dead animal implies a stronger living one that killed it and that may retain some interest in it — for example, a lion. Reposing much confidence in the tolerance of a large predator for theft of his kill is plainly potentially hazardous.

But my principal question about this scavenging hypothesis is raised by what provides pleasure to contemporary people. Do you know of one royal scavenging preserve? Do you know of one club where people pay high fees in order to scavenge the leavings of others? Is not the status of ragpickers, "bag ladies," urban scavengers, the least enviable in the social system? Do they compare in any way to the hunters with their ceremonial red jackets, their complex leatherware, their costly guns, their killing grounds? No. The two groups are incomparable. One is envied, the other not, even though in a simpleminded sense the scavenger's job is safer, easier, and closer to home.

But one is fun, the other isn't. One yields pride, the other resignation. I think this reflects an evolutionary heritage that focused most passionately and skillfully on hunting, and only from necessity and episodically on scavenging.

Most people are unlikely to be fervent about this seemingly technical academic argument. But it may guide us as we try to examine what contemporary behavior is pleasurable — to earn an insight into what worked for us in the past and perhaps, in some complex but durable way, selectively gained a foothold in our nature. Only a few people enjoy being hit with whips. Nearly all enjoy gentle caresses and sexual intercourse. Why? This is "natural" — the result of our evolutionary nature. There is something intrinsically sensible in the idea that what pleases nearly all people must have helped most of their ancestors endure. It seems likely that the way people choose today to acquire wild food reveals something about how we used to get it in the past. The low status of scavengers in societies as disparate as Belgium and India (where the caste system formalized it ruthlessly: they were the Untouchables[20]) suggests that this is a compromised form of survival.

Compromised, and no fun.

Gone to Market for Hearth Food

If scavenging for food is not fun, shopping for it often is. Outdoor markets and ambitious food shops are widely attractive to both purchasers and voyeurs. If such shops don't permit hunting, they offer gathering, in a garden even more plentiful, various, and colorful than any imagined Eden. Contemplating, comparing, choosing food obviously involves elaborate and absorbing skills and enthusiasms.

One of the most interesting markets in the world is the Tsujuki fish market of Tokyo. By four o'clock in the morning, a vast congress of buyers and sellers converges around what seems to be a virtually complete aquatic museum of natural history. Because so much fish is consumed raw in Japan, as sushi and sashimi, choosing it is a vital part of preparing it. A sushi chef can stand or fall on the freshness and quality of what he buys as well as on how he prepares it. The market is intense, varied — a phenomenal display of demand for what people can and want to eat and the ability of fishermen to find and provide it.

The Tsujuki provides a snapshot cross section of Japan's dinner that day. With the inexorability of digestion itself, the improbable, exuberant spectacle happens every morning. By eight-thirty the heavy traffic ebbs. The retail trade begins. Then the thing to do is have a sushi breakfast in one of the restaurants nestled at the outskirts of the market, where its participants repair after their late-night negotiations.

Perhaps it is because I am a grocer's son, but there has always seemed to me to be a special and significant drama to markets. They encapsulate well much of what people are doing and efficiently dramatize whatever flora and fauna of the region pertain to human society. But I mean markets, not supermarkets or groceries where you see and smell packages. There is a firm difference between the clinical rows of boxes at the MallMarket and the piles of cardamom, oranges, mangoes, and fifty-seven varieties of rice in the Bombay market or the one in the Old City of Jerusalem, or the spectacular jumbles of Ibadan or Accra, or even the comparatively wan earnestness of the Greenmarkets in New York City.

To a traveler, some of the difference is undoubtedly the result of the exoticism and intensity of new environments. Nevertheless, there is also a difference in the naturalness of the heaps-of-herbs market versus the wall-of-boxes store. One is gathering at its best, the other is administration. Of course, good markets are also well managed and there is a clear and traditional order to them. They may be visually lively and seemingly fresh, but the arrangement of stalls, who occupies them, and under what terms is not casual. The markets convey a sense of deftness and directness — the person behind the counter today may have yesterday been behind the plow. This somehow rounds out the meaning of the food. It was never possible to charge very much at the Automat, however good the food.

Nude Food

The distribution system pioneered by Huntington Hartford of the A&P stores in the United States has enabled more people to enjoy healthier, more abundant, more various, and more interesting food at a relatively low markup than other extant systems. The US industry norm is that net profit hovers around 1 percent of volume. However, as the century draws to a close, the most progressive and successful chains draw particular profits from traditional, primordial, boutique-type sections of their stores: in-store bakeries, fish markets, prepared-food sections, custom butchers. Produce is increasingly displayed in hearty and relatively dramatic ways. Theatrical lighting designers have entered the grocery business. Sensual visual appeal replaces perfect clinical geometry as the style of presentation. A grim blend of sub-Bauhaus aesthetics with perfect row-house hygiene yields to vivid and lucid displays of naked food. Voilà! Tableaux of suddenly rediscovered artisanal culinary drama: the baker baking, the butcher slicing, the barbecue chef assessing the food, the smoke, the heat.

In these lusty sections, the markup is much higher than in the grocery Bauhaus. The operators of industrial-style food stores were surprised that people enjoy ways of selling food that are nostalgic, even primitive. But the marketers have been adept and are adapting. The industry is changing. Shoppers are willing to pay extra for what they perceive as interesting and robust food whose origins and preparation are accessible and plain. Not only "natural" food connects, but seemingly "natural" ways of selling it.

A fruit-and-vegetable store called Balducci's in the Greenwich Village neighborhood in which I once lived redigested itself into a beyond-scale temple of food. Nonetheless, it retains some sense of a neighborhood feedlot (though now a rich neighborhood). Busloads of tourists come from the suburbs to explore food shopping that is sensually intimate. It is a sensory success. The memory recurs to me of the effectiveness of the Food Halls of Harrods in

London. This is the luxurious upper-class shop marked by traditional English reserve in most other areas. But its celebrated food shop is visceral — hanging game unplucked, colorful, flagrantly dead and elegant; fish swimming in ice at arm's length; cheese odorous and unpacked; unrinsed wild mushrooms pyramided in their traveling crates. It is a sentient, dramatic shop, the jewel of the enterprise, borne of passion not propriety.

If people feel there is a danger that food will exterminate rather than succor them, they will want to control the process of feeding themselves and thus enjoy what they consume. It becomes at once pathetic and reassuring that the word "natural" on a food product is supposed to be an endorsement. It is pathetic because what else but natural things should be permitted to enter the stomach? At the same time, it's reassuring because people want contact with elemental substances along with the pleasure they enjoy during their pit stop — smell, taste, flair, aggressive surprise, anything. The stomach — that turgid bottom-line arena of encounter between person and environment — will do its work, no problem. But before that obligatory chemistry, there's an opportunity for play. Enjoying food.

Lively people become tax collectors. What they eat in order to survive must also yield some tax. The tax is pleasure. Not just from candy, either. Think about your best dinner during the past seven months. It was mainly not dessert.

Cooking with Gas

Hunting, fishing, gathering, gardening, and shopping for food provide pleasure. Obviously, so do cooking and serving it. Here is the end point of the underlying mammalian transaction, the POP — the point of purchase. For the hungry person it may be better to receive than to give. But an elaborate suite of pleasures is associated with feeding other people. Virtually everywhere, there is a colorful mixture of art, technique, economy, and tradition. This is called cooking — the art of how food is prepared.

How people fashion the substances that sustain them is of deep interest to them. There is usually an added extra ingredient; the herbs, spices, and other flavorings, how and when they are added, and the various methods of preparation. Take a common and drastically simple foodstuff such as lima beans. Try to predict how many genuinely different recipes will exist for it in the world. It is likely you will underestimate severely. There seems to be no limit on the quite urgent aesthetic ingenuity of cooks. There is also surprisingly little real loss of already successful recipes.

Culinary knowledge has been maintained as lore and tradition. It is a pervasive, unquestionable element of daily life. Formal schools for cooking are a relatively new addition. Apprenticeship has been the customary way of training professional handlers of food. There are also systems of inherited status, such as the Indian caste arrangement. The principal route for learning about food ran through the home kitchen, across the dining table, or by the fireside. The extraordinary variety and invention in the foods people produce are revealing. They confirm the role of pleasure in both production and consumption. They underscore the significance of pleasure in determining what people decide to do with their time and energy. Food is not just part of the veterinary process of feeding people. It is the starting point of recurrent pleasure.

Not all is artful folderol and cultivation of the mouth's muse. There is nutritional justification for major elements of interesting cuisine. Beans must be cooked or they can be dangerous. Yogurt contains enzymes that allow people who otherwise couldn't to digest milk solids. Roasting pork to a tasty turn kills potentially dangerous parasites. Garlic and onions add decisive tastes to food and provide a variety of medical and antiseptic benefits.[21] Piquant marinades are interesting to taste and also tenderize and even "cook" some foodstuffs.

Nevertheless, pleasure counts big. Like music, which is not necessary for survival, food, which is, can be fun to make. This is genuinely optional pleasure. It is unlikely that we are genetically urged to cook. No chromosomal whispers are known to lure us to the stove. Cooking depends on our control of fire, an ability we acquired relatively recently in our history; it is not probable that there has been genetic selection for good cooking, at least in the modern sense. But for better providers of more interesting food — yes. Better hunters and gatherers will set a better table. Skillful butchers, skinners, peelers, salad makers, and nutcrackers would then as now benefit themselves and those who ate their food with a real advantage in both the productive and reproductive systems.

Fire and cooking sharply heightened the ways to enjoy the pleasures of food. They must have enhanced the impulse to create and share these pleasures. Cooking was the social equivalent of the wheel. Our exquisite and dauntless sensitivity to tastes and smells, which impelled, governed, and guarded our consumption of food, now could be turned in a symphonic way to its production. The stakes were suddenly higher. If the way to a man's heart was through his stomach, the way to a woman's was through her broiler and her breadbasket. Once communities expanded, particularly after the emergence of agriculture and pastoralism, feasts became a hard central feature of social interaction, especially between and among families. As Lévi-Strauss instructed us, the sharing of food was next in importance only to incest prohibition. The exchange of mates between families was the only process more significant for human evolution than food sharing. But it was also wholly associated with it;[22] the wedding dinner established a circle of implication and meaning.

The new methods of food production increased supplies markedly. The new social density they permitted and required also turned food into the focus of much of the domestic and familial diplomacy around which social life now turned. Skill at producing pleasure at the table had a new meaning for social status, for marital arrangements, for political and similar alignments. It defined and supported the network of female alliances so crucial to sustaining and monitoring the social group, because women managed the distribution of food.

Recent discoveries suggest that hunters, gatherers, and, later, foragers lived with considerable and unexpected complexity. Excavations in Denmark reveal that foraging groups some five thousand years ago were quite large. It appears that they were both affluent and sedentary. They successfully made the transition from a culture dependent on the reindeer. They settled near water, hunted large sea prey such as porpoises and whales, and collected shellfish and fish[23] — this provided the bulk of the diet — much like contemporary Greenland Eskimos, who take 75 percent of their food from the sea. Interestingly, it has been estimated that prudent hunting among the Aleutian Islanders would have required a core group of some six to eight families involving about seventy-five people.[24] This already presupposes a fair amount of cooperation, mating arrangements, and the like.

Of course, cooking was available to add complexity and taste to food. Like the 1820s Manhattan dinner described by James Fenimore Cooper, dinner around the campfire, in the tent, cave, igloo, or copse, both defined social life and stimulated the enjoyments of the mouth. Compare the dinner of five thousand years ago with the newly traditional barbecue, with its particular primordial attention to the taste of smoke — grapevine, mesquite, apple, hickory, charcoal, always surrounded by the magnetic aroma of charring fat.

New foods and more food meant more opportunity to create more tastes and new ones. Hence, more and new pleasures. Now — then — not only food but also its taste could be exchanged. The currency of the pleasures of the mouth increased in complexity. More syllables permitted more vocabulary, which made speech more elaborate and, hence, eloquence more conspicuous. The language of food and its complexity also developed new norms of complicated excellence. Not only cooks but sailors explored the spice routes.

Society Was in Ferment but 3867 BC Was Still a Good Year for Burgundy

Something else may have been added at that formative time too. Booze. The anthropologists S. H. Katz and M. M. Voigt of the University of Pennsylvania have speculated that the development of agriculture was decisively stimulated by the discovery that when the treated and mashed seeds of grain lingered with liquid the mixture fermented to became beer. Despite the common suggestion that beer was first produced some 5,000 years ago, an earlier date of 8,000 to 10,000 years ago is suspected by Katz and Voigt. Some of the earliest pots of that period reveal the trace of beer. They surmise that this was such a desirable product that people made sure they had the grain with which to make it.[25] They also speculate that the desirability of the liquid directly stimulated humans to cultivate grains that till then had been gathered in the wild. If agriculture was an emotional step backward for humans, moonshine eased the transition.

Women were principally responsible for this innovation. In pre-Columbian Peru women made the beer *chichia* by soaking some grain, chewing it to begin the fermentation process, and then returning it to the original pot. If we take seriously the general enthusiasm of contemporary people for alcohol, we can conjecture that those ancestors of ours would hesitate to stray too far from their stash of beer fixings, in contrast to those foragers who liked to move on. Perhaps alcohol was an unexpected ancient inducement to settle down. Virginia Badler of the University of Toronto has discovered traces of wine in fourth-millennium containers associated with the Sumerian traders of the Tigris and Euphrates valleys. These containers were found in dwellings of some opulence — which suggests that then, as now, wine was associated with the good and satisfied life.[26] My suspicion is that there will be future discoveries showing the presence of potable winelike beverages even earlier in our history; the beginnings of agriculture probably mark the onset of the wine trade. Our ancestors were physiologically much like us, and likely to respond as we do to strongish drink, which is one of our favorite pleasures. How many contemporary Americans — or English or Italians or Chileans or Australians or practically anyone else — would willingly move to a wholly "dry" jurisdiction?

Some major and very populous groups — Muslims, some Fundamentalists, some Hindus — have strong inhibitions about consuming alcohol. Often the prohibitions relate quite directly to one theological assertion or another. Believers disdain the fruit of fermentation because they accept that God wills them not to drink. Faith is the deciding factor. As the British wine scholar Hugh Johnson has noted, the Islamic restriction on alcohol had a theological origin rooted in particular problems of social disruption during the time Koranic lore was being established; evidently, a fracas in Medina led to Muhammad's instruction from the archangel Gabriel (with whom he had several interviews) to forbid both wine and gambling, which were the work of the devil.[27] Drinking in certain other social groups, too, is an indulgence often associated with improper behavior. It appears to threaten the sense of controlled obedience that worthy believers try to maintain. At the same time, sizable numbers of people abstain from alcohol for reasons not necessarily related to religious authority. It has been estimated that some 40 percent of Americans are teetotalers.[28] Many of these people may simply not like alcohol or enjoy the effect it has on their experience and behavior.

But if Katz and Voigt are correct, this did not pose a problem to our forebears. Perhaps then there wasn't (and to this day there isn't) a necessary connection between religious belief and strict temperance. The opposite may even be true. This is suggested by Hugh Johnson's comment that the word "divine" is related to "*de vin*" — of wine — and the fact that there is frequent use of wine in religious ceremonies or festivity. There is a consistent if sporadic religious commitment, at least by the Catholic church, to the grape, even though its mind-changing properties may affect behavior in potentially impious ways. A number of important liqueurs, such as Benedictine and Chartreuse, are produced by monks. It was the Franciscan missionary Fra Junípero Serra who introduced the grapevine to California around 1770; and the Christian Brothers still produce brandy there. Champagne was perfected by the Benedictine Dom Pérignon. And admirers of the lusty Rhône wine Châteauneuf du Pape should thank for their enjoyment Pope John XXII, who evidently as a matter of some needy priority established vineyards near Avignon when it became politically necessary to relocate the papacy there for a while.

In Veritas, Vino

Obviously, wine plays a sacred role in various religious practices — most dramatically in the Holy Communion of Catholicism. (Johnson notes that white wine was used originally, to avoid the problem of garishly stained religious garments.) In various Jewish ceremonies and festivals, prayers marked by wine are in order — for example, during the Passover seder. Schnapps — whiskey or brandy, but anyway, a dark, strong liquor — was a common and I think typical feature of toasts and celebrations in my recently arrived immigrant family. Among Protestants as well as other groups, toasts with wine or stronger fare — such as fierce mao-tai in China, or vodka in Russia — are common. Particular religious festivals are often associated with alcoholic drinks, such as eggnog or grog or glug at Christmas.

This is not to suggest that any or all of the religious groups that use alcohol in one way or another intend to stimulate drunkenness, profligate expenditure, or some other imprudent or irresponsible behavior. But many religious authorities not only condone but also promote at least the modest use of alcohol in the context of legitimate and sometimes sacred occasions. This implies an understanding of the simple fact that people are likely to enjoy it in an acceptable manner. Alcohol in small amounts invariably provides some pleasure to virtually everyone and stimulates a sense of convivial comfort with fellow consumers. At the very least, the association of alcohol with religious celebration reveals the good "marketing" sense of the supervisors of religious groups. They have it within their grasp precisely to decide what is acceptable and what is not. In general, they have decided to allow alcohol.

Were it true that religion is the opium of the people, as Karl Marx announced, then alcohol is the neo-opiate at the core of many religions. Of course, it is not so simple, since religious ardor has a drastically more serious point and broader mandate than promoting a feel-good enthusiasm at ritual meetings. But one step at a time; a good time is had by all at a modest local gathering fueled by a touch of alcohol. It seems to offer a congenial overall setting for more serious observances. It is also an implicit reassurance that the system of dos and don'ts that religions invariably promote is neither dully heartless nor wholly opposed to pleasure. Ethanol helps the clenched fist open to God.

The buzz of booze is a plus. Sacred affairs and normal daily life come into agreeable contact across the cortical tissue when we are stimulated into affability and comfort by flavored alcohol — the ancient liquid friend. From infancy on, human beings are uncertain about unfamiliar people. But as I have noted, usually the first firm drink at the cocktail party suffuses the victim of personal uncertainty with some confidence that he or she is at least an adequate person, able to survive this sudden tournament of strangers. Human beings no longer live in communities of ninety souls. A major job requirement in industrial communities is that it is often necessary to confront strangers. This is why alcohol has often been so important in business — the two-martini lunch was principally about fear. Not license. Not pleasure. But alcohol *seemed* to help. Probably it did for a time, whenever there were strangers on the horizon. But once it became quotidian, day-in-day-out, no. Enter the alcoholic, stage right and left. And this is why Arthur Miller's surgically revealing play about his character's death would have been trivial had Willy Loman been a drinker, not a salesman.

God, This Is a Tasty Riesling!

Even the gods may join in. I've described how before a feast or funeral or wedding or installation of a chief or just a bash, West Africans will pour a libation of gin or other liquor into the earth, for the ancestors (who are also gods) to enjoy. Then they are part of the party. This is less the worship of ancestors than their inclusion. The liquor helps complete the circle. In its sudden warm way, alcohol expands the comfort zone. The party now includes the dead and the future. The members of the party can embrace the convivial event confidently and with a sense that the social world, even the heavens, are populated with friends. When a West African baby is "outdoored" — brought outside the house for the first time and hence into the wider community — several drops of water and several of liquor are touched to the infant's tongue, to instruct it early about this evidently important difference. The water of our vastly ancient aquatic origin. The alcohol of our brand-new settled farmer's still.

Small, even introductory amounts of alcohol appear to possess the power to re-create the affable, familiar certainties of the meal around the fire at the mouth of the cave. It is hardly surprising that some religious institutions benefit from this property. It is probably also no accident that the major organized religions originated around the turbulent period of history in which people began to depend on animals for work and for predictable food, and on foods they cultivated and ate — some of which they fermented in a multitude of ways and then drank! Agriculture was and is a difficult way of life — which is one reason people leave it and stream to what are often dauntingly unpromising cities, where even catch-as-catch-can life appears to be more appealing than farming. This begins to explain why barely 3 percent of Americans grow all the food for the USA and much for other countries besides. Though there are other, rather heavy political reasons — for example, the disproportionate power of rural voters — I suspect it is also an underlying and basic reason why the rich societies in Europe, North America, and Japan so extravagantly and peculiarly subsidize their farmers. They have to, because otherwise people wouldn't farm.

It was no accident that the origin of agriculture was associated with the emergence of organized religion and the probably coterminus development of the arts of fermentation. Something had to be done to lighten the present and future of the lives of farmers. Booze helped. But when the average American, Briton, and Belgian has to drive over forty-five miles back and forth to work each day, the old arcadian inebriation is no longer Falstaffian and appealing. The car is the enemy of the cocktail. The pleasure of release, at home in the farmhouse, from the constraints of long growing seasons and the hazards of nature is replaced by terror of the sound of screaming rubber and collapsing metal.

To this day, there remains an association between spirits, especially wine, and home. It appears that 75 percent of wine in the United States is consumed in homes, and of those occasions when it is, 82 percent center on sharing food.[29]

Yesterday, Six Hundred People Dropped By for Dinner

When I was a college student I worked as a kitchen helper — dishwasher, actually — at a construction camp in Frobisher Bay in the Canadian Arctic, where the Distant Early Warning radar line was being built. In the social assembly of the dining area, the chef was the ardent, temperamental master with the power of employment over people and a firm grip on the mood and rhythm of the kitchen, to say nothing of its product. All three individuals who had the post during the two summers I worked there exhibited a quantum difference from anyone else in the kitchen in their sense of sèlf and their willingness to define the lives of others. Of course, this was partly a show of the industrial-relations kind, partly simply their jobs, partly idiosyncratic, and partly the romanticization of the Leader, the Chief, the Chef.

There was also the huge practical matter that this man was responsible for ordering well in advance appropriate and sufficient food, which was flown in at great expense from lower Canada and then had to be converted into some eighteen hundred meals a day acceptable to a crowd of hardworking and demanding individuals marooned in this outpost for at least six months at a time. For entertainment, movies were shown twice a week at the United States Air Force base, which was the core of the operation. There was a weekly softball game for those who could tolerate the battalions of mosquitoes that took advantage of the two warmish months of summer. There was no alcohol. While there were some Eskimo families in the area, a detachment of Mounties enforced a firmly announced ban on fraternization.

But there was food, which played a more salient, dramatic, and even poignant role than in the average factory cafeteria. These were men placed in a demanding situation in order to earn exceptionally large sums of money. In return they placed commensurate demands on the kitchen. They came to expect food that suited their newly acquired income status. This was exaggerated by what was presumably an emotional neediness produced by the isolation, the unusually bleak social circumstances, and the fact that they were financial prisoners of the camp.

Therefore the dining room was no dainty tearoom. It was an aromatic, turbulent arena. The contract arrangements under which the DEW line was being built took account of the fact that no one had built such structures in the Arctic before so there were many unknowns. Hence the deal was cost-plus — that remarkable situation in which the more money the contractor and associates spend, the more profit they retain. Thus the kitchen was under little obligation to be thrifty — which, paradoxically, increased the pressure under which it labored. What, only one kind of roast and no shellfish and no steak for lunch? No meringue pie, only dreary fruit tart? Spaghetti with no *big* meatballs? After all, cost-plus. Everyone seemed to arrive at the same time and the line had to be served rapidly and fully. Though we dishwashers were not directly concerned with the clientele, it was also clear, since we were in the kitchen, how firmly the chef had to coerce not only his staff but also the food.

It is interesting to watch cooking for six hundred. It is rather like the reverse of archaeology. You see the various layers of taste and structure added to the food as it is prepared and then cooked, and it becomes clearer — the quantities are so graphic — how the tastes and textures of food are taken apart by the diner, even if he doesn't specifically or even generally understand the composition of what is being eaten. It is a lively, taut business in which time, taste, heat, texture, and appearance are always in a close connection that the cook must watch like the mugger his mark. It is fast-moving predictive chemistry, because the cook is supposed to know the outcome, which is what the recipe is for. But the recipe is not enough, because, of course, the ingredients are still forms of life — they are more or less fresh, too watery, too grainy, the fish is unduly fragrant, the beef has had too much exercise, the vegetables have relapsed into tasteless cells, the oven has a dead spot in the right corner. Cooking for six hundred is a corrida with many small bulls and an exigent audience. The chef now has a few hours in which to defuse the problems. Unlike the conductor, who achieves his music immediately, the orchestra of food is on two-hour delay. And the chef must taste it in advance, before it is ready.

Building a Library of Tastes

Good cooking involves the solution to a mouth-puzzle. This is the essence of the food passion: how to create or re-create that special sense of a particular food imagined or once tasted — for example, the Salzburger Nockerl served at a lush hotel at which I had lunch after visiting the Max Planck Institute in Sieweisen in Bavaria, or the shrimp remoulade at Galatoire's in New Orleans, or the garlic potatoes at Nick's Diner on Ilfield Road in London in the late sixties.

Had Beethoven been deaf from birth, he could not have thought his music through. Cooks must consume as skillfully and knowingly as they produce. Even if they learn from and enjoy reading cookbooks — which I do, having been captured first by the books of Elizabeth David — they nevertheless must have tastes in mind and experience to fit to the emerging story on the page. And this does not happen in a cultural vacuum. Presumably, the best stake out a place in whichever tradition of cooking they locate themselves. The Renaissance French did not think good taste in food was inherited, as were courage and the right to bear arms. It required a setting for its exercise.

Making good food involves tasting it intelligently, again understanding its immediate sensory archaeology. As part of some research in 1990 on the Four Seasons hotel group, I interviewed Bruno Loubet, the wonderfully passionate chef of the Four Seasons restaurant at the Inn on the Park Hotel in London. At twenty-eight, he had already gathered the first Michelin star for a London hotel restaurant, and each week created a novel *menu surprise* that neither he nor his staff could recite until he began inventing it around three-thirty on Monday afternoon. But the tastes and the invention came from his mother and the food of his youth in rural France. He remembered well, and presumably watched, and the heat and range of his interest kept the memory of long-ago food vivacious.

The food epiphanies to which I've briefly referred, and mercifully many more, are the opposite of my stations of the cross. Chefs create them, and while there is no doubt some trick and routine and fakery to all of it, finally the chef is confronted by his small family, the order for a table of six regular customers, just himself, or six hundred Arctic workers in Frobisher Bay. The taste and meaning must measure up.

There was no question that the chef in our Arctic kitchen forcefully commanded the isthmus between emotionally needy hunger and the accumulated lore and art of mass catering. Finally, the meal was his aria, even though there was a supporting chorus and noisy orchestra. His audience was of individuals, too. Even if hundreds ate the same food, each mouth had its own reception for the general product. As Brian McNally, who has operated some conspicuous "hot" restaurants in New York City, has said, restaurants "involve engaging in an intimate act in a public place."

Just so. Eating involves placing rather complex substances into a bodily orifice, changing their state, and incorporating them into the body — surprisingly intimate, considering all the matters of manners that arise: don't slurp, don't burp, don't chew noisily, or do, depending on where you are. It is no surprise why this is a matter fraught with emotionality and symbolism. Even fast-food restaurants must compensate for their bureaucratized cuisine — no cooks there, just teenagers with checklists — with an elaborate array of colorful and presumably evocative symbols: the famed arches, a southern colonel, Roy Rogers, Burger Kings and Dairy Queens. As Calvin Trillin has despairingly put it, many restaurants are "themed." Serving essentially industrialized food in environments made redolent with clear meanings, they use architectural spice, however simple, to conceal a prosaic menu. The point, obviously, is to augment the potential coldness of the experience with an apparatus of emotionality that satisfies extranutritional needs and punctuates dining time with colorful experience.

I return in my mind to a hotel restaurant I was urged to visit in rural Japan while writing on Japanese food. The chef had trained in France and produced outstanding and interesting Franco-Japanese food displayed with unusual artfulness. The food was indeed interesting and inventive, if also prodigiously expensive.

But most arresting and even alarming about the entire experience was the chef's chef d'oeuvre. It was a model in pastry and icing about five feet high enclosed in a glass case at the entrance to the restaurant, a replica of the Church of Sacre Coeur in Montmartre in Paris. (That's the white one, perched on the hill, with improbable minarets; it looks more like a massive dream-state visitor from another planet than a church in urban France). Here was a wholly bizarre confectionery echo, in flour and sugar, of an already improbable architectural object. Thus was the marriage of two culinary cultures celebrated. The ardor and ambition of the cook had been preserved in this quite remarkable and unexpected form and the spectacle was justifiably famous. The model was quite perfect — controlled insanity — and it was a reminder in its intensity of the chef's station at five minutes to noon and five minutes to six PM in the kitchen at Frobisher Bay.

It's Not Negotiable

Obviously, all practitioners of the arts that please the senses are to some degree committed to an aggressive understanding of sensory physiology and psychology. But painters, sculptors, and musicians need not always please — they may shock, revolt, trouble, abuse, irritate. They may shout or drum or stamp their feet at their audience. They may assault the audience's certainties and excite their fears and ridicule their deepest morality. The dramatist may unhinge their expectations of life by the suddenly plausible behavior of outrageous or despicable characters.

But the chef, or the winemaker, or the confectioner — they must please. Otherwise, in any kind of open market they will not survive. The mouth is less tolerant than the brain or whichever organ of the body assesses politicians. To prosper where there is choice, the cook must yield up foods that taste good and seem healthy — unless his product is supposed to be punishment, as in prisons or some hospitals, or in the schools for children of affluent families in nineteenth-century England. There the deliberate goal is to permit no pleasure. The absence of it certifies the guilt or lowliness or poverty of the hapless diner.

Once again, pleasure becomes a coin of the realm, if only in a negative sense. From one report,[30] even the traditional last meal of a prisoner condemned to die in the gas chamber of San Quentin in California must be consumed in a bare room containing only a toilet, and while the diner is standing, holding his tray. In addition, because of regulations governing pre-executions, the individual may wear only underpants and socklike footwear. Providing the last meal — up to fifty dollars is allotted — is presumably a form of compassionate gesture. But the conditions under which it is consumed emphasize the punitive nature of food in this extreme and dramatic situation. It is also pertinent that the individual in the episode described — who was reprieved at the last hour — had requested that his fifty dollars be used to provide ice cream to other death row inmates. Food as emotional currency. This was refused by the authorities. The doomed convict instead ordered full-dress pizza for one.

And here we have the other side of the family dinner, the bistro lunch, the lovers' duet dinner of warm assertion. In between these extremes is the primary issue, of food, survival, and the avoidance of hunger, which is satisfying enough in itself.

What unites these approaches to food is the volatile element of pleasure that food provides to the central nervous system and the bubbling, ramified pleasure it provides within the central social system. A number of times a day, people have the opportunity to turn necessity into virtue, to convert nourishment into an aesthetically interesting intimate drama, to use the instruments of taste and smell as skillfully as musicians use their ears. It is a remarkable luxury. There is always something new and arresting and traditional and tasty stewing on the stove. You can smell it from here.

SIX

The Senses: Everyone Has a Native Guide

WITH HINDSIGHT it's easy to see how preposterous that arch-Cartesian René Descartes was when he announced, "I think, therefore I am." What is surprising is how influential his assertion remains, and how complacently the description *sapiens* still attaches to the *Homo* of our zoological name.

Some acknowledgment of the power of the senses has to augment that name. Descartes should have advertised something like, "I think, therefore I am . . . confused about my complicated passions." Perhaps he did say this and the final phrase was lost by the scribe or removed by an editor. His phrase as it has been canonized is one whose misleading implication is equaled only by its pomposity and folly.

In this chapter I explore the senses, the pleasures they provide, the arts they sustain, how they merge with notions people have about rationality, logic, formality. Humans are wise, sapient, and thoughtful. But humans also swim in a sea of sensibility, of sensuality, of inner and outer observations, of judgments formed by sight, smell, touch, vibration, hearing, thirst, the passage of time, temperature, movement — a rich array of sources of information and hence guides to action. If people are skillfully thoughtful, the principal basis of their judgment still results from the work of the senses. People are not dedicated computers designed to think dispassionately, without anger, amusement, or partisan verve. The senses affect all thought. The senses guide all the action that results from thinking.

Repeat, repeat: The brain evolved to act, not to think. Brain tissue was added only because particular individuals were intelligent about their environments and each other. They were eager and able to combine effective management of their lives with successful courtship, mating, and reproduction. The senses were and still are the essential guide to thought. They form the irreducible platform upon which all judgment rests. Our capable brains developed because they effectively evaluated a flood of incoming sensory data and made successful decisions about what to do.

The senses came first. Making sense of them followed. This is mainly what people are sapient about.

Homo sentiens sapiens — this is our real name. Before we gentrified it to pretend to lives of low-voltage sweet reason in polite society.

The relationship between pleasure — basic physiopleasure — and the senses is obvious. Nevertheless, there is, here, a closer link than usual with pain, as well as with fantasy, with ideopleasure. The senses orient the organism with the information it requires to survive and prosper. Pain is an obvious warning of danger. Pleasure is an obvious if often more complex green light. It is a robust signal that whatever produces it is desirable for the organism. The health consequences of sweet and of bitter tastes reflect this clearly.

How does a contemporary industrial society decide how its members can identify, receive, and enjoy pleasure? In regard to pain there is an array of notions of what is acceptable and what is not. Insurance companies and juries even try to fix a dollar amount on the cost of pain. (Franz Kafka was an insurance adjuster whose literary life was presumably affected by his job.) Can the balance between pleasure and pain help define how societies should be organized?

This is in essence the same kind of question as the one posed earlier about diet. Remember? Is the chronic problem people in

to defend against challenges from other males interested in political power and sexual status. So primate copulation reflects social success in the past, as well as foreshadowing genetic success in the future. If, as Henry Kissinger noted, "power is the great aphrodisiac," at least for male primates it is likely that power has to be largely satisfying in its own right, because the act that is its consummatory shiver occupies such a minuscule period of time. Or (assuming that primates indulge in this kind of calculation, which is doubtful) perhaps the pleasure of sex is so startling and so dramatic that it more than justifies the extensive folderol that accompanies it. In any event, we can be quite certain that male primates do not know that sex leads to birth and that the satisfactions and rewards of parenthood are associated with the pleasures of intercourse. It is one of nature's oddities that there is little directly perceptible connection between the desirable and striking act of sex and the vital matter of raising the next generation. Except among humans, of course, which changes the story altogether.

We will return shortly to the human coital condition, but let us first consider what might be the evolutionary role of orgasm for all primate females, including people. For males orgasmic pleasure is associated with ejaculation, which is an irreplaceable feature of conception and reproduction. For the female, however, there appears to be no direct reproductive advantage of orgasm. It is obviously not necessary for conception because primate copulations often are far too brief to induce female orgasm. Yet conception regularly occurs.

There has not been a gender-equal connection over extensive time in the physiological link between orgasm and conception. For the male, yes. For the female, no. Primate anatomy *is* primate destiny. Sexual life seems unfair for female primates, at least insofar as the connection between orgasm and conception is concerned. I've already indicated that female primates appear to enjoy intercourse. Doris Zumpe and Richard Michael of Emory University have described primate females who reach back energetically to grip their partners at the moment they ejaculate, while Suzanne Chevalier-Skolnikoff has observed orgasmlike female responses under a variety of conditions, including several heterosexual episodes.[32] However, these few data are inadequately weighty given the evolutionary and biological importance of what they might imply.

Human females have orgasms — in many cultures, often and regularly; other primate females have them infrequently, if at all. In this respect women are more biologically different from the other primates than men are. That is, in the great chain of sexual being, men are behaviorally closer to other primate males than women are to females. This difference is fascinating in its own right and also because it illuminates differences in how, when, and with whom men and women enjoy erotic pleasure.

Reproductive Strategy on the Home Front

In general males are willing and eager to have sexual relations with as many females as they can. In the pure state of nature this is the most effective reproductive strategy they can employ. They can reproduce half their genes in half a minute and move on. Without the availability of effective contraception or abortion, each sexual act stands an appreciable chance to result in a child.

But for the female the stakes are incomparably higher. A half-minute of sex can result in a full generation of pregnancy, breastfeeding, child care, and parenthood. It seems indisputable that differences that survive in male and female sexual choices have resulted from countless generations of natural and sexual selection. These have in turn resulted in the survival of contemporary people whose lives still reflect those formative times.

I've discussed this matter of sexual strategy before, in other contexts. The same comparisons can be made about that concentrate of pleasure, the orgasm. Men have orgasms readily and very quickly. Women have orgasms carefully and slowly. Men can be stimulated by quite impersonal stimuli such as pornography or peering at the bodies of strangers, while women appear to respond more warmly to personal and psychological circumstances with sharply fewer partners.

Females hardly ever engage in gang rape and group sexual abuse of the opposite sex while males do so with some frequency, particularly when there are preexisting male bonds such as those that link members of athletic teams, fraternities, or military units.[33] Male pleasure happens quickly and impulsively, female pleasure more slowly and with circumspection. While men not uncommonly suffer from premature ejaculation, particularly when partnering an unfamiliar woman for the first time, women hardly ever announce a similar complaint. The usual adjustment thoughtful couples must make is to delay male orgasm while the female is affectionately stimulated. For example, this is formalized in central Polynesia among the people of Mangaia Island, where young boys are instructed in the appropriate luxurious erotic arts by older women. Incompetent male performers in this society are likely to lose their partners to more adept consorts.

But this level of sexual pedagogy is unusual. From a review of available sexual data from the majority of human societies, it appears that in general "men take the initiative and, without extended foreplay, proceed vigorously toward climax without much regard for achieving synchrony with the woman's orgasm. Again and again, there are reports that coitus is primarily completed in terms of the man's passion and pleasures, with scant attention paid to the woman's response. If women do experience orgasm, they do so passively."[34]

In the broad intercultural context, this is hardly surprising when we recall that some of the societies represented by this evaluation are of the sort that practice clitoridectomy and similar violations of women's opportunities for pleasure. Such practices reflect a general insensitivity, and presumably also active reluctance to encourage women to enjoy sexual pleasure. A couple who in the evening have paid for the feast celebrating their daughter's sexual mutilation are unlikely at night to retire to their marital bed avid for shared orgasmic fun. Public values and private experience become difficult to distinguish. The cultural world continues to turn while the husband turns away too soon. Countless lives have been blighted by such mute disconnection. The gross national pleasure is far lower than need be.

And what is gained? By whom? Who the hell made up this plan? Who sustains it?

Furthermore, what exists is not just the result of cultural values that disregard female pleasure. If female pleasure must be coaxed and in an important sense *earned*, then females' lack of pleasure in intercourse must reflect males' incompetence and ignorance — their inability to understand the sexual, physiological, and erotic needs of women. Hence they act unsatisfactorily.

But how and where would men learn better? Literacy is a recently acquired general skill that most people in the world still barely have and use, and anyway, as we have seen, even ongoing schools do not offer much to read about female sexuality. There are no signs on the horizon of a widespread tutorial system for young men in which erotically experienced women take part, such as among the Mangaian Islanders. No obvious forum exists for exchange of decent and constructive information among young men. Where is a predictable and nonprurient opportunity for the men of a society to learn about the sexuality of the women among whom they will spend their lives?[35] Even where there are relatively active educational programs of sex education in secondary schools, their principal justification and emphasis is on responsibility for preventing disease and pregnancy. Artful discussion about enjoying the pleasurable capacities of the body is rare. Even in thoughtful communities, such colloquy would run the risk of stimulating parental and religious opposition.

Young men in most cultures have little chance to learn about the sexual "design difference" between men and women. This has directly affected the most private and poignant of intimacies. It creates a barrier between men and women in precisely the encounter in which barriers are least appropriate. There is a missing major lesson in erotic physiology. Both men and women may fail to understand the physical reasons underlying what they do and what they don't do with each other sexually. Bitterness and blame, and avoidance altogether, are likelier outcomes than thoughtful efforts to understand the banal, impersonal, biological basis of sexual asymmetry.

Time as Hymen, Time as Organ

The relatively cautious way in which women approach sex reflects the substantial potential of its consequences for them. Metaphorically, just as the hymen is a physical barrier to potentially hazardous pleasure, the sexual response rate of women is a behavioral barrier, a temporal barrier. First the flesh resists, then the spirit. The result of both is to inhibit, delay, and avoid commitment.

Far more consequential than the hymen is another physiological indication of this. The tip of the penis, which ejaculates, is the most erotically sensitive part of the male body. However, the vagina, where conception begins, is less pleasurably sensitive than the clitoris, which has little directly and functionally to do with reproduction. As we know from the enforced experiment of the miserable mutilations discussed earlier, women can reproduce without the clitoris. For men, orgasm and reproduction are largely inseparable. For women, orgasm and considerate affectionate partnership appear to be vitally connected, if not inseparable. This means that the pleasure of women is more socially mediated, more complex, presumably more emotionally and physically elegant.

A huge difference. *Vive la différence?* This is very awkward. But the difference lives, with many consequences for the pleasure of men and women.

Old fogies will remember the controversy about vaginal versus clitoral orgasms. Following Freud's mislead, many commentators asserted that female orgasms experienced during penetration were more mature, more serious, than those that happened when mainly the clitoris was stimulated. Freud's surmise was not wholly eccentric at that soon-after-Darwin time. If sex had to do with natural selection, then what most effectively abetted reproduction should earn highest status in the natural hierarchy of desirable practices. Clearly orgasm from penetration was more likely to lead to conception than when the clitoris alone was stimulated manually, orally, or with some device or another.

Freud's assumption was that nature "got things right" in a straightforward way. Therefore vaginal sex should provide peak experience. He was wrong. He did not have the benefit of later work on female sexuality, particularly from Alfred Kinsey and, most significantly, William Masters and Virginia Johnson, who showed how much more effective the clitoris was in promoting orgasm than vaginal penetration alone. Certainly he did not consult a sufficient sample of women willing and able to talk knowledgeably about their sex lives to know how important clitoral activity was to sexual satisfaction. Obviously, he was not only limited by the information of the time but also by his own presumably typical male experience. We can speculate with confidence that if the men of Mittel Europe had orgasms most commonly when their right elbows were caressed for fifteen minutes before penetration occurred, Freud would have looked for an equivalent condition among women and would surely have identified the clitoris as a vital elbow analogue.

Mother Nature and the Executive Dildo

Nature did not get things right, at least by the look of it. It failed to equate male and female sexual rhythms and routines. Most important, it evolved significantly different capacities for pleasure in the bodies of people who are otherwise powerfully united during sexual congress. A humble but revealing demonstration of this is the garden variety dildo available at corner drugstores everywhere in the industrial world. For obvious sentimental reasons, this device is shaped more or less like a penis. It is, however, usually somewhat streamlined. Perhaps modesty compels a smoothing out of the more Paleolithic bumps and ridges of a completely faithful replica.

But the most telling fact about many of these devices is that they vibrate. Indeed, they are usually called "vibrators" — even, inexplicably, "executive vibrators," in the case of the more luxurious models. So they are not really direct substitutes for penises at all, because while real penises may be quite animated and their owners highly energetic, one thing they certainly don't do is vibrate. And they don't vibrate, furthermore, at around the frequency of a hummingbird or bumblebee.

The inescapable interpretation of the vibrating dildo is that it serves a vital function in stimulating the clitoris. Otherwise, there would be no need for vibration and the instrument could simply be raised and lowered to simulate intercourse successfully. But this is not its principal pattern of use. Other massage devices that are round or flat and not penis-shaped are also popular and presumably serve the same purposes as the more symbolic cylinders.

The marketplace speaks. Perhaps men wishing to enjoy companionable quality time with well-satisfied female partners could profit from five minutes of research and reverie in front of a generous inventory of executive vibrators.

The Mystery of the Migrating Clitoris

But why did nature go so wrong? Why separate the organ that most pleasurably rewards female sexual behavior from the one that accomplishes the task of conception needed for survival (which is the whole point of the exercise)? Why didn't nature unite the heart of pleasure with the key to reproduction the way the tip of the tongue responds to sweetness to secure fruit?

There are several possible explanations. One depends on the same evolutionary principle that resulted in useless male nipples. All females have nipples and they are vitally necessary, so the genetic information about establishing them is passed on willy-nilly to males. However the more "costly" physiology that would actually cause them to produce milk is not also passed on. There is not only a normal curve of variation within each sex, there is also one that embraces both of them. So some characteristics that are vital for one sex may tag along with the other, even though they merely boast the form, not the function. The same principle may apply to certain emotional and cognitive processes; one sex may specialize, while the other receives some spin-off benefit involving the characteristic to a lesser degree. This may account, for example, for differences between males and females that persist in various tests of cognition, perception, and personality even after test makers and educators try to reduce these differences by squelching questions that obviously distinguish between the sexes.

The case of the clitoris is interesting. It appears to have retained its intense and dramatic function. But it has migrated to a part of the body where it has to be stimulated through conscious effort, not mainly as a feature of intercourse itself. This seems to mean several important things. One is that positions of sexual intercourse that permit manual stimulus of the clitoris (and breasts as well) — particularly the one in which the male penetrates the vagina from the back side — may be more "natural" to the extent that they are more pleasurable to both sexes, and to the female particularly. Front-to-rear is, of course, the customary position taken by the other primates, and there is reason to believe it hardly offers a perfect sexual idyll, certainly for the female. But it may be a more promising variant for humans than for monkeys. Perhaps the so-called missionary position — male atop female, face to face — derived its ironic slang name because it interfered with more entertaining sexual positions in conflict with a Christian ethic that viewed sex mainly as a reproductive duty, not an opportunity for real pleasure. Recall Saint Paul and his cheerless enthusiasm for the ascetic mode. Note too the astonishing Christian conviction that Jesus did not suffer from Original Sin because his mother was a virgin and he was not therefore the defiled product of sexual pleasure. So the female clitoris and its lively stimulation be damned, literally as well as symbolically!

Despite its erotic reputation, the missionary position is an inefficient stimulus for the clitoris. As Kinsey found, the overwhelming majority of women who experienced orgasm in intercourse had also enjoyed or required stimulation of the clitoris and labia. Perhaps this most common Euro-American coital position satisfies some men's needs for dominance, some women's for passivity, or is merely a sign of custom and physiological ignorance. It may also be a formidable barrier to female pleasure and to the mutual enjoyment sought by couples who want to accept differences in how men and women respond sexually and then build on them consciously and constructively. There is a further benefit to the rear window of opportunity. If, as some researchers suspect, there is in fact such a location as the "G-spot" — a point where the vaginal canal is particularly sensitive, so that vaginal orgasm is more readily experienced — then rear entry will maximize strong pressure on this region from the penis and enhance pleasure all around. Here, at last, "express the animal in you" becomes appropriate — for this is the customary sexual posture of primates who have organized their sex lives without benefit of missionaries.

Everywoman's Mate Meter

I have left for last speculation about the most behaviorally subtle and probably most significant reason for the evolution of the migrating clitoris. This is that its evolutionary movement to its somewhat out-of-the-way location and its retention there help females identify which partners care about them, understand them, and are willing to delay or truncate their own sexual pleasure so that their partner experiences it fully. The clitoris is not only an organ for enjoying pleasure; it helps assess how effectively a man shows affection. As with so much else human beings do, here is a complex method of behavior that enhances or replaces what in other animals is accomplished either directly through physiology or with some fairly simple action — such as the peacock fanning his immense, sexually attractive (to female peacocks), and otherwise useless plumage. So just as a marginally stronger shade of intense color may be what allows one peacock to be chosen over another, so even a slight increment of male sexual sensitivity may make the critical human difference.

What is fascinating about this possible function of the placement of the clitoris is that important determinations about sex, mating, and the life cycle itself are based on *pleasure*, not on pain, or resources, or family standing, or religion, or the like. The dinner is judged mainly not by the sizzling main course, crisp salad, or fruity dessert, but by the zip of the champagne.

Of course, the opportunity for women to form such judgments depends on the kind of community in which they live and what social values determine about their rights to pleasure. For example, among the Mehinaku Indians of the Brazilian Amazon, there is no word for the female orgasm and it is not a sexual expectation of women. Rather, sex is strongly related to the exchange of resources, particularly fish. Attractive females enjoy many lovers, whose gifts to them are assets for their extended families.[36]

Sex in exchange for resources may actually be less problematic to communities than sex in exchange for pleasure.[37] For example, there are indications that an important reason behind the persecution of European "witches" — and the execution of possibly a million of them — was the belief that certain women were dangerously licentious, liable to entertain demons, and likely to subvert the decorous social order. A spasm of antipathy to real and, more important, fantasized female sexuality yielded various inquisitions that began in Provence in the early thirteenth century and did not formally end in Europe until some five hundred years later. The last witch was burned in Scotland in 1728.[38]

The power of pleasure can be very volatile and very disturbing, as all lovers can understand. When the partners are seen as appropriate to each other's class, religion, ethnicity, race, and the like, then their marriage is made in heaven. The bells toll for the prince and new princess as they pose radiantly on the cathedral steps. But "in the wrong hands" passionate love can produce the bitterest of conflict and total incomprehension between the lovers and those around them. Romeo and Juliet are finally powerless against their entire worlds. Countless novels, from *Lady Chatterley's Lover* to *Native Son*, together with stories of people — such as the Duke of Windsor — who abandon empires large and small because of the love they experience with a particular person, reveal the strength of the evolutionary message about pleasure achieved through love. Countless adulteries, countless broken marriages, countless hectic lives, and countless happy endings emerge from sexual connections that prompt the partners to conclude that the pleasure they feel physically is a stunning predictor of a desirable future, well worth whatever convulsive uproar must be endured on its behalf.

Here, as elsewhere, the female has the more serious and complex task of assessing this pleasure and its role in her life. She must form and re-form the larger picture and adjust it for the passage of time and the varying circumstances in which she and her partner might spend their time. In the story told in "Paradise by the Dashboard Light," the raucously brilliant song by Jim Steinman that was recorded by Meat Loaf, a man is seducing a woman. The process is described (by the baseball hero and announcer Phil Rizzuto) in adolescent male terms — getting to first base, second base, round-ing third, heading for home. Suddenly, the music stops. The woman calls an abrupt halt. She heatedly queries: "Do you love me? Will you love me forever? Do you need me? Will you never leave me? Will you make me so happy for the rest of my life? Will you take me away and will you make me your wife? . . . I gotta know right now."

"Let me sleep on it," exclaims the evasive, equivocal male. She refuses sexual access until he promises to be with her "till the end of time." In the bitter final verse, the new husband desperately shouts, "Now I'm praying for the end of time." The promise of the relationship and of the duet of pleasure at its center is not matched by the real quotidian life within which they exist.

The dizzying spell of love-at-first-sight is exhilarating, its pleasure often overwhelming and general.[39] But it can also in effect be nature's trap, a dramatic way of establishing the bond supporting reproduction. It may begin and end as a relatively swift and intense episode. While it may or may not endure in intensity or form, it may nevertheless result in a childbirth that commits one or both partners to nearly two decades of effort and resources. Nature's trap may also be its finest hour. As Schopenhauer remarked, the desire for intercourse is the "genius of the genus."

A mix of psychological forces and passion combine in a potent cocktail with the physical pleasure of sexual consummation. The result is the continuation of the species through a process that is nothing less than the most elaborate kind of Pavlovian reinforcement over time. Certainly, the prevalence of abortion and the controversy surrounding it reflect the power of the sexual eagerness that makes abortion necessary in the first place.

Reproduction is not the only or the inevitable outcome of love-at-first-sight and other similarly intense forms of infatuation. Homosexual people experience such feelings. So do infertile people and those who use contraceptives. So do married people who stick together through ennui, rage, contention, indifference. So do people who want nothing from the relationship but the relationship itself. So do people who leave their mate amid the flurry of a love affair with a new partner who promises galvanizing life-changes, and a dramatic sense of opportunity and emotional renewal.

The Story of the Centuries! Read All about It

Ponce de León believed that if he secured a potion from the Fountain of Youth the overwhelming irritation of death could be avoided. Food chemists seek the magic ingredients that will allow people to eat tasty food that is fatty and sweet without also suffering the health drawbacks they carry. There seem to be as many hangover remedies as communities using alcohol.

Contraception is probably the most important antidote yet discovered to the realities of nature. It is difficult to imagine a more significant influence on the ongoing behavior of men and women. Without question, the availability of effective contraception — particularly when it is controlled by females, who have most at stake from pregnancy — has proved decisive in fundamentally (and probably permanently) changing the link between pleasure and consequence, between sex and social structure, and, certainly, between men and women. Contraception directly affects the relationship that is at the core of the evolution and continuity of the species, that has the most enduring and long-lived impact on society, and that motivates and satisfies one of the deepest emotional needs of people. The Fountain of Youth remains elusive, but the Fountain of Sex has been found. Certainly during the 1960s and 1970s, after the pill became widely available and before sexually transmitted diseases were of major cautionary consequence to erotic enthusiasts, it also seemed as if the Fountain of Pleasure had been discovered too. Many people had more frequent and varied sexual encounters with other people, both before, within, outside of, and after marriage. The synchrony between new contraceptive technology and an unusually large, healthy, relatively uncensored group of baby-boomers yielded an unparalleled parade of frank fashions in clothing and behavior. Visual, physical, and symbolic pleasures were more lustrously and openly available than in the decades before.

What did this involve? And what did it imply? Let's put this in the very broad perspective such a large matter requires. The English anthropologists Vernon Reynolds and Ralph Tanner have mounted a sustained and thoughtful assertion that the principal function of religions throughout the ages has been to regulate reproduction.[40] This was a matter of critical importance during most of human existence, when groups were small, survival was precarious, and each new mouth to feed was eventually more than compensated for by the two new hands that could work to feed it. Sport sex was a waste of energy and time and could be disruptive to stable reproductive families. Masturbation was clearly of no use, and it is even possible that the loss of some semen could affect the chances of males poorly nourished and under survival stress to father children. The argument put forth by Reynolds and Tanner is complex, elaborate, and controversial.[41]

One of their pertinent assertions is that religions first arose not to inhibit pleasure, but in response to its power. Without contraception, sex between men and women offers a high probability of producing children. Therefore, it is of little surprise that sex, marriage, and family life are principal foci of the intense interest of religious institutions. It is also significantly if puzzlingly revealing that the most dramatic figures of the Roman Catholic Church —its saints — have been overwhelmingly unmarried and presumably virgins.[42] It seems remarkable that the symbolic heroes of the church have so rarely been those men and women who raised the large families the church has at the same time encouraged.[43] Or is sexual pleasure a harsh and major disqualification from professional reputation and success in an institution explicitly dedicated to families and the increase in souls? This is perplexing if not also startling in such a pronatal institution.

Contraception is an act of public and personal responsibility. In addition, it facilitates personal pleasure-seeking. And it clearly undermines the sovereign role religious institutions claim over the behavior of their followers. We need again look no further than the Roman Catholic church to appreciate how broadly the instructions of priests about contraception have been ignored by women who are able to experience both socially acceptable behavior as well as privately enjoyable pleasure. That this has had an impact on the overall authority of the church goes without saying. A rather similar situation, involving abortion, has escalated in various religious jurisdictions into major political as well as sacral controversies. The fact of the matter is that the dual options of contraception and abortion have offered men and women an unprecedented opportunity to engage in social interaction and sexual exploration and enjoyment.

Physiopleasure. Psychopleasure. Sociopleasure. Even the literal fear of God has failed to stanch the tide of discontent with religious prohibitions established during a different period of history, a time when such prohibitions presumably had benign impact on the reproductive destinies of men and women and their social lives. A revealing index of the Catholic church's difficulty in making theological assertions about contemporary sexual behavior is the unprecedented difficulty it is experiencing in finding enough priests willing to remain celibate. And as the world's families become smaller, fewer parents who want grandchildren will be willing to embrace the notion of one of their limited number of children joining a priesthood dedicated to nonreproductive celibacy.

A la Recherche des Actes Perdus

Clearly there has been some decline in the importance of historic religious rule in many societies. The late twentieth century is, after all, not the Middle Ages. Certainly there are more pluralistic secular trends even in relatively traditional societies. The speed and density of communication and travel between cultures have produced an inevitable interruption between traditional dogma and contemporary behavior. (Though not everywhere, of course; for example, there has been a Muslim resurgence in orthodoxy difficult for an outsider to compare with earlier periods of history.)

But this discontinuity of history does not also mean that the impact of even earlier, prehistoric rules associated with sex and reproduction has vanished. For one thing, the very existence of the widespread demand for abortion indicates that people continue to have sexual relations without the calculations and foresight contraceptives often require. I have pointed out elsewhere that the worldwide growth in legalized abortion occurred *after*, and in good part *because of*, the availability of the contraceptive pill — in the late 1960s and 1970s.[44] My central notion is that once females became responsible for contraception, countless men — more men than ever — abdicated any responsibility for the results of sex. They no longer felt an obligation to marry women who were pregnant. We know that as many as 40 percent of marriages in the early part of the century, and in centuries before, occurred when a pregnancy was established — a not-unreasonable empirical basis for considering a marriage. Then changing roles of women and men rendered such imposed marriages less acceptable ethically and politically. The option of abortion became more vital. It has everywhere become more frequent. For example, according to Planned Parenthood of New York, at least 40 percent of women in New York City will in the 1990s become pregnant once or more by the age of twenty, and some 50 percent of these pregnancies will terminate in abortion. Among white middle-class women, it is expected that virtually all will end this way.[45]

And in the year 2000? Is there sufficient reason to expect substantial change? Certainly new contraceptive technology may have a decisive effect, particularly the RU 486 formulation that stimulates relatively safe and painless miscarriage some few weeks after pregnancy begins. This is an especially promising candidate to produce major new impacts, more, in my opinion, because of its behavioral nature — it acts well after the act, when circumstances are plain and definable — than because of its strictly medical efficacy. Behavior is the issue here.

Even so, who would have expected the contraceptive pill to have been a cause for heightened demand for abortion? The five-year contraceptive implant into women's upper arms introduced at the end of 1990 is likely in my view to widen the gap of mutual obligation between men and women in the reproductive sense. It is also too soon to know what the impact will be of the fact that the implant is discernible in the arm, even if barely, particularly when its user is lying on a bed. A scarlet letter? In the past, contraceptives could be a woman's secret. What will women lose and gain through exposure of their reproductive state?

It's So Romantic

Each sexual episode has its own fashion, rhythm, and meaning. But a common factor also underlies the situations I have been discussing here. Private lives may be evanescent and idiosyncratic.

The physiopleasure of sexuality remains an attractive and often overwhelming feature of intercourse. Nevertheless, it is the psychopleasure of the classical spasm that continues to animate women — often drastically against their own interest — particularly ones young and inexperienced. What Brecht in *The Threepenny Opera* called "that old love-tickle" is as much about the sense of self and destiny as it is about the body and what it does. Sex without contraception is closer in prospect and fact to what sex is about — bonding, babies, and the unscrutinized, shifting personal epic called passion. As a young New Yorker told a journalist: "You know the danger, but you want to know the experience, as a woman, and there are those incredibly excited male hormones rubbing against your leg at lunch."[46]

Which church has something — and what — to offer adolescents in place of this? The excitement of the psychopleasure of participating in nature's most important single action overwhelms all else, including the injunctions and lessons by theory and example of an otherwise reasonably effective school system and pattern of parental care. Even though an individual may, on reflection, decide that a sexual escapade was undesirable and out of phase with her life, the array of pleasures delivered by participating in the inexorable pageant of sexual reproduction is often wholly convincing. Why is the bride traditionally supposed to be so radiantly happy if not because she is exactly in synchrony with nature's passionate imperatives, comfortably nested in a celebrating community? On the wedding night, she will at last experience private pleasure (if that is what in fact it turns out to be; see above for a discussion of male sexual incompetence); and for the first time she will begin to establish — with her gifts or hope chest or bride-price or whatever — a public version of the inexorable pageant. Contemporary behavior tied to emotions associated with the practical success of evolving *Homo sapiens* enjoys an advantage. The participants are — as students say — pre-prepared.

A physical analogue may clarify this. I have already noted that there are many more male homosexuals than female ones, and that one reason is that male homosexuals act more like heterosexual men, who are relatively promiscuous, while homosexual females act more like heterosexual females, who are less so. But there may also be another simple if unquantifiable physical reason, which is that male homosexuals can more directly enjoy sexual behavior that is like copulation than female homosexuals can. Unless women use artificial devices, they cannot simulate conventional intercourse, whereas men can, either orally or anally. This is, of course, clearly speculation. Nevertheless, perhaps homosexual physical pleasure may rest on a platform of evolutionary propensity, much as all other pleasure presumably does, too.

No Sex Please, We're British

This was the title of a long-running London theatrical farce that played famously to busloads of English people and foreign visitors. The clear implication was that one element of national character is its sexuality — its commitment to eroticism and freedom of happy sexual encounter — as well, presumably, as its cultivation of the sexual arts and pride in perfecting them. In this fanciful world of crude stereotype, Latin men are stellar lovers and Latin women sultry provocateurs, whereas English men are bashful and schoolboy-inept, while their female compatriots are anatomically reluctant and as sexually cold as a Shropshire autumn fog. French women French-kiss and wear maddening lingerie and stilt-pumps. English women wear knickers and sensible shoes and shake hands while blurting, "How do you do?" On and on.

The stereotypes are not interesting but their existence is. These are essentially crude if perhaps wishful summaries of how much and what kind of sexual pleasure different human groups are willing and able to enjoy. This appears to be a problem for varying social commentators, such as censors, religious zealots, and advocates of libidinous adventure. It reflects a chronic tension between social order and erotic fun and flair. For example, while the public rooms of a traditional Iranian rural household may be populated by women wearing the chador and acting in a drastically chaste manner, upstairs, on display in the sleeping alcoves, are *Playboy* centerfolds and other unexpectedly stimulating images.[47] Sex is always complicated, always interesting, always an issue.

Obviously, various communities, cultures, nations, social

classes, and the like do differ in the style and intensity of their sexuality, just as they differ in other ways, too. Nonetheless, virtually all have some active sexuality and some array of values and procedures that, finally, even strangers and outsiders can understand. The power of the pleasures — physical, psychological, social, symbolic — that sexuality provides continues to do effective battle with countless hindrances, ranging from priesthoods that advocate celibacy or sex without countraception to the real possibility of death itself among the communities afflicted with AIDS. To understand the power of sexuality, it is necessary to expand the conventional notion of the pleasures with which it is associated beyond the lubricious, the genital, the spasmodic, the skin. Sex is surrounded with the social and psychological forces that have powered human survival and that continue to symbolize human continuity. That, of course, is why religious groups have such an understandably strong and often ambiguous connection to the pleasures of the bed.

But the sovereign force is no longer inexorably tied to the outcome to which it was once directed. Rather suddenly, the relationship between the elaborate and colorful forms of sexual pleasure and social obligation has altered drastically. Once more we encounter a striking clash between what we became during the cave-dark nights of millennia and what we can do in modern times.

The Dirty Big Secret

When we put this in the perspective of the Christian religious tradition that has animated the industrial way of life, we see how dramatically the meaning of sexuality has changed. Augustine thundered that it was precisely Adam's sin, of pride, of lust, of conjuring freedom, that condemned us all: ". . . the willful choice of the first man and woman changed the nature of nature itself, and all humankind thereafter suffered and died." Furthermore, the historian of theology Elaine Pagels goes on to recall Augustine's assertion that "it was human choice — Adam's sin — that brought mortality and sexual desire upon the human race and, in the process, deprived Adam's progeny of the freedom to choose not to sin."

There were critics of his stern view, perhaps most refreshingly the young Italian bishop Julian of Eclanum, who wrote at around the same time that "God made bodies, distinguished the sexes, made genitalia, bestowed affection through which bodies would be joined, gave power to the semen, and operates in the secret nature of the semen — and God made nothing evil."[48]

But Augustine prevailed over such congenial innocence. He successfully linked an array of irksome circumstances — ranging from the pain of childbirth to the helplessness of infants, even to the existence of thistles — with the sinfulness of the "boundless sloughs of lust and damnable craving" associated with sexuality. Pagels decides that the reason that the notion that "suffering and death are the wages of sin" has remained popular for some sixteen hundred years is that it offers an explanation for dolorous human conditions and hence reduces the sense of helplessness — even if the alternative is a strong sense of guilt.

Though buttressed by history, popularity, and the repeated utterances of the church, this view seems unnecessarily bleak and defeatist, and even heartlessly eccentric. It is also hopelessly inconsistent with what is known about the evolution of human physiology, the role of sexual selection in it, and the comparisons that are made legitimately with other animals who often act rather like us but without benefit of clergy.

Nevertheless, there is a powerful overhanging question here: why has the Christian tradition accepted such a fearful attitude toward sexuality, embraced such guilt, and yet been so active in organizing and operating the world?

The question becomes even more interesting in the context of my earlier proposal that pleasure is an evolutionary entitlement and that therefore people should expect to enjoy sexual pleasure as a right and feature of natural experience. But how on earth can this be accomplished pleasantly against the current of the broad river of guilt in which the population is immersed up to its waist, if not its eyeballs?

Now, suddenly, we see the gravity of this matter of pleasure, particularly the sexual kind. Is it so disruptive or frightening that even an idea as grim, bizarre, and unprovable as Original Sin is weightily and successfully employed to blight whatever sense of freedom potential pleasure-seekers may muster? Can this justify telling even young children they suffer from Original Sin? And yet does not the existence of effective contraception drive a deep wedge between the past and the present? I think so. Nevertheless, the ongoing and bitter controversies about related issues such as abortion reveal that while technology may change, people do so very slowly, if at all.

And what a drama this has been, too. We evolved in a sexual system that produced enough offspring born to capable families for our tribe to increase. Then our tribe *really* increased. The new pressures of agricultural population and opportunity appeared to stimulate the emergence of genuinely inventive and surprisingly fanciful theories of social control, often based on the idea of God. The main ethical systems of the world were developed to deal with the challenge — or crisis — of agricultural life and scale. But now the industrial system, and in particular industrial discoveries about contraception, have made many of these pastoral themes more or less irrelevant. Suddenly there is a promise of boundless prosperity in pleasure. Yet much of the ancient censoriousness persists, oftentimes fiercely. Is this a quiet, haunting message from *Homo sapiens* to human beings, from ourselves to ourselves, about the still-looming possibility that sexual pleasure requires a firm context, that it has, like sugar, to be part of some thoughtful pattern of diet?

FIVE

BigMouth

HUMAN BEINGS are like other mammals in that they often receive their first food directly from their mother's body. But it is difficult to imagine any other mammal having such variety, complexity, and intensity of experiences surrounding food. No other creature on earth enjoys as much as people do so many kinds of pleasure from food — simple, complex, real, symbolic, basic, luxurious.

A Martian surveying the planet's cafeteria while the daily human meal is served would surely be stunned by its size and overwhelming variety. Much of the menu is determined by climate, geography, cultural tradition, and hunger. Nevertheless, people enthusiastically select an immense amount of what they eat and drink because they enjoy it. From the fiery peanut stew poured over pounded manioc in Lagos to the fried cubes of bean curd glistening with sweet-spicy sauce in Szechwan to a mousse of flounder garnished with specks of black caviar in Brussels, food is interesting, entertaining, almost flagrantly varied. It is an absolutely central feature of vivacious life.

Transactions surrounding food and drink are the glue of the social system. Few important events, even funerals, fail to become the occasion of a toast, a meal, a snack — of taking something from the environment and cooking, spicing, slicing, brewing, or fermenting it, and then placing it into the mouth. A Thai custom is that before a person dies he will collect several dozen or so of his favorite recipes in a booklet to be distributed at the funeral.[1] Hence the feast of delicious food continues even after death. This love of the legacy of food surely supports the vibrantly engaging food of Thailand. The dead literally feed the living as skillfully as they can.

The Mouth Organ Is Not Silent

The mouth is the organ of speech. But it is also the recipient of a vast sensual diplomacy. No other organs, not even the genitalia, are the subject of such concentrated and varied attention, experimentation, etiquette, and congeniality. Precisely in materialistic societies — which have generated bountiful wealth — people attend public feeding places at which they uneconomically consume food whose cost to them is several times the cost of the ingredients themselves. They are voluntarily paying for the pleasures provided by the cooks, servers, designers. They are being pleasured by taste, originality, perhaps a sense of the exotic and luxury, by the intimate architecture of their experience, and, centrally, by the hubbub of social life that is the mark of a successful restaurant.

No one except a tyrant enjoys an empty restaurant. The cool exclusivity it can provide is far less important than the sturdy, busy civility of a popular bistro or the intense clatter of a dim-sum parlor or the easy, familiar affability of the local diner. The pleasures of the mouth seem to be enjoyed best amid a community of acceptable folk.

When people are prosperous and have the choice, they increasingly choose public dining over private. In 1990, US families that earned over $70,000 a year spent an average of $3,500 on restaurant meals. This is $400 more than the $3,100 they bestowed on their grocers.

Perhaps earning all that money is time-consuming and these people are too pressed for time or unskilled to prepare for themselves the standard of cuisine they expect from the world. So they pay others to offer it to them. But if they are so short of time, why do the costliest meals usually take the longest? Since dinner out is often the evening's total entertainment, we have to assume people are choosing to enjoy food amid a convivial public.

Nevertheless, they are also enjoying clearly physical pleasures. I have already described how humans evolved to eat almost anything. We are omnivores with adaptability and some discernment. This is obviously one reason for our ability to migrate to virtually every corner of the world and still find dinner. With the same assertive bio-flair of the female rabbit who ovulates when she copulates, not only are we able to eat a great variety of foods, but we also *enjoy* it. The taste buds are an effective survival tool. They draw us to enjoy what we need to survive. This is presumably also why, once basic hunger is allayed, people appear to be willing and able to sample a considerable variety of different foods and different preparations of them. Even a society traditionally thought to be rather insular, Japan, newly boasts in its major cities a rich and accomplished sample of styles of cooking from dozens of countries.

The aesthetic and sensual pleasure people enjoy from food and drink is utterly clear. And novelty, too, is attractive: the latest style, the latest tradition, the latest look — all draw the diners.

Elegant variation is the staple of the nation's menu. This relatively recent trend has its limitations, however. As Paul Rozin of the University of Pennsylvania has suggested, it is the very fact that we are omnivorous that allows us on one hand to sample this elegant variation but on the other to suffer possible discomfort or even death caused by unknown foods.[2] Food can also be a weapon, so there is some advantage in being familiar with it, in order to detect when it may be poisoned. An alternative protection in paranoid or dangerous communities is to employ a taster — a common if perilous occupation in despotisms. For example, Saddam Hussein of Iraq employed a taster who was his chef's son.

Another limitation on choice of food and how it is prepared has to do with contamination and disease. Many elements of the Jewish system of kosher food have been related to health and avoiding potentially hazardous foods, such as shellfish and pork, where refrigeration was unavailable. The widespread use of wine with food reflects the simple fact that fermentation turned grape juice into a safe drink, which water may not be; wine was also used as a disinfectant in surgery. And concern about contamination can suffuse an entire society. For example, a principal function of the Indian caste system is to regulate who may prepare the food that particular castes may consume. Thus, Brahmins may only eat food prepared by other Brahmins. While there are a host of religious, attitudinal, and economic factors in the system overall, one core historical function was to try to cope with the vital issues of health and cleanliness in a tropical environment which heightens their deadly importance.[3]

The human menu has changed for a variety of reasons, such as more effective distribution of conventional seeds, agricultural information, and products, as well as the ecological imperilment of various flora and fauna. Since the advent of agriculture and now industrialization, people have actually reduced the variety of foods they eat. Because of technical and cultural limitation of what they can or want to produce, people use only some fifty animal and six hundred plant species out of the thousands that hunter-gatherers had available to them and evidently used. There is a compromise between fewer raw materials and a greater number of variations in preparing them. More has to be done with less. Art and imagination compensate for less natural variety.

A good simple case in point is tofu, or bean curd. This is a foodstuff that is laughably uninteresting in its original state, so bland and plain that, as I've observed elsewhere, "it seems the ideal product of a futuristic dictatorship committed to the denial of fun — the perfect food for a country managed by depressed chemical engineers who relish standardization."[4] Yet this simple substance becomes an extraordinary array of sharply different and attractive foods in the quick hands of oriental cooks. Here is an example of my version of Romer's Rule (which is that animals adapt to change through small mutations, such as acquiring darker skin color when a habitat becomes dry and brown, rather than through major changes, such as developing wings to avoid a predatory enemy). Cultural variation "takes up the slack" to maintain a common and satisfying human balance with the environment and within it. The elegant variation produced by cooks compensates for the loss of sensitivity and access to the plethora of foods that were available to the hunter-gatherer. Culture replaces nature, using "all-natural" ingredients.

Many elements in the food chain produce pleasure. Some are obvious, some are unexpected. It's obvious that people enjoy sharing the food they have — cooking it for one another, exchanging it, delighting one another with it. Less obvious but also potent is the pleasure evidently involved in sharing the acquiring of it — particularly in hunting and fishing, but also in gardening and shopping, in what the ecologist-farmer Wendell Berry has called "the frankly emotional . . . pleasures of nature and pleasures of work."[5] A royal hunting ground or prized salmon river is as agreeable and interesting a feature of life as a jumbly farmers market in Siena or one of the strikingly skillful food shops — most large cities have at least one or two — in which the appearance of the items offered is almost as promising as an advertisement for fireworks. Or, the pleasure may be more austere, as in the locally famous cheese shop in Cavaillon where in the right-hand window trim rounds of new subtle goat cheese are displayed on golden straw as sparely as jewels.

No, there's a world in food, a world of food, a clear-cut world of connection between the body and the world. There's a seasonality, a scarcity, a harvest, a time for the perfect lingonberry or *langoustine* or corn or shad roe or oyster. Two or three or four or more times a day, a fortunate primate can investigate a library of edible and potable options. The menu will depend on climate, purse, taste, avidity, leisure, the company, health, fashion, taboo — as many factors as matter in anything. Nonetheless, however the decision is made, finally food will be brought to the mouth and ingested. A verdict of some sort will be rendered. Life will be sustained for some more hours. Another course will have been enjoyed in a lifelong dinner.

You see it when construction workers turn the edge of their work site into a dining room. All of them are eating a different thing as they sit on the sidewalk, on stacked Sheetrock, on an emerging wall. What people eat is as different as their fingerprints. The restaurant menu is a proof of human variability, of the expansiveness of what people enjoy. Why else is it so big? The average modest New York neighborhood Chinese-restaurant lunch menu for $4.25

boasts some fifteen choices of entrée, three kinds of soup, three kinds of rice, and often a choice between a soup and an egg roll. Mathematically, many choices for $4.25. Exactly 710. The restaurants do well with this. People enjoy the food, the price, the choice, the whole operation.

This is quite comprehensible, when adults are doing the choosing. Why do infants prefer some foods to others? As I have already noted, it perplexed me that my child preferred one kind of pureed vegetable to another. No one earnestly taught him, because no role-model adult consumed such charmless muck. So whatever could be the reason to choose between the squash with rice and peas with potatoes? Simple. Preference. Pleasure. The beginning motions of a trajectory of taste. He would sooner not eat than eat something he would sooner not eat.

Martin's Herring Store

Why is a professional anthropologist going on so about food? In a study of pleasure one has to. I have other reasons too. I will elaborate. I begin with my childhood, because my father owned a grocery store in Montreal. His name was Martin, his store "Martin's Herring Store." His claim to expertise with this highly adaptable swimmer was presumably a way of attracting the largely Jewish Eastern European immigrant customers he sought. For them this tasty and durable fish had played a historically significant role in their diet in "the old country." So cavernous barrels of various styles and intensities of preserved small fish buttressed the back of the store, presumably to draw the aficionados through the rest of the offerings on their way. There were also tubs of olives, many kinds of beans, dried fruits to compose the tureen of compote, slabs of astonishingly tasty halvah, intense kosher sausages, and brooding rounds of cheese. It was a fascinating world to a child, of edible items bearing with them the tastes and history of mysterious other places.

Then the store prospered. It was gentrified to "Martin's Self-Service Groceteria." Now nearly all the items were packaged except for fruits and vegetables, which I would occasionally be permitted to buy wholesale from the French-Canadian farmers at the Saint Lawrence market, a brief bicycle ride away. The best was the corn, which erupted in August, plush and plenty. Everyone became a corn connoisseur for a few weeks. Then the store was driven out of business by the changing residential patterns of immigrants. A Greek man bought the lease.

Food was both business and pleasure. I seem to have carried on the family trade in this respect. Having been on the business end of the cash register for a while, it has always seemed to me to be a matter of social responsibility that people be fed good, tasty food when they pay for it, so I have always regarded good and fair restaurants and shops as a major communal resource. When I lived in London, I would frequently submit critiques of restaurants to *The Good Food Guide*, which was first established by gourmet English socialists to help overcome the legendary indifference of their compatriots to the pleasures of food; as I have already boasted, eventually I was asked to become a covert inspector for the *Guide*.

This personal history has helped me establish a baseline for discussing food, which is that its taste, its nutrition, its value, and the ambition and accomplishment of its preparation are all vital features of a community. Shops, restaurants, markets super and simple, compose a major part of the array of resources with which a community deals with daily life. Along with its drinks, such as wines and beers and other spirits, the food of a community is one of the easiest, most sensible, most interesting, and least antisocial means of enjoying pleasure.

There is a politics of food, just as the matter of the enjoyment of sex has forever — at least since Eden, Mother Eve, and apple-of-knowledge pie — been a political question. Is food (and drink, its kissing cousin), like sex, a provider of pleasure that must be curtailed or somehow *controlled?* Is it possible that the contemporary drama about food as a source of personal extermination is nothing but a new version of the sermons about hellfire and brimstone that surround the stimulation of genitalia? Is Mephistopheles about to suborn the mouth as well as the penis and vagina to do his morally violent worst? Do the bacon and eggs — fat, cholesterol, no fiber — of the next day's breakfast correspond in turpitude to the lubricious one-night stand? Are the morning-after eggs Benedict the moral equivalent of the strip-down, tumble-down night before?

If I pose these questions rather dramatically, I do so within the graphic context of the history of an organism that managed to make it shameful in some beds for husband and wife to see each other's nude body; that legislated prohibition of any alcohol at all; that currently insists that Iranian women, among others, conceal even their faces in public. Why should food be different? Perhaps it is — or so it seems from the success of McDonald's, which provides fatty cooked animal protein with vast success and whose double-humped-M logo surely owes more than a smidgen to the image of heroic breasts: the distillation of Dolly Parton.

Then again, perhaps it does not. But perhaps the mammal remembers.

The Good Book Comes in Two Versions: Diet and Cook

Sexual caper even with oneself usually takes place in private. This obviously explains in part why it is a popular focus of general fascination. But much eating takes place in public. Increasingly, fast-food and similar restaurants feed many people who would previously consume food at home or dining out with people who knew them — the communal long tables of the Basque restaurants of San Francisco or the large, round family tables of any Chinatown come to mind as models of what was once the predominant way of "eating out." At home, the family dinner was ubiquitous and a focus of the day. James Fenimore Cooper described a typical Manhattan residence in the 1820s: "The eating or dining room is almost invariably one of the best in the home. The custom is certainly of English origin, and takes its rise in the habit of sitting an hour or two after the cloth is removed, picking nuts, drinking wine, chatting, yawning, and gazing about the apartment."

People normally know what, where, and with whom other people eat. But they are usually in the dark about the nature and intensity of their sexual activity. The joy of sex is concealed, the joy of eating is obvious.

Nevertheless, there is considerable inhibition about eating, too, when food is very abundant. In principle a person can have nearly unlimited sexual activity — with a spouse, one or more lovers, or through masturbation — without deleterious effects either physically or economically. There may be real risks, such as of disease or unwanted pregnancy, but these are largely preventable. So there is little incentive for people to boast about how little sex they enjoy. The contrary is much more likely.

But the pattern is quite different with food. In the wealthy countries, inhibiting the pleasures of eating has become a widespread pattern. This is mainly for obvious reasons associated with health risks from excess weight, high-fat diets, and the like. A surprisingly pervasive tension about the pleasures of eating is graphically and simply reflected in bookstores. An army of luxurious cookbooks and meal memoirs faces its enemy army across the aisle, the diet book brigade. Caught in a relentless vise between pleasure and prudence, a plurality of the economically privileged population is on a permanent diet. I've noted the effective flattery "Oh, you've lost weight" — a comment that in other historic circumstances was a mark of sympathy and dread. People among the wealthiest on the planet fly to very costly spas, where they are fed painfully austere portions of food while also enduring the exercise and trailblazing routines a Kalahari Bushman hunter-gatherer has no choice but to accept if he is to live until tomorrow. This practice is interesting not only because it may effectively reduce weight and improve health. It also secures social status. The endeavor is seen not as preposterous but as earnestly worthwhile. It is a secular replacement for going to Lourdes or Mecca. It reflects well on the campers, on their morality and sense of personal discipline. Unhappy and ravenous campers perhaps, but virtuous paragons whose morality is a shield against mortality.

In contrast, fat people are discriminated against because it is assumed they lack backbone. They are self-indulgent. They are self-destructive. They enjoy bad food and too much food too well. Clearly they don't exercise. They are vehemently lazy. Their cholesterol levels are shameful. Their fiber intake and their moral fiber are both zero. Medical statisticians and moralists alike define them as surefire quick losers in the war against mortality. They do not have the warrior leanness and hardness on which people can depend. They enjoy intake more than output. They bear the equivalent of the scarlet letter on their indecently curvaceous jellybellies. Since they probably drink as well as gorge, they add medical complications and moral peril to calories.

One caveat: we are concerned here principally with members of wealthy societies, in which excess, not scarcity, is the problem. In communities in West Africa where the commitment to leanness has not become a medical issue, a political "big man" may be a literal big one also. In the community in which Martin's Herring Store prospered, the ample bellies of uncles were actually called "corporations," as if the fat they stockpiled was a store of assets — which they in fact would be in a community facing potential starvation.

Some may legitimately protest that plump people suffer from metabolic defects or a genetic predisposition to fatness and that the austerity of a saint would still leave them with unduly curvy bodies. Such factors undoubtedly underly the body shape of a substantial number of people, who are doubly and unfairly punished by the effects of extra weight as well as critics' disapproval of their allegedly poor moral character.

This medical explanation accounts for some people. But the issue is much broader. I've noted that human beings, as well as other mammals, appear to be genetically keen to store fat in times of surplus. University of Michigan geneticist James Neel has rather convincingly proposed that there is a "thrifty gene" that prompts the human body to retain extra food rather than dispel it as waste, in order to prepare for the "boom-and-bust" cycle that creatures dependent on nature must be able to endure.

No Stop Signs at the Table

In addition to this genetic mechanism, which does exist, there is another, which doesn't: a clear-cut cue to stop eating. Animals in the boom-and-bust world of hunting-gathering must stock up when they can. So a lion operating during a time of scarce prey will eat up to 40 percent of his body weight when he strikes lucky — his belly will even drag on the ground for a time. But he probably doesn't have a dinner engagement with his boss that evening, and in fact he may not eat again for a week. So putting on weight is a sign of health and effectiveness. It reveals that the useful and conservative system of fat retention is working just fine, as is a functionally understandable enthusiasm to make calories and hay while the sun shines.

Not only that. When the body is deprived of food, it prudently reduces its metabolism to get by on less. However, if its usual quantity of food is restored, the metabolic rate does not respond promptly — one reason why crash dieters often regain weight they have lost, and more. The body's system is biased toward sustaining life and being healthy, not losing weight and looking chic. This underscores the plight of the crash dieter.

Virtually everyone has the thrifty gene to some degree. It, rather than some more idiosyncratic genetic characteristics, underlies widespread changes in body size. For example, in 1905 some 5 percent of the US population was overweight. By 1985 this figure was 40 percent! Such an enormous increase in four generations cannot be accounted for by genetic change in the character of the population. It is far too sudden for that. The more obvious cause for the physical growth of the body social in industrial countries lies with ampler and richer diets, particularly in terms of animal fats. For example, in 1850, fat made up 18 percent of the diet in France, while in 1989 it constituted 42 percent; French consumption of red meat increased from 97 pounds in 1936 to 243 pounds in 1980. In 1989 the Greater London Council estimated that 75 percent of the city's residents suffer from diet-related disease during their lifetimes. Boyd Eaton of the Emory University Medical School ascribes three-fourths of deaths in Western industrial countries to causes related to way of life.[6] Germans consume more than 600 milligrams of cholesterol a day, though the upper limit recommended by nutritionists is between 250 and 300 milligrams. Some 75 percent of German adults have subjected themselves to weight-loss diets. The traditionally healthy Japanese diet is changing too; some 25 percent of it is now fat, the upper limit of acceptability. Fast foods are also enormously popular in Japan, among young people in particular. Recall that when McDonald's opened its first outlet in Tokyo, so many hamburgers were sold so quickly the first day that the cash register burned out! A sociomedical problem, *homanji*, or fat children, has appeared for the first time. And, as I've mentioned, the most luxurious and prestigious Japanese beef is almost indescribably fatty even by comparison with prime beef in North America or Europe.

Of course, dietary change is not the only major cause of such physical change. There is also a sharply reduced need for physical exertion in order to make a living and get through the day. Hardly any physical effort is necessary to acquire food. Many restaurants now deliver prepared meals, from sushi to veal rollatini to pizza to Chinese food. People walk much less, watch television rather than square dance, depend on escalators and elevators not stairs. Weight gain can even be affected by the reduced energy needed to operate a computer rather than a manual typewriter. Homes have dozens of small motors that reduce the amount of bodily work necessary to maintain safety, cleanliness, and comfort. Modern motorcars make much personal transport almost totally physically effortless. To use their bodies vigorously, people these days have to produce a bizarre and specialized behavior called exercise. This can be a challenging activity, a chore, a social opportunity, or a pleasure. However, it is often something undertaken for its own sake — not to mow the hay or chop the firewood or stalk the gazelle or thresh the grain or scrub wet clothing on a washboard.

Many people exercise only because they think they should or must. No pain, no gain — no survival. They enjoy no fun. They are shaking their fists at epidemiological data, at the lean and mean Grim Reaper.

Holy War at Dinner: The Extermination Model of Food

The war between the cookbook army and the diet book army continues. The battlefield is the body. Reasonably enough, because the body is the principal cause of the war in the first place. The conflict is between the enormous and unremitting physical and social pleasure food and drink provide and the weight of prudent medical opinion and simple experience. The temptation is so great, so pervasive, and so inexpensive. Can there be other sins — for example, sexual ones — as easy and convenient to commit and as cheap as buying a pound of butter and spreading it deliciously on fresh sourdough or whipping it into mousse or frying one soft-shell crab per generous tablespoon?

With so much tasty food available so easily, what is remarkable is not how many affluent people are overweight, but why there are aren't millions more. Why isn't a food-driven country such as France entirely populated by people the shape and size of its Michelin man, the jolly figure of the tire company whose annual restaurant and hotel guide is a vital icon of sublimated national gluttony? It is also interesting that France has a relatively low incidence of cardiovascular disease, though its diet is similar in cholesterol and other characteristics to that of Americans, who suffer far more from this affliction.[7] One serious explanation comes from R. Curtis Ellison, chief of the Section of Preventive Medicine and Epidemiology of the Boston University School of Medicine. The principal distinction, he suggests, is the greater consumption of wine in France. He relates the different health experience to the well-documented protective function of moderate amounts of wine, about two or three glasses per day, which reduces cardiovascular risk.[8] Consumption of large amounts of garlic may be involved as well — it appears to reduce cholesterol.

Surrounding food is an endless battle involving pleasure, calories, vanity, the fear of early death, lust for taste, and sociability. It has come to seem ever more theological, particularly in North America. The higher the death rate from food-induced diseases goes and the more rampant becomes the information about the extermination model of food, the more pervasive is the explicit conflict between meat and morality and between pleasure and prudence. Traditional supermarket products such as pastas irrelevantly boast that they are cholesterol- and sodium-free. Advertising copy about olive oil no longer rhapsodizes about the antique terraced groves of Liguria in which the fragrant source of the golden liquid is hand-picked. Instead, there is a grim medical report about saturated fats and the inner tubes of the buyer's arteries.

If in the name of science you eavesdrop on people talking in restaurants, you may hear them calculating which food is good or not for them, rationalizing the high-calorie animal-fat food because it's a celebration or a holiday. They decide, "Let's splurge on calories" — splurge, that is, on intake, not expenditure. Whatever their decision, it is clear they are wholly aware of the medical and moral meaning of the food they will consume. One person in the restaurant business told me that females frequently consult the dessert menu first and plan the rest of their careful binge accordingly. The writer and broadcaster Martin Goldensohn has commented that married men's eating of high-cholesterol food when they are away from their considerate and careful wives is a contemporary form of male infidelity. And even when fast-food outlets do offer low-fat, nutritious food, there is clear marketing evidence that customers continue to choose their traditional favorites.[9]

At the end of the twentieth century, the apple is widely regarded as a healthy food — vitamin-filled, fibrous, clear-cut, virtuous. But what if Adam had offered Eve an agonizingly rich apple *pie*, nearly hot, either with taut *crème fraîche* or sharp cheddar cheese?

In any event, even vaguely informed consumers contemplate the dilemma: should they sin by eating the hot apple pie with cream or cheese, die earlier, and probably go to hell? Or should they reject the dessert — any dessert — and linger firmly with a glass of spring water, extend their life, and get to heaven?

It is necessary to extend Bertolt Brecht's aphorism "a man is just the food he eats." Now, people's *souls* are the food they eat. It has gotten devilishly complicated.

Playing the China Card

If the mouth were a male sex organ, it would be erect all the time. It appears that people are in high and chronic readiness for the pleasures of food. This poses a particular problem for members of communities with ample food and no sense of oncoming scarcity. Is there a model to follow that will both yield pleasure and protect health? Or is the only plausible alternative to adopt stringent diets bursting with fiber, complex carbohydrates, just the odd morsels of meat, fish, and poultry, and microscopic traces of fat. One such diet, proposed by Dean Ornish when he was at the UCLA Medical

School, restricts animal and fish protein to 10 percent of daily intake — and there is some evidence it reverses cardiovascular damage suffered by heart-attack victims.

Possibly such a draconian diet is desirable for people already victimized by a lifetime of high-fat eating and in dire need of remedy and repair. However, there is some indication that whole cultures can develop patterns of diet that provide enjoyment and endurance at once. Two come to mind, the Italian and the Chinese. The Mediterranean diet of which the Italian is an exemplar uses much fresh fruit and lots of vegetables, little butterfat, much olive oil, and carbohydrates such as pasta, polenta, and risotto, fish when available, and relatively little meat. Because of strong local culinary traditions and regional pride, international fast-food restaurants have fared relatively poorly in Italy and the result of these and other factors is a health profile unusually positive in comparison with other industrial countries.

But perhaps the most interesting and significant healthy diet is the Chinese.[10] It confronts directly the desire for pleasure in food within the confines of economic constraint. First of all, it is an immensely successful cuisine, feeding as it does one quarter of the planet's population in Asia on a daily basis, and countless other people, too, who enjoy it virtually everywhere in the world. As well, because of historic famines and the pressure on arable land, food in China has unusual social importance. A common morning greeting is "Have you had rice yet?" or "Have you eaten?" And there is an extensive traditional lore that surrounds Chinese cooking — for example, about foods that are "hot" or "cold" — with implications for health and social solidarity.[11] Food has an importance equaled by the traditional skill of its chefs.

During my first meal in China, a central value of Chinese cuisine was clearly if simply revealed. This was at the Fragrant Hill Hotel on the outskirts of Beijing, near the Summer Palace. The menu handed us in the dining room was long and detailed, and the English translation was the second half of the document. The first entries were predictable and understandable enough. Appetizers, soups, beef, pork, seafood, fish, vegetables, and then — *Food*. Food was noodles and rice, the substantial carbohydrates. This was the essence of the meal and it was named for the generic substance. In common and traditional Chinese cuisine, all the other items — apart from the appetizers — were principally used as flavorings for whatever grain was being consumed. Unlike Euro-Americans, who will usually order Chinese food with one main protein item for each diner, Chinese people will extend the pleasure value of their rice or noodles by adding to them small portions of the special dishes. And this is why these preparations are usually so clearly and highly flavored — they have a lot of aesthetic work to do, much flavor to deliver. The sharp salt or sweet or spicy or otherwise highly sauced food rewards the diner with sufficient oral pleasure to make the bland rice or noodle staple tolerable. The chefs have responded at once to the need for pleasure and the constraints of China's economy by producing a vocabulary of dishes that ensures a lively dinner.

Because the food is usually chopped into small bits, it is quick to cook, retains its fresh food value, and is frugal with scarce cooking fuel. Because the small pieces each have a large surface area relative to their bulk, they can absorb and carry much more flavor than if they were in large portions such as steaks or filets or whole chicken breasts.

Several vital social features of this cuisine also help sustain its popularity. It is crucial that the food is shared. Rather than separate dishes arriving as the individualistic property of separate people, one per person, here there is a rush of different plates offering a variety of experiences. These are shared out either informally by the diners or by the host or hostess, who will wields that "big spoon" and urges guests to sample the array.

Another aspect of the social meaning of Chinese food is that because the food is shared, diners are obligated to attend to the intake of others and adjust their own choices accordingly. As I have noted, the most desirable and honorable guest at a Chinese dinner doesn't reveal his favorite food by eating much of it. He eats least of what he likes most. He must orient to the group. Also, the ethically ideal table shape is round, so that everyone is equidistant from the food, which is usually on a lazy Susan in the center. This emphasizes the democratic nature of the meal and the interdependence of the diners.

The net impact of the balance between carbohydrates and other foods, the negligible amount of dairy fat consumed, the colorful variety of choices, and the large component of freshly cooked vegetables result in a diet that delivers a large number of calories but by comparison with, say, the American or Belgian diet, leads neither to obesity nor cardiovascular damage. It is also possible that the ambiance of the Chinese meal makes what they eat particularly satisfying. People can eat less than they might on their own — no clean-plate club in China. Because the meal form is so satisfying, there is a relative lack of emphasis on desserts in Chinese cuisine. Traditionally, people would finish with soup or rice. This recalled deprivation and affirmed that during this meal they had eaten amply. The economic factor plays a role here. Nonetheless, fresh fruit is often the only dessert offered by even ambitious restaurants in China, and by overseas Chinese elsewhere who suffer no shortage of food whatsoever.

I Hereby Sentence You to Dinner in the Cafeteria

It is merely banal or redundant to announce that nutritious food should also be tasty and offered to diners under agreeable conditions. But this hasn't governed the catering for countless schools, prisons, hospitals, and even private kitchens in which convenience, habit, and sufficiency loom larger than pleasure and invention. I was once told by the Vancouver architect Arthur Erickson that he wanted very badly to design a hospital, along the lines defined by the classical Greeks. Sick people should have the most beautiful architecture, the best clothing, the most interesting artwork, and the most delicious food. After all, they are ill and need it most. An elegant idea, it took the industrial world's medical system many years to realize that a sense of treatment as punishment was not helpful to patient recovery. Meanness can cost more, too, because patients recover less quickly.

There is little reason why the same Greek principle should not extend to the healthy; pleasure is not only desirable but, as I have tried to define it, is also an evolutionary entitlement. Not only that. Where food is concerned and simple survival is not the issue, its taste and meaning, and its art, may loom far larger than nutrition. This can run easily to foolish extreme. The remarkable American gastronomic writer M. F. K. Fisher describes how during the fatal reign of Louis XVI of France, humble cow's milk became a fine delicacy when it was expressed and presented by aristocratic ladies. Evidently, the more adventurous not only offered the milk but provided their admirers with porcelain drinking cups made from impressions of their breasts.[12] The gruff Napoléon who followed later on and who had other priorities soon extinguished this folderol of food. But the principle of embellishing nutrients stands. Pleasure remains a principal goal.

Gone Fishin'

It has been wistfully observed that the heart is a lonely hunter. But human beings are not lonely hunters or lonely gatherers. While the move to agriculture some ten thousand years ago required our ancestors to complicate their social arrangements drastically, even hunters and gatherers lead strongly complex social lives and in general are intensely cooperative when they gather food. By contrast with the animals closest to us, the other primates, we are highly cooperative food gatherers. Once they are weaned, the other primates tend to acquire and consume their own food — though they will communicate with each other about fruiting trees[13] and will occasionally — among the baboons, for example — cooperate to catch and eat a small mammal such as an immature gazelle or other primate. Nevertheless, as adults they are principally independent operators who each eat what they can individually acquire.

Not so people. Not only do we cooperate but we enjoy it. In some contexts this we call work and in others recreation. For example, hunting and fishing remain the two most popular participant sports in North America despite the cost, inconvenience, and danger, as well as the legally restricted return even skillful predators may earn. (The Canadian government has estimated that the average sport fishing enthusiast spends about $350 to catch a single salmon.[14]) In an almost wholly industrial society in which 90 percent of all trout consumed in America are raised on farms, and despite ever-scarcer land and growing criticism of gun-using hunters, squads of eager men and, in some cases, women wake before the autumn dawn to squat in cold, damp blinds hoping to outwit ducks or to engage in spylike sorties in forests hiding leaping deer.

Such groups possess signal emotional meaning for their members. One hunter in British Columbia described the meaning: when he drank rye whiskey, he customarily purchased Seagram's VO; but when he went hunting with his chums, they drank only Crown Royal, the ranking premium brand. In American society, male hunting and fishing groups (as well as regular gambling cliques) offer one of the few examples of enduring groups that cut across the lines of social class. So a bank manager and a dentist and a mechanic and fireman may hunt together, though they will be far less likely to belong to the same golf or country club.[15]

My proposal is that the emotional satisfaction of cooperatively acquiring food, in nature, stimulates voluntary and often intense solidarity between men — the communal activity Wendell Berry refers to and calls a source of "pleasure . . . so to speak, affection in action."[16] They continue to enjoy this, however inconvenient the process and however costly per pound the ultimate yield of protein. It feels good to people when they do it now, when it's a luxury, because it felt good when people did it back then, when it was a necessity. Food gathering — what was acquired and how — was obviously critical to survival. The emotionality surrounding such cooperative gathering of food was part of the selective evolution of our species, like the emotionality surrounding courtship and sex. People who enjoyed each other and the process of cooperative food gathering were more successful than loners or noncooperators. This was part of the package of successful behavior and adequate nutrition transmitted to the next generation.

It is surely significant that people with all the money necessary to feed themselves and those they care about more than adequately nevertheless seek to reserve to themselves the privilege of the chase.[17] I have a cottage in New York State in an area rich with trout, deer, wildfowl, and rabbit. Hundreds of thousands of potentially valuable acres are kept pristine so that the members of dozens of hunting and fishing clubs can on a relatively few occasions during the year re-create the secretive strategies of the Upper Paleolithic less than two hours from Times Square. My outsider's sense is that the members think that what they are doing is close to the sacred, a luxury beyond dollar calculation. One legal deer per year, some trout, some noisy birds — worth it, worth it disproportionately for the *pleasure*.

There is controversy in anthropology about the status of the hypothesis that hunting had an overwhelmingly decisive physical and emotional impact on the evolutionary scheme. A strong and technically skilled group of scientists have asserted that early human beings secured most or much of their meat by scavenging — by taking or stealing the prey killed by master hunters such as lions. They base their interpretation of the archaeological record on detailed and exquisite study of, for example, the microscopic marks made on fossil bones found near human sites — marks that appear to suggest, among other things, that the teeth of other animals made the first or main impression on these remains.[18]

They have a point. There is evidence from various other fossil finds and from contemporary ethnography that reveals that people were and are opportunists.[19] They will take quick advantage of another species' kill if the killer is gone or can be driven off. Leopards and hyenas can be made to flee, though lions are reluctant and may become prey themselves if the human hunters are sufficiently numerous and confident.

Nevertheless, there are some problems, too, with this notion. One is, of course, that dead animals, particularly in the hot climate in which we evolved, would be dangerous to eat if not quickly consumed. Presumably for this reason, many animals, including domestic cats, will not eat a prey animal they have not themselves killed. This reflects an evolved inhibition, complex but understandable. As well, the existence of the dead animal implies a stronger living one that killed it and that may retain some interest in it — for example, a lion. Reposing much confidence in the tolerance of a large predator for theft of his kill is plainly potentially hazardous.

But my principal question about this scavenging hypothesis is raised by what provides pleasure to contemporary people. Do you know of one royal scavenging preserve? Do you know of one club where people pay high fees in order to scavenge the leavings of others? Is not the status of ragpickers, "bag ladies," urban scavengers, the least enviable in the social system? Do they compare in any way to the hunters with their ceremonial red jackets, their complex leatherware, their costly guns, their killing grounds? No. The two groups are incomparable. One is envied, the other not, even though in a simpleminded sense the scavenger's job is safer, easier, and closer to home.

But one is fun, the other isn't. One yields pride, the other resignation. I think this reflects an evolutionary heritage that focused most passionately and skillfully on hunting, and only from necessity and episodically on scavenging.

Most people are unlikely to be fervent about this seemingly technical academic argument. But it may guide us as we try to examine what contemporary behavior is pleasurable — to earn an insight into what worked for us in the past and perhaps, in some complex but durable way, selectively gained a foothold in our nature. Only a few people enjoy being hit with whips. Nearly all enjoy gentle caresses and sexual intercourse. Why? This is "natural" — the result of our evolutionary nature. There is something intrinsically sensible in the idea that what pleases nearly all people must have helped most of their ancestors endure. It seems likely that the way people choose today to acquire wild food reveals something about how we used to get it in the past. The low status of scavengers in societies as disparate as Belgium and India (where the caste system formalized it ruthlessly: they were the Untouchables[20]) suggests that this is a compromised form of survival.

Compromised, and no fun.

Gone to Market for Hearth Food

If scavenging for food is not fun, shopping for it often is. Outdoor markets and ambitious food shops are widely attractive to both purchasers and voyeurs. If such shops don't permit hunting, they offer gathering, in a garden even more plentiful, various, and colorful than any imagined Eden. Contemplating, comparing, choosing food obviously involves elaborate and absorbing skills and enthusiasms.

One of the most interesting markets in the world is the Tsujuki fish market of Tokyo. By four o'clock in the morning, a vast congress of buyers and sellers converges around what seems to be a virtually complete aquatic museum of natural history. Because so much fish is consumed raw in Japan, as sushi and sashimi, choosing it is a vital part of preparing it. A sushi chef can stand or fall on the freshness and quality of what he buys as well as on how he prepares it. The market is intense, varied — a phenomenal display of demand for what people can and want to eat and the ability of fishermen to find and provide it.

The Tsujuki provides a snapshot cross section of Japan's dinner that day. With the inexorability of digestion itself, the improbable, exuberant spectacle happens every morning. By eight-thirty the heavy traffic ebbs. The retail trade begins. Then the thing to do is have a sushi breakfast in one of the restaurants nestled at the outskirts of the market, where its participants repair after their late-night negotiations.

Perhaps it is because I am a grocer's son, but there has always seemed to me to be a special and significant drama to markets. They encapsulate well much of what people are doing and efficiently dramatize whatever flora and fauna of the region pertain to human society. But I mean markets, not supermarkets or groceries where you see and smell packages. There is a firm difference between the clinical rows of boxes at the MallMarket and the piles of cardamom, oranges, mangoes, and fifty-seven varieties of rice in the Bombay market or the one in the Old City of Jerusalem, or the spectacular jumbles of Ibadan or Accra, or even the comparatively wan earnestness of the Greenmarkets in New York City.

To a traveler, some of the difference is undoubtedly the result of the exoticism and intensity of new environments. Nevertheless, there is also a difference in the naturalness of the heaps-of-herbs market versus the wall-of-boxes store. One is gathering at its best, the other is administration. Of course, good markets are also well managed and there is a clear and traditional order to them. They may be visually lively and seemingly fresh, but the arrangement of stalls, who occupies them, and under what terms is not casual. The markets convey a sense of deftness and directness — the person behind the counter today may have yesterday been behind the plow. This somehow rounds out the meaning of the food. It was never possible to charge very much at the Automat, however good the food.

Nude Food

The distribution system pioneered by Huntington Hartford of the A&P stores in the United States has enabled more people to enjoy healthier, more abundant, more various, and more interesting food at a relatively low markup than other extant systems. The US industry norm is that net profit hovers around 1 percent of volume. However, as the century draws to a close, the most progressive and successful chains draw particular profits from traditional, primordial, boutique-type sections of their stores: in-store bakeries, fish markets, prepared-food sections, custom butchers. Produce is increasingly displayed in hearty and relatively dramatic ways. Theatrical lighting designers have entered the grocery business. Sensual visual appeal replaces perfect clinical geometry as the style of presentation. A grim blend of sub-Bauhaus aesthetics with perfect row-house hygiene yields to vivid and lucid displays of naked food. Voilà! Tableaux of suddenly rediscovered artisanal culinary drama: the baker baking, the butcher slicing, the barbecue chef assessing the food, the smoke, the heat.

In these lusty sections, the markup is much higher than in the grocery Bauhaus. The operators of industrial-style food stores were surprised that people enjoy ways of selling food that are nostalgic, even primitive. But the marketers have been adept and are adapting. The industry is changing. Shoppers are willing to pay extra for what they perceive as interesting and robust food whose origins and preparation are accessible and plain. Not only "natural" food connects, but seemingly "natural" ways of selling it.

A fruit-and-vegetable store called Balducci's in the Greenwich Village neighborhood in which I once lived redigested itself into a beyond-scale temple of food. Nonetheless, it retains some sense of a neighborhood feedlot (though now a rich neighborhood). Busloads of tourists come from the suburbs to explore food shopping that is sensually intimate. It is a sensory success. The memory recurs to me of the effectiveness of the Food Halls of Harrods in

London. This is the luxurious upper-class shop marked by traditional English reserve in most other areas. But its celebrated food shop is visceral — hanging game unplucked, colorful, flagrantly dead and elegant; fish swimming in ice at arm's length; cheese odorous and unpacked; unrinsed wild mushrooms pyramided in their traveling crates. It is a sentient, dramatic shop, the jewel of the enterprise, borne of passion not propriety.

If people feel there is a danger that food will exterminate rather than succor them, they will want to control the process of feeding themselves and thus enjoy what they consume. It becomes at once pathetic and reassuring that the word "natural" on a food product is supposed to be an endorsement. It is pathetic because what else but natural things should be permitted to enter the stomach? At the same time, it's reassuring because people want contact with elemental substances along with the pleasure they enjoy during their pit stop — smell, taste, flair, aggressive surprise, anything. The stomach — that turgid bottom-line arena of encounter between person and environment — will do its work, no problem. But before that obligatory chemistry, there's an opportunity for play. Enjoying food.

Lively people become tax collectors. What they eat in order to survive must also yield some tax. The tax is pleasure. Not just from candy, either. Think about your best dinner during the past seven months. It was mainly not dessert.

Cooking with Gas

Hunting, fishing, gathering, gardening, and shopping for food provide pleasure. Obviously, so do cooking and serving it. Here is the end point of the underlying mammalian transaction, the POP — the point of purchase. For the hungry person it may be better to receive than to give. But an elaborate suite of pleasures is associated with feeding other people. Virtually everywhere, there is a colorful mixture of art, technique, economy, and tradition. This is called cooking — the art of how food is prepared.

How people fashion the substances that sustain them is of deep interest to them. There is usually an added extra ingredient; the herbs, spices, and other flavorings, how and when they are added, and the various methods of preparation. Take a common and drastically simple foodstuff such as lima beans. Try to predict how many genuinely different recipes will exist for it in the world. It is likely you will underestimate severely. There seems to be no limit on the quite urgent aesthetic ingenuity of cooks. There is also surprisingly little real loss of already successful recipes.

Culinary knowledge has been maintained as lore and tradition. It is a pervasive, unquestionable element of daily life. Formal schools for cooking are a relatively new addition. Apprenticeship has been the customary way of training professional handlers of food. There are also systems of inherited status, such as the Indian caste arrangement. The principal route for learning about food ran through the home kitchen, across the dining table, or by the fireside. The extraordinary variety and invention in the foods people produce are revealing. They confirm the role of pleasure in both production and consumption. They underscore the significance of pleasure in determining what people decide to do with their time and energy. Food is not just part of the veterinary process of feeding people. It is the starting point of recurrent pleasure.

Not all is artful folderol and cultivation of the mouth's muse. There is nutritional justification for major elements of interesting cuisine. Beans must be cooked or they can be dangerous. Yogurt contains enzymes that allow people who otherwise couldn't to digest milk solids. Roasting pork to a tasty turn kills potentially dangerous parasites. Garlic and onions add decisive tastes to food and provide a variety of medical and antiseptic benefits.[21] Piquant marinades are interesting to taste and also tenderize and even "cook" some foodstuffs.

Nevertheless, pleasure counts big. Like music, which is not necessary for survival, food, which is, can be fun to make. This is genuinely optional pleasure. It is unlikely that we are genetically urged to cook. No chromosomal whispers are known to lure us to the stove. Cooking depends on our control of fire, an ability we acquired relatively recently in our history; it is not probable that there has been genetic selection for good cooking, at least in the modern sense. But for better providers of more interesting food — yes. Better hunters and gatherers will set a better table. Skillful butchers, skinners, peelers, salad makers, and nutcrackers would then as now benefit themselves and those who ate their food with a real advantage in both the productive and reproductive systems.

Fire and cooking sharply heightened the ways to enjoy the pleasures of food. They must have enhanced the impulse to create and share these pleasures. Cooking was the social equivalent of the wheel. Our exquisite and dauntless sensitivity to tastes and smells, which impelled, governed, and guarded our consumption of food, now could be turned in a symphonic way to its production. The stakes were suddenly higher. If the way to a man's heart was through his stomach, the way to a woman's was through her broiler and her breadbasket. Once communities expanded, particularly after the emergence of agriculture and pastoralism, feasts became a hard central feature of social interaction, especially between and among families. As Lévi-Strauss instructed us, the sharing of food was next in importance only to incest prohibition. The exchange of mates between families was the only process more significant for human evolution than food sharing. But it was also wholly associated with it;[22] the wedding dinner established a circle of implication and meaning.

The new methods of food production increased supplies markedly. The new social density they permitted and required also turned food into the focus of much of the domestic and familial diplomacy around which social life now turned. Skill at producing pleasure at the table had a new meaning for social status, for marital arrangements, for political and similar alignments. It defined and supported the network of female alliances so crucial to sustaining and monitoring the social group, because women managed the distribution of food.

Recent discoveries suggest that hunters, gatherers, and, later, foragers lived with considerable and unexpected complexity. Excavations in Denmark reveal that foraging groups some five thousand years ago were quite large. It appears that they were both affluent and sedentary. They successfully made the transition from a culture dependent on the reindeer. They settled near water, hunted large sea prey such as porpoises and whales, and collected shellfish and fish[23] — this provided the bulk of the diet — much like contemporary Greenland Eskimos, who take 75 percent of their food from the sea. Interestingly, it has been estimated that prudent hunting among the Aleutian Islanders would have required a core group of some six to eight families involving about seventy-five people.[24] This already presupposes a fair amount of cooperation, mating arrangements, and the like.

Of course, cooking was available to add complexity and taste to food. Like the 1820s Manhattan dinner described by James Fenimore Cooper, dinner around the campfire, in the tent, cave, igloo, or copse, both defined social life and stimulated the enjoyments of the mouth. Compare the dinner of five thousand years ago with the newly traditional barbecue, with its particular primordial attention to the taste of smoke — grapevine, mesquite, apple, hickory, charcoal, always surrounded by the magnetic aroma of charring fat.

New foods and more food meant more opportunity to create more tastes and new ones. Hence, more and new pleasures. Now — then — not only food but also its taste could be exchanged. The currency of the pleasures of the mouth increased in complexity. More syllables permitted more vocabulary, which made speech more elaborate and, hence, eloquence more conspicuous. The language of food and its complexity also developed new norms of complicated excellence. Not only cooks but sailors explored the spice routes.

Society Was in Ferment but 3867 BC Was Still a Good Year for Burgundy

Something else may have been added at that formative time too. Booze. The anthropologists S. H. Katz and M. M. Voigt of the University of Pennsylvania have speculated that the development of agriculture was decisively stimulated by the discovery that when the treated and mashed seeds of grain lingered with liquid the mixture fermented to became beer. Despite the common suggestion that beer was first produced some 5,000 years ago, an earlier date of 8,000 to 10,000 years ago is suspected by Katz and Voigt. Some of the earliest pots of that period reveal the trace of beer. They surmise that this was such a desirable product that people made sure they had the grain with which to make it.[25] They also speculate that the desirability of the liquid directly stimulated humans to cultivate grains that till then had been gathered in the wild. If agriculture was an emotional step backward for humans, moonshine eased the transition.

Women were principally responsible for this innovation. In pre-Columbian Peru women made the beer *chichia* by soaking some grain, chewing it to begin the fermentation process, and then returning it to the original pot. If we take seriously the general enthusiasm of contemporary people for alcohol, we can conjecture that those ancestors of ours would hesitate to stray too far from their stash of beer fixings, in contrast to those foragers who liked to move on. Perhaps alcohol was an unexpected ancient inducement to settle down. Virginia Badler of the University of Toronto has discovered traces of wine in fourth-millennium containers associated with the Sumerian traders of the Tigris and Euphrates valleys. These containers were found in dwellings of some opulence — which suggests that then, as now, wine was associated with the good and satisfied life.[26] My suspicion is that there will be future discoveries showing the presence of potable winelike beverages even earlier in our history; the beginnings of agriculture probably mark the onset of the wine trade. Our ancestors were physiologically much like us, and likely to respond as we do to strongish drink, which is one of our favorite pleasures. How many contemporary Americans — or English or Italians or Chileans or Australians or practically anyone else — would willingly move to a wholly "dry" jurisdiction?

Some major and very populous groups — Muslims, some Fundamentalists, some Hindus — have strong inhibitions about consuming alcohol. Often the prohibitions relate quite directly to one theological assertion or another. Believers disdain the fruit of fermentation because they accept that God wills them not to drink. Faith is the deciding factor. As the British wine scholar Hugh Johnson has noted, the Islamic restriction on alcohol had a theological origin rooted in particular problems of social disruption during the time Koranic lore was being established; evidently, a fracas in Medina led to Muhammad's instruction from the archangel Gabriel (with whom he had several interviews) to forbid both wine and gambling, which were the work of the devil.[27] Drinking in certain other social groups, too, is an indulgence often associated with improper behavior. It appears to threaten the sense of controlled obedience that worthy believers try to maintain. At the same time, sizable numbers of people abstain from alcohol for reasons not necessarily related to religious authority. It has been estimated that some 40 percent of Americans are teetotalers.[28] Many of these people may simply not like alcohol or enjoy the effect it has on their experience and behavior.

But if Katz and Voigt are correct, this did not pose a problem to our forebears. Perhaps then there wasn't (and to this day there isn't) a necessary connection between religious belief and strict temperance. The opposite may even be true. This is suggested by Hugh Johnson's comment that the word "divine" is related to "*de vin*" — of wine — and the fact that there is frequent use of wine in religious ceremonies or festivity. There is a consistent if sporadic religious commitment, at least by the Catholic church, to the grape, even though its mind-changing properties may affect behavior in potentially impious ways. A number of important liqueurs, such as Benedictine and Chartreuse, are produced by monks. It was the Franciscan missionary Fra Junípero Serra who introduced the grapevine to California around 1770; and the Christian Brothers still produce brandy there. Champagne was perfected by the Benedictine Dom Pérignon. And admirers of the lusty Rhône wine Châteauneuf du Pape should thank for their enjoyment Pope John XXII, who evidently as a matter of some needy priority established vineyards near Avignon when it became politically necessary to relocate the papacy there for a while.

In Veritas, Vino

Obviously, wine plays a sacred role in various religious practices — most dramatically in the Holy Communion of Catholicism. (Johnson notes that white wine was used originally, to avoid the problem of garishly stained religious garments.) In various Jewish ceremonies and festivals, prayers marked by wine are in order — for example, during the Passover seder. Schnapps — whiskey or brandy, but anyway, a dark, strong liquor — was a common and I think typical feature of toasts and celebrations in my recently arrived immigrant family. Among Protestants as well as other groups, toasts with wine or stronger fare — such as fierce mao-tai in China, or vodka in Russia — are common. Particular religious festivals are often associated with alcoholic drinks, such as eggnog or grog or glug at Christmas.

This is not to suggest that any or all of the religious groups that use alcohol in one way or another intend to stimulate drunkenness, profligate expenditure, or some other imprudent or irresponsible behavior. But many religious authorities not only condone but also promote at least the modest use of alcohol in the context of legitimate and sometimes sacred occasions. This implies an understanding of the simple fact that people are likely to enjoy it in an acceptable manner. Alcohol in small amounts invariably provides some pleasure to virtually everyone and stimulates a sense of convivial comfort with fellow consumers. At the very least, the association of alcohol with religious celebration reveals the good "marketing" sense of the supervisors of religious groups. They have it within their grasp precisely to decide what is acceptable and what is not. In general, they have decided to allow alcohol.

Were it true that religion is the opium of the people, as Karl Marx announced, then alcohol is the neo-opiate at the core of many religions. Of course, it is not so simple, since religious ardor has a drastically more serious point and broader mandate than promoting a feel-good enthusiasm at ritual meetings. But one step at a time; a good time is had by all at a modest local gathering fueled by a touch of alcohol. It seems to offer a congenial overall setting for more serious observances. It is also an implicit reassurance that the system of dos and don'ts that religions invariably promote is neither dully heartless nor wholly opposed to pleasure. Ethanol helps the clenched fist open to God.

The buzz of booze is a plus. Sacred affairs and normal daily life come into agreeable contact across the cortical tissue when we are stimulated into affability and comfort by flavored alcohol — the ancient liquid friend. From infancy on, human beings are uncertain about unfamiliar people. But as I have noted, usually the first firm drink at the cocktail party suffuses the victim of personal uncertainty with some confidence that he or she is at least an adequate person, able to survive this sudden tournament of strangers. Human beings no longer live in communities of ninety souls. A major job requirement in industrial communities is that it is often necessary to confront strangers. This is why alcohol has often been so important in business — the two-martini lunch was principally about fear. Not license. Not pleasure. But alcohol *seemed* to help. Probably it did for a time, whenever there were strangers on the horizon. But once it became quotidian, day-in-day-out, no. Enter the alcoholic, stage right and left. And this is why Arthur Miller's surgically revealing play about his character's death would have been trivial had Willy Loman been a drinker, not a salesman.

God, This Is a Tasty Riesling!

Even the gods may join in. I've described how before a feast or funeral or wedding or installation of a chief or just a bash, West Africans will pour a libation of gin or other liquor into the earth, for the ancestors (who are also gods) to enjoy. Then they are part of the party. This is less the worship of ancestors than their inclusion. The liquor helps complete the circle. In its sudden warm way, alcohol expands the comfort zone. The party now includes the dead and the future. The members of the party can embrace the convivial event confidently and with a sense that the social world, even the heavens, are populated with friends. When a West African baby is "outdoored" — brought outside the house for the first time and hence into the wider community — several drops of water and several of liquor are touched to the infant's tongue, to instruct it early about this evidently important difference. The water of our vastly ancient aquatic origin. The alcohol of our brand-new settled farmer's still.

Small, even introductory amounts of alcohol appear to possess the power to re-create the affable, familiar certainties of the meal around the fire at the mouth of the cave. It is hardly surprising that some religious institutions benefit from this property. It is probably also no accident that the major organized religions originated around the turbulent period of history in which people began to depend on animals for work and for predictable food, and on foods they cultivated and ate — some of which they fermented in a multitude of ways and then drank! Agriculture was and is a difficult way of life — which is one reason people leave it and stream to what are often dauntingly unpromising cities, where even catch-as-catch-can life appears to be more appealing than farming. This begins to explain why barely 3 percent of Americans grow all the food for the USA and much for other countries besides. Though there are other, rather heavy political reasons — for example, the disproportionate power of rural voters — I suspect it is also an underlying and basic reason why the rich societies in Europe, North America, and Japan so extravagantly and peculiarly subsidize their farmers. They have to, because otherwise people wouldn't farm.

It was no accident that the origin of agriculture was associated with the emergence of organized religion and the probably coterminus development of the arts of fermentation. Something had to be done to lighten the present and future of the lives of farmers. Booze helped. But when the average American, Briton, and Belgian has to drive over forty-five miles back and forth to work each day, the old arcadian inebriation is no longer Falstaffian and appealing. The car is the enemy of the cocktail. The pleasure of release, at home in the farmhouse, from the constraints of long growing seasons and the hazards of nature is replaced by terror of the sound of screaming rubber and collapsing metal.

To this day, there remains an association between spirits, especially wine, and home. It appears that 75 percent of wine in the United States is consumed in homes, and of those occasions when it is, 82 percent center on sharing food.[29]

Yesterday, Six Hundred People Dropped By for Dinner

When I was a college student I worked as a kitchen helper — dishwasher, actually — at a construction camp in Frobisher Bay in the Canadian Arctic, where the Distant Early Warning radar line was being built. In the social assembly of the dining area, the chef was the ardent, temperamental master with the power of employment over people and a firm grip on the mood and rhythm of the kitchen, to say nothing of its product. All three individuals who had the post during the two summers I worked there exhibited a quantum difference from anyone else in the kitchen in their sense of sèlf and their willingness to define the lives of others. Of course, this was partly a show of the industrial-relations kind, partly simply their jobs, partly idiosyncratic, and partly the romanticization of the Leader, the Chief, the Chef.

There was also the huge practical matter that this man was responsible for ordering well in advance appropriate and sufficient food, which was flown in at great expense from lower Canada and then had to be converted into some eighteen hundred meals a day acceptable to a crowd of hardworking and demanding individuals marooned in this outpost for at least six months at a time. For entertainment, movies were shown twice a week at the United States Air Force base, which was the core of the operation. There was a weekly softball game for those who could tolerate the battalions of mosquitoes that took advantage of the two warmish months of summer. There was no alcohol. While there were some Eskimo families in the area, a detachment of Mounties enforced a firmly announced ban on fraternization.

But there was food, which played a more salient, dramatic, and even poignant role than in the average factory cafeteria. These were men placed in a demanding situation in order to earn exceptionally large sums of money. In return they placed commensurate demands on the kitchen. They came to expect food that suited their newly acquired income status. This was exaggerated by what was presumably an emotional neediness produced by the isolation, the unusually bleak social circumstances, and the fact that they were financial prisoners of the camp.

Therefore the dining room was no dainty tearoom. It was an aromatic, turbulent arena. The contract arrangements under which the DEW line was being built took account of the fact that no one had built such structures in the Arctic before so there were many unknowns. Hence the deal was cost-plus — that remarkable situation in which the more money the contractor and associates spend, the more profit they retain. Thus the kitchen was under little obligation to be thrifty — which, paradoxically, increased the pressure under which it labored. What, only one kind of roast and no shellfish and no steak for lunch? No meringue pie, only dreary fruit tart? Spaghetti with no *big* meatballs? After all, cost-plus. Everyone seemed to arrive at the same time and the line had to be served rapidly and fully. Though we dishwashers were not directly concerned with the clientele, it was also clear, since we were in the kitchen, how firmly the chef had to coerce not only his staff but also the food.

It is interesting to watch cooking for six hundred. It is rather like the reverse of archaeology. You see the various layers of taste and structure added to the food as it is prepared and then cooked, and it becomes clearer — the quantities are so graphic — how the tastes and textures of food are taken apart by the diner, even if he doesn't specifically or even generally understand the composition of what is being eaten. It is a lively, taut business in which time, taste, heat, texture, and appearance are always in a close connection that the cook must watch like the mugger his mark. It is fast-moving predictive chemistry, because the cook is supposed to know the outcome, which is what the recipe is for. But the recipe is not enough, because, of course, the ingredients are still forms of life — they are more or less fresh, too watery, too grainy, the fish is unduly fragrant, the beef has had too much exercise, the vegetables have relapsed into tasteless cells, the oven has a dead spot in the right corner. Cooking for six hundred is a corrida with many small bulls and an exigent audience. The chef now has a few hours in which to defuse the problems. Unlike the conductor, who achieves his music immediately, the orchestra of food is on two-hour delay. And the chef must taste it in advance, before it is ready.

Building a Library of Tastes

Good cooking involves the solution to a mouth-puzzle. This is the essence of the food passion: how to create or re-create that special sense of a particular food imagined or once tasted — for example, the Salzburger Nockerl served at a lush hotel at which I had lunch after visiting the Max Planck Institute in Sieweisen in Bavaria, or the shrimp remoulade at Galatoire's in New Orleans, or the garlic potatoes at Nick's Diner on Ilfield Road in London in the late sixties.

Had Beethoven been deaf from birth, he could not have thought his music through. Cooks must consume as skillfully and knowingly as they produce. Even if they learn from and enjoy reading cookbooks — which I do, having been captured first by the books of Elizabeth David — they nevertheless must have tastes in mind and experience to fit to the emerging story on the page. And this does not happen in a cultural vacuum. Presumably, the best stake out a place in whichever tradition of cooking they locate themselves. The Renaissance French did not think good taste in food was inherited, as were courage and the right to bear arms. It required a setting for its exercise.

Making good food involves tasting it intelligently, again understanding its immediate sensory archaeology. As part of some research in 1990 on the Four Seasons hotel group, I interviewed Bruno Loubet, the wonderfully passionate chef of the Four Seasons restaurant at the Inn on the Park Hotel in London. At twenty-eight, he had already gathered the first Michelin star for a London hotel restaurant, and each week created a novel *menu surprise* that neither he nor his staff could recite until he began inventing it around three-thirty on Monday afternoon. But the tastes and the invention came from his mother and the food of his youth in rural France. He remembered well, and presumably watched, and the heat and range of his interest kept the memory of long-ago food vivacious.

The food epiphanies to which I've briefly referred, and mercifully many more, are the opposite of my stations of the cross. Chefs create them, and while there is no doubt some trick and routine and fakery to all of it, finally the chef is confronted by his small family, the order for a table of six regular customers, just himself, or six hundred Arctic workers in Frobisher Bay. The taste and meaning must measure up.

There was no question that the chef in our Arctic kitchen forcefully commanded the isthmus between emotionally needy hunger and the accumulated lore and art of mass catering. Finally, the meal was his aria, even though there was a supporting chorus and noisy orchestra. His audience was of individuals, too. Even if hundreds ate the same food, each mouth had its own reception for the general product. As Brian McNally, who has operated some conspicuous "hot" restaurants in New York City, has said, restaurants "involve engaging in an intimate act in a public place."

Just so. Eating involves placing rather complex substances into a bodily orifice, changing their state, and incorporating them into the body — surprisingly intimate, considering all the matters of manners that arise: don't slurp, don't burp, don't chew noisily, or do, depending on where you are. It is no surprise why this is a matter fraught with emotionality and symbolism. Even fast-food restaurants must compensate for their bureaucratized cuisine — no cooks there, just teenagers with checklists — with an elaborate array of colorful and presumably evocative symbols: the famed arches, a southern colonel, Roy Rogers, Burger Kings and Dairy Queens. As Calvin Trillin has despairingly put it, many restaurants are "themed." Serving essentially industrialized food in environments made redolent with clear meanings, they use architectural spice, however simple, to conceal a prosaic menu. The point, obviously, is to augment the potential coldness of the experience with an apparatus of emotionality that satisfies extranutritional needs and punctuates dining time with colorful experience.

I return in my mind to a hotel restaurant I was urged to visit in rural Japan while writing on Japanese food. The chef had trained in France and produced outstanding and interesting Franco-Japanese food displayed with unusual artfulness. The food was indeed interesting and inventive, if also prodigiously expensive.

But most arresting and even alarming about the entire experience was the chef's chef d'oeuvre. It was a model in pastry and icing about five feet high enclosed in a glass case at the entrance to the restaurant, a replica of the Church of Sacre Coeur in Montmartre in Paris. (That's the white one, perched on the hill, with improbable minarets; it looks more like a massive dream-state visitor from another planet than a church in urban France). Here was a wholly bizarre confectionery echo, in flour and sugar, of an already improbable architectural object. Thus was the marriage of two culinary cultures celebrated. The ardor and ambition of the cook had been preserved in this quite remarkable and unexpected form and the spectacle was justifiably famous. The model was quite perfect — controlled insanity — and it was a reminder in its intensity of the chef's station at five minutes to noon and five minutes to six PM in the kitchen at Frobisher Bay.

It's Not Negotiable

Obviously, all practitioners of the arts that please the senses are to some degree committed to an aggressive understanding of sensory physiology and psychology. But painters, sculptors, and musicians need not always please — they may shock, revolt, trouble, abuse, irritate. They may shout or drum or stamp their feet at their audience. They may assault the audience's certainties and excite their fears and ridicule their deepest morality. The dramatist may unhinge their expectations of life by the suddenly plausible behavior of outrageous or despicable characters.

But the chef, or the winemaker, or the confectioner — they must please. Otherwise, in any kind of open market they will not survive. The mouth is less tolerant than the brain or whichever organ of the body assesses politicians. To prosper where there is choice, the cook must yield up foods that taste good and seem healthy — unless his product is supposed to be punishment, as in prisons or some hospitals, or in the schools for children of affluent families in nineteenth-century England. There the deliberate goal is to permit no pleasure. The absence of it certifies the guilt or lowliness or poverty of the hapless diner.

Once again, pleasure becomes a coin of the realm, if only in a negative sense. From one report,[30] even the traditional last meal of a prisoner condemned to die in the gas chamber of San Quentin in California must be consumed in a bare room containing only a toilet, and while the diner is standing, holding his tray. In addition, because of regulations governing pre-executions, the individual may wear only underpants and socklike footwear. Providing the last meal — up to fifty dollars is allotted — is presumably a form of compassionate gesture. But the conditions under which it is consumed emphasize the punitive nature of food in this extreme and dramatic situation. It is also pertinent that the individual in the episode described — who was reprieved at the last hour — had requested that his fifty dollars be used to provide ice cream to other death row inmates. Food as emotional currency. This was refused by the authorities. The doomed convict instead ordered full-dress pizza for one.

And here we have the other side of the family dinner, the bistro lunch, the lovers' duet dinner of warm assertion. In between these extremes is the primary issue, of food, survival, and the avoidance of hunger, which is satisfying enough in itself.

What unites these approaches to food is the volatile element of pleasure that food provides to the central nervous system and the bubbling, ramified pleasure it provides within the central social system. A number of times a day, people have the opportunity to turn necessity into virtue, to convert nourishment into an aesthetically interesting intimate drama, to use the instruments of taste and smell as skillfully as musicians use their ears. It is a remarkable luxury. There is always something new and arresting and traditional and tasty stewing on the stove. You can smell it from here.

SIX

The Senses: Everyone Has a Native Guide

WITH HINDSIGHT it's easy to see how preposterous that arch-Cartesian René Descartes was when he announced, "I think, therefore I am." What is surprising is how influential his assertion remains, and how complacently the description *sapiens* still attaches to the *Homo* of our zoological name.

Some acknowledgment of the power of the senses has to augment that name. Descartes should have advertised something like, "I think, therefore I am . . . confused about my complicated passions." Perhaps he did say this and the final phrase was lost by the scribe or removed by an editor. His phrase as it has been canonized is one whose misleading implication is equaled only by its pomposity and folly.

In this chapter I explore the senses, the pleasures they provide, the arts they sustain, how they merge with notions people have about rationality, logic, formality. Humans are wise, sapient, and thoughtful. But humans also swim in a sea of sensibility, of sensuality, of inner and outer observations, of judgments formed by sight, smell, touch, vibration, hearing, thirst, the passage of time, temperature, movement — a rich array of sources of information and hence guides to action. If people are skillfully thoughtful, the principal basis of their judgment still results from the work of the senses. People are not dedicated computers designed to think dispassionately, without anger, amusement, or partisan verve. The senses affect all thought. The senses guide all the action that results from thinking.

Repeat, repeat: The brain evolved to act, not to think. Brain tissue was added only because particular individuals were intelligent about their environments and each other. They were eager and able to combine effective management of their lives with successful courtship, mating, and reproduction. The senses were and still are the essential guide to thought. They form the irreducible platform upon which all judgment rests. Our capable brains developed because they effectively evaluated a flood of incoming sensory data and made successful decisions about what to do.

The senses came first. Making sense of them followed. This is mainly what people are sapient about.

Homo sentiens sapiens — this is our real name. Before we gentrified it to pretend to lives of low-voltage sweet reason in polite society.

The relationship between pleasure — basic physiopleasure — and the senses is obvious. Nevertheless, there is, here, a closer link than usual with pain, as well as with fantasy, with ideopleasure. The senses orient the organism with the information it requires to survive and prosper. Pain is an obvious warning of danger. Pleasure is an obvious if often more complex green light. It is a robust signal that whatever produces it is desirable for the organism. The health consequences of sweet and of bitter tastes reflect this clearly.

How does a contemporary industrial society decide how its members can identify, receive, and enjoy pleasure? In regard to pain there is an array of notions of what is acceptable and what is not. Insurance companies and juries even try to fix a dollar amount on the cost of pain. (Franz Kafka was an insurance adjuster whose literary life was presumably affected by his job.) Can the balance between pleasure and pain help define how societies should be organized?

This is in essence the same kind of question as the one posed earlier about diet. Remember? Is the chronic problem people in wealthy societies face about their weight and cardiovascular health the result of a mismatch between how we evolved then and how we must live now?

To that question about taste and health, we have a rather reliable answer: yes. Those pleasures can kill. How about pleasures of the other senses? Can they kill too?

From Savanna, Africa, to Savannah, Georgia

Half of the money spent in medieval European towns on public works went for the fortifying walls that encircled them. The now-charming intimacy of the communities, with their narrow streets and close-together dwellings, reflected military considerations more than the mere aesthetic and economic choices of urban planners or the design decisions of builders, architects, and the buyers of their products. Within the limits of the need for mutual protection, a range of integrated buildings emerged, from Florentine palazzi to the hilly streetscapes of a Prague. But modern people have different concerns about security and also possess effective transportation. When they have the choice, they spread out, in a more countrified manner. They choose not to huddle together. People choose to live in suburbs.

Consider. Despite the earlier ruinous effect of the Depression on agriculture, in 1945, one-third of Americans lived on farms or in towns of fewer than 2,500 people. By 1990, only 3 percent of the population was agricultural, and the number of farms had dropped by nearly half since 1960. The suburb emerged as the newly prominent milieu of choice for the country's burgeoning population.[1] In less than half a century, the suburb grew from the smallest segment of the housing stock to one significantly more populous than the city.

In 1950 some 33 percent of the population lived in cities, 44 percent in rural areas, and 23 percent in suburbia. By 1988, 30 percent were still in cities, 23 percent in rural regions. But the suburban population had doubled, to 47 percent.[2] City size remained stable. But country and suburb exchanged ranks in the hierarchy.

People began to work in suburban settings and live in more rural ones even farther out. This is a remarkable shift in life's venue for a vast number of people.[3]

It was an aesthetic change as well as a numerical one. Previously, attractive suburban life was available mainly in decisively luxurious commuter enclaves near large, established cities — in bedroom communities such as Greenwich, Connecticut, near New York City, or Grosse Pointe, near Detroit, or Pasadena, near Los Angeles. But then, convenient interstate highways facilitated large-scale mass housing innovations such as those in Levittown, New York. Rather suddenly the dream of a home of one's own became realizable — a home that also boasted a plausible resemblance to a house in the country. The trees, the lawn, the flowers, the backyard barbecue, the nighttime quiet and sense of real darkness — these were the signs of country living. What was once reserved for the envied gentry or the country bumpkin now was available to folks formerly housed in urban walk-ups or row houses on streets bare and mechanical by comparison with the soft intricacy of the mature suburb.

Suburbs and the Primitive Brain

Why did people choose this housing form? A largely unacknowledged reason, if not the main one, is that it is sensual. A house in the suburbs smelled better, it looked better, it offered a primordial sense of place; overall, it made residents feel better.

The reason people chose an essentially regressive, near-rural form during what was otherwise supposed to be a progressive industrial era was that the suburbs of Savannah or Dallas or San Diego are sensually more like the savanna in Africa in which we evolved and in which we developed the sensorium that appreciated a certain landscape, temperature, sense of place, access to potential resources, and scent and movement of air.[4] The sensory verdict on the burbs was: "good." They provided pleasure to the basic portions of the brain, the underlying tissues that govern the broadest experiences of the organism. As opposed to inner cities, the suburbs yield primitive sensory pleasures. A clue I've already noted is that even among people who are fully urbanized, nearly all dwellings contain some houseplants, often a large and complex array that requires care, thought, and resources. New techniques of roof construction and new materials make it possible for residents of apartment buildings to create roof gardens, which become a popular amenity.[5] Thus, people carefully play host to living relics of the great savanna. And they crave and pay extra for living next to parks. As the geographer Roger Ulrich of Texas A&M University has shown, there is now strong evidence of the positive emotional and even physiological impact of scenes of vegetation and landscape on people in daily life.[6] He has also reported that postoperative patients in a Pennsylvania hospital whose rooms overlooked a pleasing natural scene had "shorter postoperative stays, received fewer negative . . . nurses' notes, and took fewer potent analgesics" than patients whose rooms overlooked a brick building wall.[7] A similar finding about recovery from stress was based on studies of physiological indicators of excitation and calm.[8]

Of course, there were other vital and substantial reasons for the suburban move. The houses were good investments. Mortgage money was available, and not only for veterans. They carried tax advantages that favored people solvent enough to buy houses and that disfavored those poor enough to have to rent or peripatetic enough to want to. (In the United States in 1989, a tax benefit worth some $40 billion flowed to homeowners able to reduce their income tax by deducting mortgage interest and real estate taxes. Critic Benjamin DeMott has sharply described the class biases implicit in these tax breaks, which are in effect a welfare subsidy.[9]) Particularly during the 1950s, suburban areas offered an ample arena for the fecund American families raising a huge crop of baby-boomers. Four-children families were common. The suburbs offered adequate status, capable schools, reasonable transport to work; and the air there smelled good.

Not merely incidentally but by conscious design, many enclaves of these new suburban squires adopted tacit or explicit racial covenants that excluded unwanted groups in the population — blacks, most conspicuously, though Jews and other "ethnics" also received their share of restrictions. Racism was a major catalyzing factor in American residential patterns. But it was not the only one. Similar suburban development also occurred in Canada, Australia, and the United Kingdom, countries where, at the time, the volatile matter of racism was only a minor issue. Even ethnically homogeneous communities such as Japan displayed a comparable pattern. This is not to deny the significance of racism. But it dramatized and speeded up existing processes; it did not create them.

The Baby Orchard

These and other similarly hard reasons all apply. But, most primitively, in their exodus from the city these modest migrants sniffed the air and recaptured a modest tract of the savanna. Often they said, "We're moving for the children," which was correct — for all the children of the Upper Paleolithic, but particularly for youngsters able to tumble out of doors into a safe, interesting, and healthy environment. (After the Second World War, the British army built high-rise apartments for its troops stationed in Germany and discovered that families with children, which was most of them, experienced severe psychological difficulty if they lived on upper floors because parents could not monitor their children many stories down. With the characteristic well-meaning perversity of earnest bureaucracies, the army's solution was to subject all incoming families to psychological tests and in demonic compensation install the healthiest specimens on the highest floors. In a related finding, the French government ministry concerned with public housing concluded that there was a quantum jump in violence and other aggressive behavior once apartments rose above six stories. In Oscar Niemeyer's plan for Brasília, no housing structure was greater than six stories.)

Adults and children weave an easily generated web of social relations when they are all on the same level. They enjoy both the protectiveness of clear boundaries and the soothing blandishment of carefully nurtured vegetation. An urban level of physical danger from crime and moving vehicles is sharply reduced in most suburban settings. A highly successful developer of my acquaintance made his fortune by interviewing real estate agents and discovering that almost invariably the houses in a residential development that sold first were those with trees and on a cul-de-sac. The latter protected children from cars and the former presumably recalled the protective vegetation that proved so useful in the savanna. Forthwith, this entrepreneur built only houses with mature trees and on culs-de-sac, with remarkable commercial impact.

It's an interesting historical irony that cities were once places medieval people moved to because they were walled and relatively safe. But toward the end of the twentieth century, people fled them precisely because of danger or the perception of it. What will be the city of the twenty-first century? A regatta of private armored cars, laser intruder alarms, and freeways connecting suburbs to other suburbs? In the United States there are already more private security guards employed than public police.

But it's not automatic and self-evident that people will want to live as far from their jobs as they do and have to travel remarkable distances to earn their livings. The average American travels nearly twenty-three miles a day to get to work and the same distance back. This subjects commuters to a near-lifetime of traveling some two to three hours each day in vehicles ranging from comfortable automobiles soothed by air-conditioning, radios, and other music players to buses and trains that may be overcrowded, uncomfortable, and unreliable. It commits local and national communities to a voracious demand for petroleum. From individuals it requires a substantial sensual compromise — the commute is rarely elegant — and the sacrifice as well of irreplaceable time in order to make available to the self and the family the menu of suburban benefits. The most salient features of suburban life are its presumed consequences for health and the obvious sensory experiences associated with nature. "Suburban" is in fact the wrong, and unduly disparaging, descriptive term. "Neorural" is more accurate, "nonurban" less pejorative. Suburbs are not below anything and should not be so described.

People travel immense daily distances because they are happier living in the perimeter precincts of the urban zoo than in the zoo itself. At least they think that their lives are better there. Of course, there is often remarkable joy and stimulation in the urban core. Great cities boast their luxurious *quartiers* in which the rich and powerful reside, often on separate plots of land with gardens, and which are often planned as if they were in the country — for example, Hampstead in London, Westmount in Montreal, Pacific Heights in San Francisco. Yet many of these extraprivileged urbanites specifically also claim the extra home, the marina condo — some place, any place, away. It's always costly, but they want it and get it.

Contemporary cities in wealthy countries enjoy a historically unusual and relatively luxurious situation. Public sanitation is well controlled and water supplies are relatively safe and nonodorous. How drastically unpleasant cities were before these improvements is colorfully described by Alain Corbin: "In Paris, the chief source of water remained the Seine"[10] — which was a persistent inducement, were one needed, to drink sterile wine instead. In the extreme case of early city life, the countryside provided urgent relief that involved not only sensibility but survival. Eighteenth-century Parisian planners actually conceived of huge ventilation fans turned by the running water of the Seine; these would be set on street corners to blow away the perilous atmosphere.[11]

The desperate conditions — of visible running sewage, stinking air, and danger of disease communicated by air (after all, TB was a crowding disease) — generally no longer exist in affluent countries. But the early remedy, fleeing to the country, still does. This suggests that a similar lure still persists. Now, however, the impetus is primarily aesthetic rather than medical. Hence, the suburbs, and the second homestead movement. In practical medical terms, the deteriorated air of the city may generate less risk and physical detriment than a two-hour daily commute or a six-hour weekend journey. Nevertheless, many people who can afford this rustication knowingly choose it, at appreciable cost.

Why?

Because it is travel from the city center to the pleasure center.

Getting Back to It All

I can offer myself as a victim or example of this perhaps wasteful and certainly indulgent process. I was born in the center of urban Montreal — which I have already identified as the area accurately and colorfully chronicled by the novelist Mordecai Richler — and next moved to the center of London, where, as a student, I was delighted by the intensity and volume of experience there. When I subsequently taught at the University of British Columbia, I lived in or near the center of Vancouver — a city that at the time was almost wholly suburban; nevertheless, it never occurred to me to live away from the central area. When I moved to New York, it was to an apartment in Greenwich Village in expensive Manhattan, not any of the graceful suburbs near Rutgers University where I worked. I was a contrarian commuter, from the city to the suburbs, because I enjoyed urban life, even in New York, that deeply experimental, often dazzlingly inconvenient paradigm of urban complexity. For me, trained by and for urban streets, this was a logical home.

Logical, but not quite biological. Or so I had to acknowledge when, with a modest stash of money generated by a successful book, I acquired an ancient farmhouse with a dozen wistfully rural valley acres, barely two hours' drive from the city's core.

After sixteen years of experience with this inessential outpost of my heretofore urban self, it is still a luxurious mystery to contemplate why time weighs differently in the country, why the night is deeper and darker, why the smell of the morning air or the evening is more sweetly etched than in the city, why it is a champagne experience simply to *be* there. Why do towering trees in the dark form a pageant of reassurance and confidence? Why do racing storm clouds offer a confident insight into the natural value of tumult and a hint of danger? There is a generous power in enjoying the growth of evergreens from saplings to mature specimens bigger than a human, even though the experience of such burgeoning life underscores the diminishing interval of my own privileged visit to the planet. But that awareness in itself becomes a decisive form of affirmation, rather like those exuberant moments when our white mutt Cosmo responds in his own sensory way to rural release by running a half-dozen wide, full-tilt circles in the grass for no apparent reason other than the dogjoy of it.

My example is personal, but it is not eccentric. The busiest people in a country, its leaders, are often provided a house in the country — Camp David in the United States, Chequers in the United

Kingdom, Harpsund in Sweden. The president of France makes do with two, one near Paris, the other in the South. It is presumably assumed to be not only a perk of office but a restorative benefit to the individual. The South of France is in good part a housing development not only for the president but for successful plutocrats in the North of Europe. And a house in the country is not only a capitalist goal. When the East German government was dismantled, remarkable country lodges and extensive hunting estates were revealed as facilities of the earnest communist servants of the people. Of a Russian millionaire it is said he "has a dacha like most routinely successful Soviet citizens."[12] The lure of country air knows neither political nor ideological boundaries.

My argument is simple, but it refers to a complex process — how the human organism evaluates its immediate sensory conditions and then decides what provides pleasure and what does not. Metaphorically, the countryside produces music; the city, noise. This is the heart of the matter and an important reason for the paradoxical triumph of the automobile in modern society.

Even better than the countryside itself is a rural environment facing on water. A river, a pond, a lake, the ocean — these are magnets and highly prized. Only 4 percent of the American coastline is publicly owned; private people and interests wanted and acquired the rest. People cluster around water in strong disproportion, particularly when they are on vacation. Remarkably, people expend large sums of money and often endure humiliating and stupefying congestion to lie on beaches near oceans and experience hot sun and cool water. But they appear to find this justified by the astonishing repetitive clarity of ocean waves or the rumor of restoration that moving water conveys.

There is an obvious evolutionary reason for this. Bodies of water contain fish, shellfish, sea plants, which can be acquired and eaten. Water can be drunk, particularly when it is running and it is cold. This is why water fountains in rich countries serve chilled water, not warmed, and why people make tepid drinks cooler with ice. In the hot sun of the Upper Paleolithic, during an active bout of hunting or gathering, presumably a stream with cool water was highly regarded, to drink from and wash in or for children to play in. Certainly the taste and temperature of cool water are primevally satisfying. It is not complicated to understand why, and why thousands of generations of emergent hominids may have evolved a taste for cool water, just as we benefit from their evolution of stereoscopic vision and their acute sensitivity to the off odors of putrid meat or other foods. The pleasure-program that receives the experience of cool water and fresh air is so gratified that people are often content to do nothing else than lie near-comatose to enjoy the setting. They will also travel hours and miles to accomplish this. They must, they say, take their children to the beach, take them from the city center to the pleasure center.

It's Only Natural

It is even possible that the color of the most popular prepared human drinks — a kind of light brown — reflects a prehistoric enthusiasm for the liquid in small and precious bodies of water found in the sere tan savannas of our mother Africa. (This aperçu was made to me by the biologist Walter Pople when we were both at the University of Ghana.) Improbable? Consider beer, coffee, tea, colas, whiskey (to which caramel may be added to deepen the hue), red wine, rum (from which Frenchmen derive much of their alcohol), brandy, cocoa. These seem to be disproportionately desirable and widely distributed. Of course, there are important exceptions, such as gin and vodka (which, however, are often mixed with other liquids), champagne, milk, orange juice, tomato juice, and water itself. But Pople's suggestion remains intriguing as far as the most common manufactured drinks are concerned. It is a powerful anecdote and its scientific status has perplexed me for no less than thirty years. What do you think?

Water has advanced human purposes in other, perhaps more recently influential ways than for drinking and washing. Transport, for one. Countless cities locate on rivers or coasts because it is easier to float things and people than carry them. As for coasts, they are the first places explorers and travelers land when they visit by plan or in confusion. Also, bodies of water offer wet armament — one less city wall to build, particularly on the oceans. There is nothing behind which waterborne attackers can hide.

But beyond all functional considerations, people *like* the water. They covet access to it. If you take the hydroplane from Vienna to Budapest along the Danube, you will see the small beach houses built by people along this dramatic river, which sometimes turns so full and angry that it floods its banks and sweeps these houses downstream. They are therefore cheaply constructed for the most part, often on stilts and looking like too-small hideouts for modest giant insects. Nevertheless, there sunbathe their often naked owners, hostages to the river, who return to it despite the fact that it punishes them. Back to nature, back to naked human nature.

And river lore need not yield mainly nudity; it can generate paintings, too. I think specifically of New York's Hudson River school, which began to paint for great houses scenes of the great river and the landscape that surrounded it. Not only was this a worthy subject for oil paint, it also supported a broad worldview: "No region of America or the world is more representative of the manner in which changing cultural values to landscape helped to shape and reshape the society's aesthetic consciousness than the lower Hudson."[13] And Winslow Homer and his school touched a willing nerve with paintings of coastlines, where the ocean met man's estate.

The state of nature should and could mollify and soften the conditions of urbanity. The same broad impulse animated the Romantics in England, too, as the industrial revolution forced its clattery way upon the population of that self-consciously country-squirish population. Interestingly, at least one poet of pastoralism, William Wordsworth, saw the movement to cities and industry as an erosion of social life too. In a letter to Charles Fox in 1801, he wrote: "It appears to me the most calamitous effect, which has followed the measures which have lately been pursued in this country, is a rapid decay of the domestic affections about the lower orders of society. This effect the present rulers of this country are not conscious of, or they disregard it."[14] There is a modern-day version of this complaint — the "green" or ecology movement. This is as much a hankering for authentic, uncontaminated nature as a rejection of dangerous and profligate industrial practice.

Human beings are essentially rural animals, but this doesn't mean we like farming. Robin Fox and I called agriculture "the great leap backward," while physiologist Jared Diamond of the UCLA Medical School declared that it was "the worst mistake in the history of the human race."[15] The behavioral marketplace appears to confirm this. When people can leave agriculture, by and large they do so, and then move to cities. Cities are more fun, or seem more tractable, than farms. They offer many more opportunities to earn money, even, or particularly, for people who are very poor. Small hits of uncertain urban money appear to offer a more attractive prospect than definite but small income procured through the laborious and emotionally demanding work of agriculture.

Cities appear to offer more of the emotional opportunities a hunter-gatherer specimen enjoys than does the agricultural country. Paradoxically, there may be more hunting-gathering kind of action in the modern city than in the modern country. This helps to account for the phenomenal growth of cities when agriculture becomes more efficient, or the countryside becomes crowded, or both.

But it's a two-step. First people move from the country to the city. Another turnabout occurs when they become wealthy enough to acquire housing and personal transportation. Then the predominating housing form they choose is the suburb, while the urban core is decimated. There are numerous firm economic reasons for this. But the underlying and essential one is that suburbs capture some of the pleasurable sensual experience of rural life while they also permit access to the economic thrust of urban life.

Yet a historic compromise has devastated millions of acres of good farmland and countryside, and threatens to overwhelm precisely those agreeable conditions it was created to exploit. This residential pattern has been in large part responsible for committing whole civilizations to chronic traffic jams, energy crises, and implacable environmental degradation. In the United States, nearly half the infrastructure of urban areas services the 140 million automobiles which use 63 percent of the petroleum consumed.[16] This dependency on the automobile is almost irrevocably linked to economic prosperity in general. As the widely respected economist Albert Wojnilower has written, "in the United States . . . every new job means a new car, because most people drive to work. Fewer new jobs means fewer car sales."[17] In turn, this generates notions of national productivity standards that in significant measure reflect the essentially unproductive money cost of getting to work to make money and getting home to sleep; the gross national product includes the value of energy, roads, bridges, tunnels, tollbooths, and vehicles shuttling the twenty-three miles there and twenty-three back. But these "produce" nothing except the opportunity to go to work and go to bed. To say nothing of sponging up time — which explains why in sprawling cities such as Los Angeles, car telephones, car faxes, spoken books, and (surely soon) portable microwave ovens are such significant compensatory devices.

Better Homes and Gardens

People's partial retreat from the cities they had formerly invaded is motivated by the scent, sight, and space of the primordial environment, however lamely it is echoed on Acacia Drive in Heritage Acres. And even when people are landlocked in high-rise structures or gentle row houses, they bring plants indoors, and often animals. It is difficult to overestimate the significance of this. Houseplants, gardens, and pets exist in such rich and complex profusion that their message about the mechanical city as a comfort zone is nearly overwhelmingly subversive. The message is: we humans don't altogether like it here, unadorned. There are 500 million living creatures in American homes apart from the people.[18] There are literally countless plants. Even flowered wallpaper eases the pain of naturelessness, as do landscape paintings, and even plastic flowers. For the fortunate, a view of the park provides the pleasure.

The more affluent the suburb, the more extensive and lush are its gardens (even if they are more costly and demanding). Gardeners everywhere attune themselves to the natural process of seasons, growth, and decline when they plan and care for plants, which silently convey eloquent meaning. Propagating urban orchids becomes a personal triumph; garden tours feature pageants of roses, lilies, wildflowers, and peonies, together with the rich, fat bougainvillea of the tropics. The thick scent of blooming gardenias can even soothe the morning air on the day tax returns are due. A luxury of flowers marks the critical days of social life, such as at weddings and funerals and basic parties. Cocky dominant Edwardian males used to wear a flower in the lapel. I grow rosemary at home and often, before I leave to drive down the New Jersey Turnpike, I crush some spikes on my fingers so I have something pleasant to sniff as I cruise by the refineries. If you stroll a perky dog down the street, passersby will smile with pleasure as if you have told them a charming joke. It is possible to stare at a beautiful cat as if it were a temple dancer. And people with pets will coif them to boast at shows, walk them in the driving sleet, pay their veterinary bills with clenched teeth, and mourn with absolute knowledge of loss when loving animal companions mutely die. More people visit zoos in the United States than attend sporting events. As Henri Bergson wrote: "There are things that intelligence alone is able to seek, but which, by itself, it will never find. These things instinct alone could find; but it will never seek them."[19]

What? Bergson is essentially writing about the limbic system, the brain tissue that is the primitive arbiter of the meaning of experience. Could it be that the suburb is an arena for the play of "instinct," an unexpected symptom of emotionality and passion?

Yes. Suburbs offer escape to prisoners of rational urban technology who do not wish to carry over to the intimate spaces in which they live their private lives the economic, architectural, and intellectual conditions that define their public work.

We can glance at other species trapped in cities or what approximates them. The most successful zoos are those that release their inmates from cages and try to re-create for them the environments from which they came — zoos such as the San Diego, the Whipsnade, the Bronx, the Smithsonian, who pioneered simple veterinary civilities that now seem utterly obvious. But what about the zookeepers? Presumably people deserve comparable respect for their own aesthetic heritage, which involves an understanding of the fact that the core of the human pleasure center lies deeply in prehistory, hundreds of thousands of years ago.

Perhaps this seems merely banal and whiny. Nevertheless, it is really necessary to an understanding of why people have created suburbs. Since one reason is that they want to live in them, and to do so in an act of quite fundamental and consequential choice, we may assume that what they receive from this choice is equally fundamental. Nothing less, that is, than an effort to surround their systems of pleasure and pain with conditions that maximize pleasure and hold the urban pain at bay. These can be physiopleasures, such as smells, or psychopleasures, such as a sense of space, or ideopleasures, such as those associated with pastoral notions of rural purity and untrammeled authentic nature. Whatever they are — whatever the cocktail of pleasures that "getting away from it all" provides — country life is obviously singular and viscerally different in significant ways from its urban alternative.

To my knowledge there are no shops along country lanes selling local people potted samples of pavement or hanging containers of asphalt. There are no perfumes or deodorants called "Lincoln Tunnel at Rush Hour" or "Sultry Subway."

Rural Noise Is Crickets, Urban Noise Is Critics

Does this mean that people decide to live in cities even though they want to leave them as quickly as they can? And that there are no pleasures or benign values associated with urban life that comfortably suit the species we are? Of course not. Cities are places where people make lives as well as livelihoods. They are the location for the full exercise of a rich array of enthusiasms and broad plans.

Perhaps the smells of the city offend the physiopleasure centers. Perhaps houseplants, office planters, and hopeful struggling trees on urban streets don't quite do the trick for a visual system formed by Paleolithic African landscape. Perhaps chronic urban noise is irretrievably rough and irritating. Where there are many people, there are also many events. Some may be criminal, accidental, ugly, greedy, cruel, drunken, drugged, bloodcurdling, bigoted, tawdry. Obviously, the fear and flight programs of basic animal existence — what is that noise? beware! run! — are liberally stimulated by the remarkable density and potential danger of urban circumstance.

Nonetheless, the city is a potential feast of sociopleasure. Here is its strength and its lure. In city life the complicated eager gregariousness of an immensely skilled social species rises to the countless occasions and fashions it creates, embraces, negotiates, and often abandons. It is no accident that the ideas surrounding the notion of "civilization" are associated with the word describing the city. Urban life obligates people to accomplish the predictable and unavoidable tasks of survival, but it also generates an enormous array of seemingly inessential activities that nevertheless become vital features of the city scheme. The arts, entertainments, festivals, parades, political meetings, fashions, public dining places, even the streets and piazze themselves — all these and more become purveyors of elaborate and complex pleasures.

Pax Urbana

At the very least, people simply enjoy proximity to each other, even in the relatively anonymous and impersonal context of the streets of cities. As urban sociologist William Whyte, author of *The Organization Man*, notes about city centers, "what attracts people most, in sum, is other people." Supplying comfortable and usable public spaces creates a demand for them, which in turn yields vital traffic supporting businesses in the immediate area, and, of course, in turn creates yet more opportunity for street encounters. Based on his extensive observations of urban life and on more general data, Whyte asserts that "the central business districts are among the safest of places during the hours that people use them. Conversely, among the most dangerous are the parking lots of suburban shopping malls." Even the chronic complaint by many women about the vulgar behavior of male onlookers appears to rest on psychological not physical threat: "We have never seen a girl watcher make a real pass at a girl. . . . [Furthermore] . . . when a *really* good-looking woman goes by, they will be confounded, and they betray it with involuntary tugs on the earlobe and nervous stroking of their hair. Attractive women can scare them."[20]

Psychological harassment need not become physical to blight a woman's walk down the block. Nevertheless, it is pertinent that even among strangers there is an effective web of informal urban law. Occasionally the smooth urbanity gives violent way to ugly crime, often when the conventional sociability of malefactors is distorted because they are on alcohol or other drugs, seeking money for drugs, or fighting over trading routes and rights in the illegal drug industry. (A 1990 survey of convicted rapists in English prisons revealed that 37 percent were dependent on alcohol, while 60 percent had used illicit drugs or alcohol within six hours before commiting rape.[21]) In general, however, the huge number of impersonal interactions that can and do occur in public urban spaces appears to generate a *pax urbana* with a common style; as Whyte comments, "pedestrians in great metropolitan cities . . . act more like each other than their compatriots in smaller cities."[22]

Even impersonal chance experience in well-planned city centers provides pleasures. How much more derives from exquisite examples of the array of varied urban possibilities? The Wagner opera, the exhibition of seventeenth-century Italian drawing, a museum of fire trucks, a hangout bar for female sadists, the silk section of a fabric store in an Indian neighborhood, the overtime period of a Knicks-Celtics game, the cathedral funeral of a beloved urban power-monger, that club downtown where a taut Brazilian group plays near-dawn dance music as intricate as a rain forest. In this variegated realm, great cities are grand beyond prediction and exuberant beyond all reason. Purveyors of various pleasures earn a living perfecting the improbable — for example, by playing a Chopin nocturne celestially, or by capturing in a collection the extensive banality of matchbook covers or, more colorfully, the weather vanes of Appalachian barns.

The kaleidoscopic existence and recurrence of all this urban pleasure is nothing less than fiercely astonishing. And while there was and is a rich array of accomplished country arts — among other forms, music, furniture design, weaving, cooking, and dancing — the intensity and volume of the output characteristically differs from the urban variety. Perhaps it is because country people first do their work and then their art. But for urban people art is their work. Perhaps the most neutral definition of folk art is that it is an after-hours avocation, not a way of economic life.

None of this is meant to deprecate country artwork. On the contrary. Its relatively amateur character yields fresh and robust pleasures. Urban cultural work and rural cultural work reveal distinct foci and directions. So does public response to each. It is a staple of urban society to argue endlessly about this or that film or play or book or artifact. The sound of the critic is loud on the rialto. Art-taste may become as severe a social arbiter as tribe or caste under other circumstances. Hanging a LeRoy Neiman lithograph or earnestly playing Barry Manilow or serving a Kraft dinner can as effectively ostracize an aspirant member of a particular culture-clique as a prison sentence. A person's social comfort zone within the urban tumult may be defined by particular critical standards and arbitrary aesthetic values that have been historically associated with urban influence. The choice of pleasures of the eye, ear, nose, and mouth — and of the body, as with furniture and clothing — may determine decisively the real social place of a person or family. The social mobility that sets apart one generation from the last may be most graphically reflected in new arrangements of taste.

Making such judgments is a principal industry of the city. Critics substitute for crickets. The changes of season and flora and fauna are replaced by changes in the form, fashion, meaning, and facade of the fabricated landscape. The sensorium craves stimuli to perceive and evaluate. It wants color, shape, movement, taste, sound, perspective, proportion, sequence. If nature is too distant to provide it, artists create multiple products and fill the bill.

Ear, Ear

Music plays a role in reassociating us with our evolutionary nature, just as landscape paintings refresh our memory of the Paleolithic even though we are indoors and modern. Music has a deep human function beyond creating dress-up occasions for concert evenings. For many people listening to music yields remarkable pleasure, a trancelike involvement of seemingly inexplicable intensity and richness. Unusually skilled and powerful performers of music may achieve fame, riches, and genuinely heroic stature even if they do not use words or lyrics but depend wholly on the arrangement and phrasing of sounds created by various instruments. These sounds in themselves, in the general context of literate industrial society, have no meaning whatsoever. Their creators can be heroes of the careful adult world of French chansons, or the vigorously adolescent corps of noisy heavy-metal rockers, or the smooth and knowing café piano men in between. Perhaps particular musicians fail to understand one another, or maybe their common work has no shared meaning. Nonetheless, as a group they share a power to provide pleasure and an inescapable, vibrant sense of participation in a vital form of human intercourse.

Music is often used in religious ceremonies to generate a sense of awe and of the potent goodness of the sect involved. Indeed, the music may be the most affecting element of a religious service, as in the Catholic High Mass or the intense hymning of a southern gospel church.[23] I was fortunate to see live via satellite the remarkable and now legendary 1989 Christmas concert conducted by Leonard Bernstein in East Berlin — a performance of Beethoven's Ninth Symphony featuring players and singers from both Germanys and elsewhere to celebrate the breaching of the Berlin Wall. The combination of impassioned direction, superb music, and monumental occasion was overwhelming. Its impact was as palpable as it was symbolic. Nothing else could have generated such a summary of a human event.

How did music gain such elegantly acceptable power over the human central nervous system?

Glenn Gould Drove My Taxi

We can ask the question in another way: what can the human central nervous system create for its edification and its pleasure? Clubs magnified the power of arms, stonecutting tools abetted fingers and nails, bows and bolas augmented the throwing arm, vegetable dyes allowed interior decorators of caves amusing variety in the images they created. Likewise, presumably drums and strings permitted early human beings to control the sounds around them, both to inform others about their condition and to take charge of time by filling it with interesting sounds. In fact, a painting of some forty thousand years ago in the Trois Frères cave of southwestern France shows a figure wearing a mask and playing a single-stringed instrument. The first publicity still of the first musician? Was the mask the earliest equivalent of the modern musician's tuxedo or spangled jumpsuit — a costume implying, as all costumes do, that the wearer is in the service of a broader entity than his personal self? Is this a clue to why musicians more often than not wear special if not extravagant clothing? In other words, was music at first essentially sacred? Does it still possess that character?

Of course, we can't know what it was, but we can consider what it is.

I have already referred to the deep quiet, or so it seems, of the country. However, there is always some noise — of wind, of birds, trees creaking, the famous crickets, and the like. This is not noticeable as noise, presumably because we are evolved to, or at least able to, pay only scant attention to such recurrent, ongoing ambient sound. We know that in general the brain has the capacity to screen out a host of sounds — often nearly all — once it is clear to the organism that the sounds possess no dangerous or clearly advantageous character.

This is the neural equivalent of those flaps of flesh — the eyelids — which permit animals visual escape. The ears have no direct analogue. There is no parallel escape from sound. Even in the womb, the fetus hears a chronicle of its mother's soundscape. Jacques Mehler of the Centre Nationale de Recherches Scientifiques in Paris played to a conference I attended a recording made in utero that clearly described tinkling coffee cups, the muffled sounds of breakfast conversation, and yet another Beethoven symphony, this time the *Pastoral*. So even gestation offers no relief from sound. Neither, fully, does sleep. In 1990 the astonishing fact was published that some 60 percent of the residents of Cairo took sleeping pills — chemical earflaps — to help them fend off the unusual racket of nocturnal noise in that crowded city. But music is controlled sound, crafted to provide pleasure and create significance where there would otherwise be relative silence or random clatter.

There is the same near-miracle of kinds and styles of music as there are cuisines and variants of them. There is the same social character to music as to food. While music can be played for the self alone, there is always the likelihood others will hear it. Sound travels. Recall that human beings have overwhelmingly lived in social groups and that solitude was and is exceptional. Anyone making music is also committing a social act. Be it bunkhouse blues or a flutist in a meadow or a high-decibel teenage gang hunkering experimentally in a garage, the news and noise get out: music is being made. Even in the New York subway system, which licenses a certain number of performers to work the stations, when there is a good player or singer or group making music, people stand around in a respectful circle and quietly enjoy the oasis of melody in a jungle of sound. Often they seem lured even into tenderness by the sound, despite the harshness of the setting.[24] Furthermore, this experience has a clear binding effect among the people who listen.

Music focuses anonymous people into a sudden collectivity.[25] To a considerable extent, particularly in large cities, this is what happens at concerts. The communalism can range from the narco-tribalism of a Grateful Dead concert, to the rhythmic unity forging the listeners and dancers with an Ashanti drum band at a feast in Accra, Ghana, to the perplexing, exhilarating wonder in a gilded hall when Isaac Stern and over a hundred players newly reveal the force and urgency of a concerto that has already been played many thousands of times.

The dramatic point is that though the impact of music is, of course, often achingly personal, the contact made through the ear is also made with other people — not only the other players, but also the audience. How else, except to communicate, could players bear the exposure and scrutiny of hundreds or thousands as they moved their fingers or pursed their lips? Music is concentrated communication. It is also elegant and usually beyond words — almost primatological in its force. Like most performers, effective musicians must be energetic apes, eager to please.

Coming home from the airport from a fine trip away can be unpleasant. Traffic and rickety taxis can make the journey from JFK Airport in New York especially disconcerting. One of the best rides I had was when the driver happened to choose a radio station that was broadcasting Glenn Gould's startling recording of the *Appassionata* of Beethoven. I have a crush on Gould's playing, having grown up to understand piano through him, since he was often featured on the Canadian Broadcasting Corporation. Also, he was in my view, and not only mine, an utterly remarkable player of bizarre musical accuracy. He had a compellingly idiosyncratic view of almost every note he played and its relationship to other notes, and even to the universe. In his first performance with Leonard Bernstein of the Brahms D Minor Concerto, Bernstein said to the audience before the overture that he had never heard such a rendition of the music as Gould's, that he profoundly disagreed with it, but that he would cooperate out of respect for his evident artistry.[26]

Later on such controversy among performers would become unnecessary, because Gould, to general surprise and dismay, declared he would no longer perform in public and didn't. Remarkably, he had decided to violate the central force of music, which is its physical presence and its connection to a person or to people; that is why when stars give concerts, they are expected to sing their greatest hits — to personalize the legendary.

Instead, Gould recorded in studios and continued to produce extraordinary music, but as the follower of a muse, not a flesh-and-blood performer. His decision was drastically controversial, but he was in constant dispute with convention anyway and saw no reason to yield to it. He lived oddly, too, apart from his solitariness. For he was fascinated by isolation, an obvious peculiarity for a communicator.

Is his music so strange and wonderful because he made it for himself? I use this example, of Glenn Gould, because somehow he represents something about the role of music as concentrated communication. I am also certain that had he from the outset of his career refused to encounter audiences, his work would have failed to unite as persuasively as it did the common voice of great music and his own commanding version of that broad tone. Talent, that always odd chemical, was perhaps his birthright, but that couldn't be all. The rare experience he had so often had of luxuriously effective and generous performance was his work-right. In part he lived off it while he lived and performed in solitude until his premature death.

Avant-garde or experimental music is an effort to stretch the known boundaries of community life, not to deny that there is a community within them. It is more likely to fail if it offends the receptive capacities of the brain than if it puts off the tastemongers of the tribe. Muzak is a different beast, which is why it has a different name. It describes only a rumor. But even the rumor of music appears to soothe people rising through hundreds of feet of elevator shaft in tin cans, or to induce them to shop with more of their money than when the tape runs out.

The Artful Smudger

When the zoologist (and painter) Desmond Morris was curator of mammals at the London Zoo, he experimented with teaching several of the chimpanzees who were his wards how to paint. This occurred during the early sixties, when the controversies about "modern art" were at their height. It excited much interest. Scorners who said about Pollack, Picasso, Klee, and other nonfigurative painters, "Even my three-year-old nephew can do that," could now add to their diatribe, "Even a monkey can do that."[27] They were correct, too — because in a fascinating report Morris describes how several animals became not only quite proficient at painting but also rather passionate about the process.[28] The master chimp painter, Congo, became angrier when disturbed from his painting than from eating, having sex, grooming, or sleeping. With experience, the animals were able to produce work up to the level of a preschool child, and their products were actually distributed commercially. In their first show, the chimp paintings were displayed without attribution alongside the products of humans and evidently were accepted as appropriate for an art show. The artist Joan Miró offered Morris a Miró for a Congo. The exchange was made. Both gratefully received.

The animals were *interested* in painting, in experimenting with it, in trying colors and their arrangement. They appeared to derive what we would have to call pleasure from this optional activity — an activity, by the way, that yielded them no particular gains or perquisites beyond the value to them of the pleasure and interest of the process itself; they earned neither money nor Mirós. For example, if a chimp painter was given a sheet of paper with a design already affixed to one side of it, he would restrict his own work to the other side in an evident effort at balance. Colors would not simply be superimposed on one another by the chimps but were deliberately chosen and arrayed in definable patterns, such as in the shape of a fan. Even status and age affected the painting — higher-status animals and older ones painted larger and more forceful images.

The fascination of the public and the art world with all this was reflected in a story told me by Morris about an interview a critic conducted with Pablo Picasso during the height of the rhetorical tumult. The encounter went something like: "Mr. Picasso, there is this talk about even chimps being able to do modern art. Do you think there's something basic, even primitive and backward, in this kind of abstract work? Where do you stand on this matter of the biology of art?" Here Picasso left the room, closing the door behind him. He reentered, now bent low. He swung his arms close to the ground the way a chimp would. He uttered some chimplike sounds, bit the interviewer on the forearm, and wheeled out of the room.

End of interview. Another episode, if somewhat flamboyantly frivolous, in the story of the search for the roots of visual art. In any event, it describes the view of one producer of no mediocre elementality.

Shut Your Eyes

Given the cross-cultural ubiquity of decoration, if not of art itself, it appears there is a basic human capacity to derive pleasure from colorful or monochromal shapes.[29] Within built environments, the existence of such artworks becomes a measure of the stature, freedom, and luxuriousness of their inhabitants. At one extreme, in maximum-security prisons, there is no such thing as art. Even the walls of the structure are likely to be colored in a deliberately dull manner — battleship gray or exposed concrete or perhaps even a bilious green, such as the one carefully and chronically slapped on by the managers of the Montreal Protestant Central School Board installations to which English-speaking non-Catholics such as yours truly were assigned. Even in spots less drastic than prisons or my grade school, only in recent years, and then only occasionally, have functional structures such as warehouses and even schools and hospitals been painted with bright and vivid colors. The absence of color — of pleasure for the eye — was and is part of a calculated abstemiousness. Presumably, this was designed to induce seriousness. When the maintenance chiefs of my King Edward VII School in Montreal ordered paint, it was unlikely that ugly colors were cheaper. At issue was the vivacity of the surroundings. A point was being made. The dullness established a stern attitude to existence associated with Calvinism, Puritanism, and other styles of Protestant rebellion against the sumptuousness of the Holy Roman church and the empire with which it had been historically linked. The eyes are part of the body. Like other sense organs, they should conform to the broad austerity with which the pious life was supposed to be led.

This was not only a matter for religious enthusiasts. The history of artistic censorship in communist Europe reveals an equivalent suspicion of untrammeled visual imagination. How else can the resistance to abstract painting in the USSR be explained, when in fact almost by definition this work had no political message and hence posed no apparent political danger?

The real danger was that people would experience pleasure. Pleasure independent of any didactic purpose. Pleasure dependent only on the skill of the artist, not his or her sociopolitical agenda. Pleasure that could affirm to the person who experienced it that small, private episodes — not only large, public ones — were precious and available. This was threatening. In a stern society full of rectitude and conviction, for such pleasure there was no entitlement, evolutionary or revolutionary. "To each according to his need" did not include eye-popping fun. The brilliant exploratory work of the Russian Constructivists had to remain secret, stashed away in unmarked private homes, or be quarantined by the government, held in warehouses and in contempt. Foreign abstract work also was "decadent," in the way Jewish art was decadent for the Nazis.

What *is* this fearful decadence? Where does it come from? Is it secreted by a particularly vile gland carried only by a strain of human being as obviously ill fated but dangerous as those bearing the horns of the devil or the mark of Cain? This is a considerable puzzle. On what grounds can people say, "This painting [or tune or dance or statue] is so virally perilous that if you come into even fleeting contact with it, you will suffer a grave disease of the spirit and you will become dangerous to other people too"?

Ideas and images and assertions about human possibility —what life can be like — are often thought to be dangerous to political regimes, and certainly to religious ones. Even when there are no obvious or even subtle challenges to civil authority — such as in lyric-free serial music or abstract painting — the possibility that citizens enjoy pleasures that baffle their leaders appears to stimulate retribution with surprising readiness. The official reaction may involve censorship, denial of financial support, public ridicule, even imprisonment. The most dramatic response to the work flows from those who understand and appreciate it least.

In the Soviet Union and elsewhere, the dynamic very much depended on status. Somehow, members of elites could inspect foreign films, learn about foreign art, enjoy luxurious foreign foods and travel, with seeming immunity to the secretions of the decadence gland. Presumably, the assumption was that their power and the exemplary wisdom with which they earned it insulated them from whatever moral weakness might result from pleasure. But there had to be different arrangements for the common folk, who had in some important way revealed their weakness, if only by failing to secure power.

This process, often called censorship, exposes a central vexation of civil society: Who gets pleasure? What shall it be? Who controls it, if anyone? Are no holds barred in the strange war over enjoyment? And think of it: sometimes this battle can even take the surreal, improbable form of disagreement over artful smudges on paper or canvas such as the doodlings apes can produce, or over the particular arrangements of sounds generated by pianos, to say nothing of the howling collective voice of electric guitars wielded by postadolescents. How trivial can mortal creatures get? It seems that on this issue, plenty trivial. We see over and over again that pleasure is never trivial — even when, or particularly when, people consider it unimportant.

Coloring the Troops

Pampering the senses is not only the prerogative of government elites and plutocrats. Even in the austere, function-driven military, the distinctions of status reflect themselves in access to visual pleasure. I once had some consulting activity to conduct with a senior adviser to the US secretary of defense and visited the aide at his office in the Pentagon. The seemingly endless corridors of this vast structure are for the most part dull, uniform, remorselessly uninteresting to look at. But where the secretary and other high-ranking personnel are quartered, the corridors are as aesthetically intense as Parisian boutiques, with dozens of flags, portraits of past heroes, displays of military uniforms and accessories, group photographs of people and equipment, and mementos supplied by military allies. The same is true in other military installations, such as the service academies and base camps. It seems that a form of communal hunger for visual pleasure is greedily sucked up and intensely and representatively satisfied in the precincts of leadership. It is as if members of the elite get to eat everyone else's sugar desserts because sugar is bad for the poor folks' teeth.

In any event, it is noteworthy that even in the studiously prosaic military, color and heraldry matter. The bonds of community are expressed in shapes and hues tied to art. Pride in military craft mingles with the pleasure of the eye.

The color guard is said to have a function for morale. The flags define loyalty. The dress uniforms pump up pride. Yes, of course. But the operative mechanism is visual enjoyment. The control of such pleasure resides in those who control the system overall. It is they who decide the nature and form of uniforms, select the array of military ritual objects, and determine the aesthetic luxury or austerity of members' immediate environment. Here are the medieval sumptuary laws again, whereby only royalty could wear purple and ermine, velvet was restricted, and pleasure was explicitly linked to status, or was supposed to be: "To stem the insolent display of wealth by the bourgeoisie, kings had for centuries promulgated sumptuary laws, but to no avail."[30] The superlatively vain queen Elizabeth I wore the most sumptuous and extravagant of raiment, while her ladies in waiting were allowed only black and white.[31]

So in the military only officers may wear colorful silk cravats, gold braid is completely controlled by military status, pink uniforms are out, women wear sensible shoes and nonalarming lengths of skirt. A similar if subtler situation prevails in corporate life, in which wise young executives will not wear more elegant clothes than their bosses even if they can afford to do so. Successful men's shops such as Brooks Brothers have discernibly different categories of suits appropriate for different stages of the business career, and it is politic to observe these carefully.

Beauty is in the eye of the boss.

And the Nominees for Best Tourist Spot This Year Are: Tuscany, the Dordogne, Hong Kong, Ljubljana, Kano, Manaus, Nevis — and the Envelope, Please

The Oscar ceremony is the world's most watched regular television program apart from the World Cup Final, and tourism has become the world's largest industry. All three phenomena involve expansive concerns. Which players and films seen in nearly every country will be rewarded? Which of the world's many nations will field the ultimate team? And where will we go for holiday this year? How far? What will we see? Eat? Hear? Wonder about?

Why? Why go anywhere? Why take time, spend money, endure travel and borders, puzzle over foreigners and their weird customs and languages, risk diarrhea and worse? At the extremes, comfort and danger seem the sharpest motives. On the one hand, a tourist lies on the beach in Saint Kitts depleting a convenient banana daiquiri to soothe a spirit dawdling in an already near-comatose body. On the other hand, a paying customer skis down steep mountains — the steeper, the better — usually with some danger, and often in otherwise unpleasantly cold weather. On the one hand, a burned-out urbanite wallows like an entitled hippo in the esoteric thermal mud of an Italian spa, while on the other hand a trio of daredevils climb a sheer Colorado rock face with spikes and string.

Within the extremes are millions of people who travel away from their homes and routines in order to experience and inspect new and different places and approaches to living, eating, symbolizing, planting, dressing, building — the gamut.

This requires explanation. If, as I have suggested, we are a species evolved to hearth and home, why should we also be willing to undertake inconvenient journeys?

There are a host of possible ways of approaching this. Compare the experience of place with the experience of food. Then it becomes clear that there is a voracious appetite for variety in food, as well as an underlying attention to familiar tastes and textures. By that standard it appears reasonable that people will want to enjoy elegant variation in where they are, what it looks and smells like, what kind of people live there, and what things they do and believe. At the same time, it is obvious that most travelers also want some uncomplicated, homey comfort.

So there will be ongoing tension between these poles. For example, many tourists want to enjoy the authentic life of the place they're in. They are prepared to stride into the native quarter, try some local foods, attend some local fetes. At the same time, they may want a comfortable Hilton to return to, because relatively fastidious concerns may be difficult to shake — for example, those involving toilets and sanitation.[32] Euro-Americans find the squat toilets of North Africa, parts of China, and elsewhere particularly difficult to employ without genuine perturbation. Sharing even familiar toilets and baths or showers is uncomfortable for many tourists. Hence, when hotels are graded, toilet and bathing facilities loom very large in the makeup of the final rating. (That is why some charming and elegant hotels in France and Italy may have relatively low ranking but great appeal; the hotels are too small or frail, or their owners too recalcitrant, to install facilities otherwise ubiquitous in even modest motels of plain vanilla.)

The tension between exotic variety and old-shoe comfort is constant in the tourism world. This not only affects how intrepid and vigorous a visitor will be but also the extent to which the host will permit the guest to examine the locality. At an upscale hotel in Charleston, South Carolina, the information lady only very reluctantly parted with the name of an outskirts honky-tonk thriving with fine music and gruff, irreplaceable ambiance. Hotel concierges are understandably but tryingly eager to steer guests to white-tablecloth restaurants when they want to venture away from the space-bubble environment of their lodgings.

When I worked in China with photographer Reinhart Wolf on our book *China's Food*, it was endlessly difficult to convince our hosts to serve us the food they ate, which was of course what we had come to try, instead of the banal and frequently miserable hotel food tourists were compelled to endure. There were even, in many hotels, two dining rooms, Western and Chinese. It was both genuinely perplexing and irritating that the custodians of one of the grandest of culinary traditions were so stupid or so arrogant as to assume that they knew better than their visitors what the latter should be permitted to consume. In Hong Kong the same tradition of cooking produced remarkable fare with a sense of easy pride and convivial competence — in establishments interested in pleasure rather than sufficiency, delight rather than admonitory austerity. Perhaps the approach of both traditional and postrevolutionary China has to do with a general and understandable suspicion of pleasure-seekers; the translation of "leisure class" is "having-idleness class."[33] But depressing the enthusiasm of visitors for a place they have chosen to explore is not only financially foolish and administratively incompetent; it is a violation of sensible rules of international citizenship.

Provocative Nights at the Ice Age Motel

Tourism can be — and probably even should be — a very hot bath or a cold shower. It can envelop the visitor in a welter of compelling, soothing conditions, like the tropical beach or the plunging mountain of snow. At its most dramatic, it offers a drastic realignment of notions of space, smell, temperature, food — even of time, when enough zones are crossed. It is exciting in itself to enter an airplane in a snowstorm and exit on a Caribbean tarmac. It offers a reassuring sense of both control and adventure to check in to a small Paris hotel after an overnight flight and then inscribe that first mark of a walk into the morning city with its newly washed gutters, precise familiar architecture, and emergent clatter of cafés and shops. There is something implausibly interesting in encountering for the first time the density, poverty, and complexity of Bombay, even on the ride from the airport. There is a direct link between New York and Bogotá because many of the flowers on sale in Manhattan grow in the acres of greenhouses surrounding the Colombian airport. But the Bogotá air is very thin. Breathing and what it means and how to do it become a novelty. Even the traveler's air is variable.

Again, why bother? Recall the recent history of our species. We radiated nearly all over the globe and have managed to live near the Arctic Circle, in Savannah, Georgia, in the forests of Rwanda, and on boats in the harbor of Hong Kong. Our desire to travel recaptures and reminds us of our ability to master interesting and unusual places to live. By offering contrast, tourism not only clarifies where we live, it also in some manner defines the plausibility of escaping from where we live — we can master Siena as well as San Francisco, Tokyo as well as Toronto. That's one reason why people city-monger so much and exchange earnest opinion around the general kind of question, Would you rather live in Stockholm or Rio? Iowa or Yucatán?

This is reverie in nearly all cases. But people do acquire dwellings in places they first went to only to visit — enough of them to suggest that the confidence that derives from mastering a place is part of the tourist's reward. City- or country-mongering is a contemporary echo of our prehistoric question, Shall we stay or go? Will there be better fish or roebuck or nuts or pears three days' or three months' walk away? Will the winds of the Ice Age be less debilitating if we head south once more? Will we have fewer nerve-racking disputes with our neighbors if we go where there are fewer of them?

The contemporary choice is infinitely more luxurious. Usually there is little real danger. The extraordinary — now ordinary — fact is that an assertive species that explored successfully all over the globe when it had to for survival now willingly does the same thing for pleasure. People make a luxury out of what was once a necessity. This is like exercise or sport, in which people participate because they enjoy it or know that in some grim statistical-medical sense it is good for them. But in other times and circumstances they had to exert themselves because survival made it necessary. The pursuit of exotic travel options may be different from tennis or jogging. But like sport, travel keeps people in a kind of trim, open to the possibility of making a life and living somewhere else different, somewhere else demanding.

An immense travel industry has grown up, partly animated by a valuable ancient knack. The flesh is not in need. But the spirit is willing and able. It bubbles with curiosity and the pleasure it provides — the willingness (even ferocity, in the case of scientists and explorers) to find out something new and then control it through experience and knowledge. Though we are a conservative species, we are not a static one. Intent though people may be to know where they are and where they have been, they also want to know where they are going and where they could be going. I've been employing a similar procedure in this book. For example, in this chapter I have discussed the senses as physiologically encoded guides formed during evolution that still influence and direct contemporary behavior. They helped us explore in the past when we had to, and they stimulate us to do so in the present when we want to.

Not only do they do that. They can be embraced in the service of fiction, of philosophy, of drama, of jokes (jokes deserve a whole chapter),[34] of puzzles, of games — of a host of dances choreographed by the mind. The senses are so significant and interesting and appetitive that when nothing is happening to engage them, the resulting state is called boredom. It is intolerable. When there is a vacuum in social life and loneliness threatens, people create fictional arenas in which to socialize — in books, television, film, on stage. When there is no one home, for company we switch on the tube or radio or music or look at drawings or turn to a book or the telephone. We populate the place with various forms of talk show.

These are for the senses what gymnasiums are for the muscles.

SEVEN

The Power of Pleasure / The Pleasure of Power

I LIVE in New York City and read the *New York Times* whenever I am in town and, if I can get it, whenever I am away. Because I have lived there for more than a generation and have had a somewhat extensive and variegated professional career — a slap of good luck — by now I find that when I look at the front page, frequently I know some of the writers and the subjects of the stories, or have some direct connection to them through other people I know. So, a good friend publishes Gorbachev and knows him well. I met the UN secretary-general at the home of a man who was a major figure at the United Nations for more than three decades. A military tactic employed in an assault against Saddam Hussein in January of 1991 was evaluated during a small consultancy conference on military deterrence theory I attended at the Naval War College the August before. A US senator's vote on an important bill is of particular interest because I had a while before discussed his approach to the issue with his son, who is my son's college roommate.

The front page of record has personal meaning. It is not the unattainable catalog of acts and utterances of strangers or Martians. It is not about figures describable only as "they" — those special, distant, efficacious folk who manage the world's central action without influence from the world's groundlings, as Shakespeare called them. My familiarity with the public account of the world in which I live is comforting and pleasing.

I am realistic. I know that nearly all my contact with the matters I am describing is derivative and secondhand. I don't even have minor involvement in them. Though I gain absolutely nothing concrete from it, I nonetheless derive pleasure from my proximity to these legitimately significant issues. I enjoy the connection to the powerful forces they represent. I enjoy the power of insight, even when it derives from mere acquaintance and other accidents of personal life. Proximity to power yields pleasure. Power is attractive. State occasions draw the crowds. People who possess power appear to enjoy it, often fiercely, and they fight to acquire and retain it far more enthusiastically than they struggle to become weak or to be excluded. Power is largely a pleasure for those with it, though they are often reluctant to advertise the fact. It is interesting and reassuring for those without it too. The groundlings crowd as near the front as they can, just behind the reserved seats.

I hesitated before beginning this chapter with the three paragraphs above. I was wary that readers might think that I was boasting because I know some influential people. Or that I am pathetic because I attach myself falsely to the issues of the moment. Or that I am mean-spirited and harsh because I enjoy the power system of the world as it is rather than hating it. Or that I accept the world rather than push to change it, to improve it. Or that because I appear to accept power as a legitimate source of satisfaction, I deny the appeal of the long human quest for equality, equity, and a world founded on the assumptions of love rather than the friction between coercion and weakness.

Perhaps all these possible accusations against me are in fact true. That doesn't interest me. My intent in this account is to take my argument about pleasure another step: to describe a few ways power produces pleasure and one interesting way in which it affects the body. I will sketch the relationship of power to sexuality and describe some suggestive research on how power relations interact with hormones we all secrete.

The basic question is: Why does being up feel better than being down?

Despite Mosquitoes

Power over pleasure, over what people are able to enjoy, is a central feature of human societies. I have explored various ways in which this works. But the exercise of power is in itself pleasurable. A fundamental reason why people seek power — those who do — is that attaining power and wielding it are fun, usually very interesting, and often fascinating and dramatic. This aspect is in addition to the obvious benefits of power — being of service to other people, accomplishing goals that are worthwhile, acquiring or enjoying resources, compelling the assistance of other people, being famous, being disproportionately significant in one's group, even securing an opportunity to outwit the coldness of natural oblivion by an act or a structure — the Maginot Line, the Marshall Plan, the Jacob Javits Convention Center, the duke of Buckingham's palace.

Not only that. There is also evidence that power is good for the health and that a complicated physiology and brain chemistry are involved in struggles for status. The body and the body politic, the Constitution and the constitution, are linked in a complex but increasingly knowable way.

This complex connection makes understanding power relations more difficult. But it is encouraging as well, because since bodies are the same everywhere, at least we know that *something* unites the politics of highly diverse communities. As a onetime prime minister told me about summit meetings of chief officials: "When elected heads of state get together, they listen carefully to each other because of what they understand about each other's lives." If nothing else, the relentless demands of candidacy on a politician's body and life are readily apprehended by his or her peers, just as people who secure large fortunes understand a great deal about similar moneyed people, even if they operate in other areas of action.

Common bodily factors relating to power may be shared by people everywhere. But there is an uncommon array of different kinds of power. Different people enjoy different forms and foci of control. Each culture and each individual will have a particular and firmly etched definition. A Buddhist might define power as the capacity to melt benignly into the environment, while an ancient Egyptian will define his power by the size of his Pyramid. One modern American may define power as the ability to drive rapidly down a smooth road in a car that is almost wholly insulated — except visually — from the surrounding environment. But another modern American may feel powerful when she reaches a campsite after a ten-hour trek through brambles and mud, across rocks, and despite mosquitoes. A pianist can feel powerful after holding a pause in a prelude a split second longer than listeners expect. A college friend who is now a surgeon in Montreal once evenly told me: "What I love most about it, Tiger, is that first thin red incisive line."

What unites various styles of power is this: individuals experience a sense of efficacy within a clear place in a knowable nook of the world. They make a clear difference in a knowable way. Often this involves other people and working to change their behavior. How they respond is important too, of course, as far as the fun of power is concerned. But if power is often unpleasant, it is nonetheless omnipresent. It may occur outside the body, but it has an impact on our insides, too. The worried middle manager baffled by his chronic subdominance in the work world — by his definitely uncertain grip on power — sustains an ulcer pasture in his gut.[1] I want to discuss only a few of the elements of this elemental process, but at least a few.

When I was a high-school student, I acquired an after-school job at a photography studio down the street. The owner had a son several years older than me. One of my assigned tasks was to help him. Evidently he had not had a subordinate before, because one day he was trying out his great power and assigned me various wholly menial tasks, including, in one memorable moment, very obviously dropping something at his feet and asking me to retrieve it. I was fascinated by the peculiar impulse behind his action. There was an apparent mixture of sadism, bossiness, and a sense of personal satisfaction as a half-smile played on his face. What was this all about? And why didn't I punch him in the faintly smiling teeth — which was what I wanted to do — before I quit the job?

LIONEL TIGER

The Modern Emperor Is Supposed to Have Clothes but No Power

In democratic countries and during a democratic era there is understandable ambivalence about power, the ambition to acquire it, and what often goes along with it. The obvious social climber, the self-gilding nouveau riche merchant, and the vain, uncouth arriviste who deliberately "married money" are figures to mock and avoid. The jangle of their gold chains is a signal to flee. Such characters distort the conventions of civility; they are simply too candid. When the writer Norman Podhoretz wrote *Making It*, a memoir in which he approvingly described his "climb" from working-class Brooklyn to Manhattan's most vibrant literary salons, he was widely vilified for the aggressive candor of his account. Certainly some of his indignant critics were folk who had covered comparable ground without revealing their route or even acknowledging the journey. But he had openly spilled the Brooklyn baked beans. No self-congratulatory hubris is allowed in the fragile world of achieved preeminence.

The appropriate conventional response to success is reticence, not a dance of pleasure or a whoop of approval. Sheer enjoyment of the exercise of power because of the intricate challenge it may offer or because of the noisiness of its effects is unacceptable. In that sense, power is like beauty. It is close to a cardinal sin for indisputably beautiful women or handsome men proudly to describe themselves as luxuriously attractive. Usually they must grouchily bemoan the immense difficulty their glowing perfection causes them when they want to be taken seriously as philosophers or ecologists, when potential mates are intimidated by them, and so on. They cannot glory obviously in their obvious glory, without exciting obvious envy and also moral animosity.

The same reticence applies to seemly people with power. In the name of modesty and the antipleasure principle, they are obligated to describe their eminence and effectiveness as the fruit of earnest diligence, as the capstones of a sense of responsibility, as exquisitely demanding work. After the English publisher Robert Maxwell had completed an intricate and demanding negotiation in 1991 to buy the *New York Daily News*, which would have otherwise been forced to close, he announced: "I never celebrate. This is a sobering additional responsibility to take on 1,800 people's jobs and the survival of a monument."

The principle is, no pleasure for its own sake, especially when it occurs during the exercise of power. Fun is removed. Function is what is left. There must be redeeming social virtue. Success is supposed to come to people because they want to do useful jobs well, and for a proportionate wage, and because they are *good* at what they do. It is decent and honorable to want to serve communities, families, and good causes. But just as outright greed for personal gain or ambition for self-aggrandizement are unsavory and quietly unacceptable in upstanding company, it is also not cricket to celebrate overtly the interesting pleasure of straddling the head of the boardroom table, of being the focal point of couriers and lawyers with contracts to sign, of sketching the firm design of a structure that will envelop and affect people for fifty years, of waving as you make your way off the helicopter that has just arrived back at the White House — and waving freely, because one aide is carrying the case of state papers and another the bag of windbreakers, country corn, and a military novel.

If the protagonist openly revels in the pageant of power, he or she shares disapproval with figures as diverse as the hard-driving mogul, the wealthy miser, the politician who will make any compromise to win every vote, and the yuppie committed to a private ballet of personal acquisition. They do not occupy the same moral universe as the self-sacrificing Mother Teresas. There is even, as the literary critic Benjamin DeMott has indicated, an elementary unwillingness in the United States to acknowledge the realities of social class with which power is associated, certainly as these are portrayed in popular movies.[2] This is a broad evasion of the consciousness of inequity. In the Land of Opportunity nobody's address should be fixed, particularly on the wrong side of the tracks. If everyone is supposed to have equal opportunity, then all statuses are incipient. Hence, all positions are in flux. Therefore, none are crucially important because they are only way stations.

Bay Cay Bay Jay

This view of the power structure is a fantasy. Among other indexes, income and health statistics belie it immediately. Other societies are more candid in their self-assessments on this matter, even one so close to the USA, both physically and structurally, as Canada. For example, it was acknowledged early on in Canada that ethnic position and social class formed a "vertical mosaic," not a melting pot.[3] The fixities of status were consistent and durable along racial, ethnic, and social-class lines. Certain races and ethnic groups had higher or lower status to begin with. Corresponding economic advantages usually reflected the initial pecking order. Programs of affirmative action and the like are efforts to restrict and compensate for this reality. Clearly, the heat of racial politics in the United States suggests that disadvantaged groups understand this very well, even if the dominating groups do not or are in any event ill disposed to articulate it. Yet within disadvantaged groups themselves, hierarchies may emerge that depend either on shades of skin color or other determinants of status — for example, among black college sororities and fraternities.[4]

The relationship between the accident of birth and the facts of economic life remains highly charged and controversial.[5] European politics reflects traditional class inheritance quite directly. Where recognized aristocracies exist, royal and noble families will obviously affect social hierarchies in an ongoing way. Even in republics such as France or Italy, aristocratic lineage remains a factor (though not an overwhelming determinant, as it may once have been) affecting the eventual placement of a person in the social system. A favorite French description of visibly enviable people is that they are *b.c.b.g. — bon chic, bon genre.* Fashionably chic and wellborn. A springtime stroll around the seventh or sixteenth arrondissements of Paris will reveal quickly an apparently highly disproportionate incidence of exquisitely dressed women with blond hair, blue eyes, and a visible air of certified entitlement because of who they are, how they look, who they know, and what they buy and taste. It is fascinating that even the monumental convulsions of transition to the industrial way, except where there have been communist or similar revolutions, have not dislodged the privileged families of yore in any way commensurate with the sheer scope of the changes that have occurred.

Attacks on aristocracies and privileged classes understandably focus on the wealth they control and the consequent political and economic power they continue to wield. But the upper crust also have the best pleasure, the most inherited reclusive beachfronts, the most arrestingly sumptuous paintings to inspect at breakfast, the most durable trousseaux of stocks and bonds to bend to their discrete dynastic programs. As "legacies" — offspring of alumni — they enjoy the readiest access to scarce slots at desirable schools that train the next generation in the latest methods of securing comfy, enjoyable livelihoods.[6]

Such good fortune is exposed to frank public view at some risk. Power is consistently both attractive and frightening, admirable and alarming. Governmental arrangements are often designed to create a "balance of power" so that the evidently great human appetite for assertion — particularly among people who are in that trade — can be limited by the impersonal obligations of law and custom. As I have tried to show, personal decorum in many cultures also involves sharp restriction on any obvious display of the nature and extent of power a person commands. There is even stronger sanction against the frank display of pleasure in the efficacy and trappings of power.

Power: use it but defuse it. Act like Mr. Universe wearing a monk's robe. Show no sign of enjoying those rippling muscles.

First Class Is First-Class

I don't usually get to fly first-class, but when I do it is interesting to try to analyze its appeal, since the fundamental product — bodily transport from one place to another — is the same for all passengers. Is it the extra space, the better food, the free and reasonable wine, the quieter part of the cabin, the opportunity to disembark first? Or is it the overall *meaning* of the situation — its social cachet, its intimations of personal worth?

The semantics are plain enough. First class is just what it says, while the usual names of the middle group reflect the economic values of the community — executive class, business class, corporate class, and the like. (I once gave a talk to some managers, including managers of airlines, and complained that there was no "professor class." Why wasn't there? A man from Air Canada thought this was an amusing idea, but I have yet to see any proprofessorial action.) Obviously, there are practical reasons for preferring first or business class. A trip I took to Tokyo unexpectedly in first class because of overbooking elsewhere yielded a much fresher passenger at the other end than on occasions I've taken that trip, or ones equally punishing, in steerage. Space, quiet, food, attention, all that. But more elusive, and also more interesting, is the pleasure yielded by status and its impact on physical well-being, particularly during a physically demanding task such as flying across a working day of time zones.

My interest is not wholly sumptuary. There are intriguing data about the relationship between the comfort of the body and social status. These may bear on the configuration of airplane cabins and similar arrangements of people according to one social order or another. Let me explain.

When commercial air travel began, every passenger was in a real sense first-class. Since flying was expensive, adventurous, and unusual, everyone who flew felt privileged, challenged, special, and succored in some way. The first passenger planes even had berths for long flights. Airships followed the image of deluxe travel by water-ships. In time, the air cabin was divided into two classes: first, and tourist or economy. Even in this latter class, cachet and opportunity for self-respect were so special that the dual system worked. Later, however, travel became more banal and common, particularly with the development of the jumbo jet. Since economic life, particularly as pursued by business organizations, now depended more than ever on the human mobility that airplanes permitted, more and more people were obligated to fly to do their work or their employers'.

But they were not "tourists." And the description "economy" surely should not be associated with a functionary so important that an employer was willing to fly his or her body hither and yon to make money or take action on behalf of the entire company.

Hence, business class, for people whose travel was often — overwhelmingly often — paid for by their employers. However, these employers appear to have been unwilling to foot the bill for the disproportionately high fares airlines were charging for first class. The most senior managers may, also, have been unwilling to lose the opportunity to distinguish themselves and the owners, who all flew first-class from the middlers assigned to seats in business or executive. At least these latter compromises were superior to economy. Social space was supplied. Psychic status was defined. Everyone's body still landed at the same time. But the journey, not the arrival, mattered.

A cheeky story about the president of a foundation suggests the complex meaning of status here. In another country there is a prominent foundation named after the family that very generously endowed it. Its operating president is an obviously effective but somewhat imperial scholar. One day the scholar was in the waiting room of an airport in a foreign city, en route back to the headquarters country of the foundation. In the same waiting room happened to be the scion of the family, still immensely wealthy, that had endowed the foundation. Until the flight was called, they talked earnestly about foundation affairs, whereupon the scion found his seat in the economy section, the scholar in first class.

The employee needed the affirmation and comfort of first class — and also, he was not personally paying for them. The man who in effect was paying for both seats presumably enjoyed giving away wealth more than receiving physical comfort and pleasure. He certainly had no need to derive his sense of personal station from the airplane seat he occupied, if only because everyone in the cabin crew would know who he was because of his famous name in a small country. Nevertheless, his and the foundation president's choices reveal the perceived value of differences in status. They become sources of personal satisfaction, perhaps more important ones than the specific physical improvements in the conditions of the journey.

My travel on private planes has been unduly restricted by the whimsical fates. Nonetheless, it is clear that here is a genuine sign of human progress. There is none of racing to meet a departure time, of checking in, of waiting, of trepidation about being caught in the middle seat. The best way is to have the limousine drive right to the aircraft while the luggage transfers itself into the hold, and then there is freedom to move around the plane. Depending on the thoughtfulness of the host, there is a miscellany of food and drink and, then, on the other end, the limousine right there on the tarmac so the soft and easy ride continues.

It is pleasant, fun, a clear-cut bonus to be fortunate enough to travel in such a style. It is also radically costly, and more often than not the private plane is going where public ones go too. So the overriding reason for the expensive, exclusive choice is the pleasure and convenience of the pampered passenger. It is therefore small wonder that corporations that own jets refrain from plastering on them the logos they so exuberantly display every other chance they get. What if a shareholder or customer or pension fund manager happens to be stranded in a wait-list line and through a window observes these knights of the commercial realm sashaying onto their sleek chariot? No, it is better they remain anonymous. This is almost more fun anyway. Envious and curious onlookers now must wonder who these special people are rather than *know* they are merely eager servants of Exxon or Renault or Nabisco.

Serotonin Cocktail at the Monkey Bar

Leonard Woolf, of Virginia and other fame, wrote a volume of autobiography called *The Journey Not the Arrival Matters*. How you get there is more important than where you're going. There is a discernible difference between a piece of toast in steerage and the same nibble at the captain's table, even though a nutritionist might contend otherwise. But a psychologist will say the difference is obvious — but why it is, is not quite so obvious. Something happens to people in high places and in low, with an impact that seems almost bodily. I have introduced the idea that the power associated with status is very pleasurable even though there may be cultural constraints on displaying and even enjoying such pleasure. There is a reason for patterns of status, there is an obvious evolutionary reason for the desire for high rather than low status, and there is now emerging a clearer picture than ever of the effect of status on a person's body, psyche, and sense of place. Now I want to inspect the point of contact between the boardroom and the chemistry lab — the relationship between an individual's body and his or her social status.

Fascinating experiments at the UCLA Department of Psychiatry and at the University of Iowa show that high status in monkey and human groups changes brain and bodily chemistry. These studies offer very clear suggestions about the physiological component, the physicality, of status. They sketch the possibility, if not likelihood, that high status in itself results in bodily and mental states that are pleasurable. The implication is that sitting in first class or business class on an airplane is in itself a physiological pleasure because of its symbolic meaning. Symbols deliver secretions.

The pioneering major work on monkeys has been done by Michael McGuire, Michael Raleigh, and Gary Brammer at UCLA Medical School.[7] The first demonstration (to my knowledge) of a physiological correlate of status among humans was by the political scientist Douglas Madsen of the University of Iowa.[8] These are their findings.

A secretion called serotonin has been shown to play an array of roles in health and behavior. It does various things in the body. With seeming perversity, its existence appears to foster improved circulation in healthy blood vessels, while in sufferers of heart disease it squeezes off blood flow and may be associated with chest pain and even heart attacks. It has been shown to be associated with a variety of behaviors, ranging from deep depression to criminality to self-destruction.[9] One definite function, through its level of concentration in the bloodstream, is to assist the transmission of messages to the brain — to the basic primitive organizing and operating parts of the neural network.

McGuire and his colleagues at UCLA discovered that the dominant animal in each of nineteen groups of vervet monkeys had a consistently higher level of serotonin concentrated in its blood — nearly 50 percent higher than the other members of the group. This is an unusually sharp difference in the averages of physiological values. Once the researchers found this correlation, they could use blood tests to predict which member of an otherwise unknown group was its leader.

How did this come about? The answer is more important and consequential than it may seem at first, and this requires a word of explication. The dominant working assumption of people studying the interaction of the body and behavior has been that differences in physiology cause differences in social behavior. The opposite interpretation, that the inner state of an individual is caused by external circumstances, has been given much less credence. In the case of serotonin, individuals born with it or somehow bringing a higher level of it to the group were the ones who became dominant. What was inside was the main cause. This was the first idea.

A fleeting digression will help explain the significance of this. The same kind of explanation has been very generally — and with untold social consequences — applied to psychological testing. For example, the working assumption behind standardized IQ tests, as well as similar tests such as the SAT is that they display the native cortical skill of the individual — that they reveal the innate equipment rather than the social or economic or similar conditions within which it functions. The lines of influence flow from the inside out. The tests are supposed to identify what is in effect the biological essence of the individual. They are designed to get to the heart of the matter.

As with all such tests, their producers and most of their users assert that they are "culture-free," unaffected by social class, religion, ethnicity, race, and so on. This is a surprising claim to emerge from a social-science community that by and large does not accept that biology has much to do with behavior — biology is, of course, the other side in the chronic argument over whether "nature" (biology) or "nurture" (culture) determines human behavior.[10] This same community — particularly many anthropologists, such as Clifford Geertz — asserts that human culture sharply and decisively distinguishes us from other animals. It is therefore surprising — if not also bizarre and, indeed, goofy — that members of the academic community who hold these views about culture should embrace (and use in their own academic procedures, such as the college admissions process) an evaluation of human skills that is supposed to be "culture-free."

I don't think IQ and similar tests work from the inside out. Evidently, the impact of serotonin does not work that way either. In another series of experiments, McGuire and his associates allowed a group of male vervets to stabilize so that a definite dominance hierarchy and leader were identified. Blood assays were taken on all members. Then the leader was removed. The researchers found that beginning about seventy-two hours after the exile occurred — during which period there was intense and typical primate politicking — a newly dominant animal emerged. It appears this individual was most often the one able to endure the uncertainty and tension of the struggle for status — the individual with a form of equability prevailed. After the struggle, the blood-serotonin level of the newly dominant animal began to increase to the decisively higher level of the former leader. Moreover, when this hapless character was installed alone in a cage, his serotonin level soon dropped to the usual one of subdominant group members.

Mirror, Mirror, in the Cage

A touch of surrealism was added to the story: a similar drop in serotonin level occurred when the leader was housed alone in a cage with a one-way mirror that reflected his image back to him. When he produced the colorful dominance display that had hitherto struck terror among his fellow males, the impudent monkey in the mirror not only failed to show subordination but produced an equally formidable dominance display too![11] With no ass to kick, the big shot's serotonin ebbed away. This result also occurred when he was housed with females only, without the males with whom he would normally joust for status. It appears the finding does not apply to females, among whom power interactions have different meanings, with different results — ones that are less dramatic both physiologically and in terms of behavior. In general, females do not occupy clear positions in the dominance hierarchy found in natural groups, which almost always include adult males. It would be interesting to test females in all-female groups, to see what role, if any, serotonin and other substances play in the system. In any event, as you will see, it is clear that the cooperation of powerful females is vital for males who secure dominant status.

The meaning was plain. An internal physiological state associated with power was the result of social behavior, not the other way around. Outside in, not inside out. The research group has also found that in college fraternities officers show serotonin levels on average 20 percent higher than nonofficers. Experiments with leaders and nonleaders of teams of college sportsmen yielded similar results.[12] Douglas Madsen of the University of Iowa has also found clear evidence of the same phenomenon among college students assigned complex experimental tasks.[13]

The McGuire team, in this case led by Michael Raleigh, conducted yet another vervet experiment, one that strengthens their case but also raises some additional important issues.[14] After setting up a relatively informal enclosure on the Caribbean island of Saint Kitts, the team divided the animals into twelve social groups, each containing three adult males, at least three adult females, and their offspring. Once the monkeys in each group established a dominance hierarchy, a baseline level of serotonin was determined. Then the dominant male was removed and at random one of the other two males was given either a drug that enhanced serotonergic activity or one that reduced it. The upshot of several phases of the experiment was that in all cases the males given enhanced serotonin levels became dominant, while the other males, who received the serotonin inhibitor, were subdominant. And when the originally dominant males were reintroduced to the group — lo! behold! — they became dominant once more, even though by now both other males had had the taste and experience of dominance.

There are several other interesting aspects of this experiment apart from its main implication, that administering a drug can markedly affect a political system. One is that the high-serotonin individuals were considerably less aggressive than the low-dominance individuals. They engaged in more sociable behavior — that is, in male bonding, and in more mutual grooming. And, perhaps most important, they were able to secure the cooperation of the high-ranking females in defining their dominant positions. In effect, dominance had much to do with the carrot and less, evidently, with the stick.

Roger Masters of Dartmouth College and his associates have published concordant work on the facial expressions of human politicians.[15] Those who smile more, do better. Carrot again, not stick, and presumably an activation of the pleasure system rather than the pain process. Smiling could be a critical factor in attracting the support of voters, women as well as men. Constituents may be irritated or intimidated by grim-faced leaders but reassured and enhanced by the smiling variety. Of course, forced grinning feeds into the stereotype of politicians at their most insincere. Nevertheless, there is probably a vital truth here, which is that the pleasure systems have a role in choosing people of power — just as the happy, smiling face is an asset to entertainers, who must control the attention and enthusiasm of their audience to do their work.

What is not as clear is what distinguishes the individuals who assume dominance from those who do not. But there are some clues.

A Hit of Tryptophan

The clues have to do with pleasure, among other things. Serotonin is broadly associated with another internally circulating substance, tryptophan, whose presence has been shown to decrease fear and anxiety in monkeys. It is also associated with an increase of benign social behavior. In humans it has been linked to relative ease in falling asleep; milk contains a hit of tryptophan — one reason warm milk is sometimes recommended as a soporific. Among people, heightened aggressiveness, general irritability, and disruption of sleep have been experimentally linked to reduced levels of serotonin — as have mania and depression.[16] In addition, there appears to be an association between PMS — premenstrual syndrome — and unusually low levels of serotonin in the days before the menstrual period.

The central fact is that a substance that the body generates is stimulated by an individual's social position. When that substance reaches a certain level, the individual exhibits characteristics of comfort and good health. Blood pressure is likely to be moderate. The individual sleeps easily and is calm. He or she enjoys better physical and, presumably, mental health than individuals lower in the hierarchical system. High status under natural conditions yields good health and a broad comfort zone. The recent work of the UCLA group underlines the proof of this particular pudding: that artificial enhancement of serotonin is necessary to affect an individual monkey's political position, ease, and probably enjoyment of life — for males, at least. Females appear to operate in terms of a much-longer-lived and far more complex system of dominance.[17] Either natural social life or a human chemical can do the trick. But, of course, monkeys have no human chemicals in their medicine chests.

This is a highly provocative finding. The implications for humans leap to mind — particularly since, as we have seen, there appears to be a somewhat similar serotonin-based system that operates among humans. Will presidential candidates gulp serotonin pills as they prepare to smile their way through their thirty-second commercials? What happens if *everyone* in a group is artificially medicated, pumped up to feel like the leader?[18] Or is serotonin like certain drugs that require greater dosages to achieve the same effect as time goes on? Perhaps you will be able to be king or queen for a day on a serotonin high, but not for a lifetime. In the absence of the chemical, the primates on Saint Kitts returned to their original, rather durable social orders. The natural unmanipulated behavior of the group produced the internal physiology — the main finding of this line of study. Perhaps, after all, it is not something with which to monkey.

The Pressure of Depression

Power and high status are associated with pleasure. Weakness and subordination are associated with depression, if not also with a more complex array of factors. An extensive literature both confessional and scientific describes how readily people can become prone to depression when they suffer severe reversals in economic, political, sexual, and social life. This occurs both among humans and other species, and by now we have an inkling of what some of the bodily mechanisms are.

Of course, it is hardly an eccentric observation to note that individuals, of any species, will feel bad when things are going badly for them. Low status is one form of things going badly. But is it inevitable? Is there no other way living creatures can sort themselves out than in hierarchies that yield pleasure for those who lead and various kinds of depression for those who must follow?

Let's step back from the obvious and be deliberately naive about this for a moment. Why *is* depression associated with low status? Couldn't it be that individuals low in a hierarchy enjoy the luxury of having decisions made for them? Couldn't they be comforted and relaxed because their time and energy are being directed by others? Is this not preferable to taking personal responsibility for the quality of their choices and enduring constant indecision about them?

Apparently not. In a very early and prescient argument, Joseph Price of the Maudesley Hospital in England suggested a clear link between the loss of status and depression.[19] Since then there has been a generous body of work on the subject, with indications that everything from divorce to the loss of a job to the hazing associated with entry to military college leads to changed neurophysiology and vulnerability to depression. And as Michael McGuire has commented, avid contests focused on the privilege of becoming subdominant are exceptionally rare if not wholly absent in nature.[20] A possible temporary exception is provided by bourgeois and aristocratic youngsters, who sometimes decide that in downward mobility lies the true heart of life's concealed darkness. But this is usually an evanescent phase of unusually fortunate people who may be correct in their analysis but who fade in their ardor. In general, contests are about moving up — there are no fierce struggles over who will have the privilege of being Numero Due rather than Uno.

An extreme example of how loss of status affects humans is the surprisingly sharp impact retirement has on men. They die twice as often in the first year of retirement as in the second. There is a shock to the system, literally, from the decline in position, income, importance, and ability to contribute — to participate in interesting things and have the fun, challenge, and irritation of activity. Obviously, over time, an adjustment occurs, but only if death doesn't catch the retiree first.

This is hardly surprising. Powerful and relatively well-off people enjoy clear advantages over the less powerful, the less well-off, or those suddenly consigned to the oblivion of no function. But it means something that the internal physiology associated with this well-being is quite directly linked to social position, to what we may call power in the broadest sense. Just as obviously, powerful people may become as depressed and fraught as the next person. Some individuals may demand a level of approval, income, power, attention, and the like that condemns them to a perpetual struggle against their own chronic dissatisfaction with whatever great or minor accomplishments or conditions already attach to them.

But their lack of contentment with what they have does not imply they would be happier with less. After all, they could always choose more modest means of life if they wanted to. Some sports who take the Gauguin route or variants of it do just that. But few do so. It is a pattern more marked by its rarity than its frequency. Renunciation remains exotic. It is usually associated with religions rather than with control of resources. It rarely characterizes people who crash like eager elephants through the jungles of wealth and power.

Neurotransmitters in the Heads of State

Let's consider further the link between pleasure, physiology, and power. My Rutgers colleague David Schwartz some years ago conducted a study of leaders in various avenues of life — business, law, politics. His findings contradicted the notion that high-status life was demanding, full of tension, eroding, unsettling. As a matter of fact, high status was associated with the calm and healthful conditions that characterized the potent people I described above. Some individuals appeared to be to the manor and the chairman's office born. They were intrinsically, physiologically, leaders — their very body cells seemed to be healthier and more effective. They ended up living longer, with less illness, less tension, and more pleasure than people of lower status. Their family lives were relatively settled and their careers proceeded smoothly and prosperously. They slept more soundly than the average person, had better diets, and exercised more. Certainly, some people are bigger or are faster runners than others, or louder singers, or apparently smarter at math, or better able to coordinate their eyes, their hands, and a tennis racket. This raises the possibility that these high-status folk were simply healthier than other people. Therefore, it seemed that health was a very salient cause of elevated status.

But the new findings suggest an opposite or at least more complex interpretation: that the elite individuals only become healthier *after* they become elite, almost *because* they become elite. In other words, them that has, gets. An ancient, verifiable principle, consistent with common sense, common observation, and basic biosocial theory.

And yet a mystery remains: why do they and not others win those high spots? This is more difficult to pin down. Perhaps another glance at other primates may provide a clue. Since we share one of the important substances, serotonin, perhaps we share some of the behavior that produces it and is influenced by it.

According to McGuire and his associates, among monkeys there appears to be some real connection between serotonin and how successfully the animals cope with the insecurity generated by changes in the dominance system. Those with something like "nerves of steel" are relatively untroubled by the confusions and uncertainties that result from disputes over status and the changes that occur when the former leader is removed from the group. Calmness confers a political advantage when there is trouble afoot. And calmness is associated with serotonin in the animals who eventually win out. They endure confusion better and appear to process confusing and disturbing information better. Perhaps they feel better under pressure and remain more effective during it. When "all about them are losing theirs," they retain an ability to assert themselves with sufficient clarity so that other animals take notice and respond deferentially. That is, perhaps they experience confusion as less unpleasurable and less unpleasant than their fellow group members. Perhaps they even enjoy the gamble and the rush of the open-ended contest. They seem more comfortable and confident even about awkward and difficult situations and are able to turn this to good political advantage. Grace under pressure, nerves of steel, taking the heat — the cliché of your choice may reflect a manner of response to a chronic situation in both animal and human groups: political change and uncertainty. And perhaps the politician's perennial campaign smile suggests, or is meant to imply, that he or she enjoys the quest for power and is also happy to see you and your offspring. If the display is successful, you will believe it.

When the dominant monkey with the elevated serotonin is removed from the group, it takes roughly seventy-two hours before the serotonin level of the newly dominant animal is clearly discernible, approximately fourteen days before it reaches the height at which it will remain. Presumably the future leader is the least displeased by the indeterminate situation, the best able to watch and wait, and the most adroit at impressing his competitors — a "take-charge" monkey.

A comparable mechanism may operate among humans, since many of the other circumstances are similar to the monkey business. For example, people respond with increased heart and blood-pressure rates when they interact with people of higher rank. They are more tense than when they encounter people of similar or lower status.[21] Status differences translate into physiological ones. Both lower status and uncertainty about status are physiologically disturbing. They are also likely to be psychologically disquieting. Individuals best able to endure this and even in some sense enjoy it — the cut and thrust of the power struggle — may turn out to be the individuals who win out in the struggle. Not being unduly under stress, being patient, finding the situation intriguing —these characteristics may be enough to shorten the steps to power. Perhaps more than the fear of failure, more even than the allure of resources, the pleasure of power — which translates into physiology — and enjoyment of political ruckus become factors in the outcome of contests for predominance.

What's the story? Better yet, what's the secret? Of course, and unhappily, I don't know. There is at least one clue, which is that it seems that "in humans, the activity of the enzymes involved in the synthesis and degradation of serotonin appear to be under some genetic control."[22] Perhaps some individuals are naturally better able than others to produce and maintain effective levels of serotonin (and, undoubtedly, similar substances, too) — an ability that allows them to evaluate calmly and eventually influence the process of uncertainty before a social order is established. They begin with an initial physiological advantage because they have a readier capacity to secrete serotonin. They don't have the serotonin itself.

It has to emerge in real social interactions with other people who lack this advantage or enjoy it less luxuriously.

Perhaps they are better able to form social coalitions and take the long view while also continuing to focus on their own political agendas. And to come back to pleasure again, perhaps they enjoy the whole process more, which reduces its toll on their energy and their level of anxiety. Perhaps in turn they can reassure other people, make them feel better about the ongoing changes, and prosper politically as a result. Smile. You're on camera.

These are not definitive explanations. But we are very much still on the threshold here of a new and potentially important exploration of the link between power and physiology. We don't know what we'll find, but it is scientifically exciting that there seems to be something there. And it would be no surprise, to me at least, if pleasure in power is related to its physiological basis and to its impact on social behavior.

Watch this space.

Power Pleases. Absolute Power Pleases. Absolutely.

I've emphasized the relationship of power to its physiological component. The physiology appears to be an important clue to the basic nature of power and to its function in human society. It is a factor both poorly understood and unduly underestimated. Even people with power may feel unable to enjoy it and instead will talk of "being of service," "giving something back," supporting the nation, the old school or college, or whatever. They are hardly able in a relatively censorious, puritanical culture to advertise candidly their enjoyment of the limo and driver, the private jet, the endless messages, the appeals for time and attention, the testimonial banquets, the diplomatic pouches, the faxes, the calls on secure phones — all the extraordinary attention and care paid to people with power.

Such drama marks all levels, from the apparatus of colorful respect surrounding heads of state or royalty, to the astonished deference shown by the weak to a gangland boss, to the embracing admiration offered a religious guru by his or her enthusiasts. It can be the power of a musician controlling the scene in a stadium holding a hundred thousand people or the television personality waiting confidently during the almost sacred moments before the red light flicks on atop the waiting camera and she says, "Good evening," to twenty million people. It can be the power of a financial manager who knows that a huge industry is being acquired and that the thousands of people busy within it do not understand the volatile nature of their immediate future. It can be the power of the general and the minister of defense who have decided to set major lethal forces in motion, highly secretively, with stern purpose; now they are in the tense, tight circle of the knowledgeable, the elect. It can be the power of an artist who redefines in a discernible way how some feature of life is described and valued. In whatever sphere, it is the role of the powerful person to be in touch — in contact — with an opportunity to make a difference, be a player, make a choice.

When we lived near the mouth of the cave, nothing escaped the notice of anyone. Leaders of the group and all its members were attuned to all of the elements of its life. When societies became large it was easy for leaders to fall quickly out of touch and be obligated to operate at long distances both temporally and physically. Diplomatic dispatches could take weeks, state visits were long and demanding, the mail was slow. Battles began in the morning so that a good night's sleep could be had by all. The obligations of power were circumscribed by circumstance. The separate pleasures, of leisure and power, were both available.

Electricity changed this decisively, of course. Telephone and telegraph increased the density and speed of communication and the tasks of leading became more intense, involved a broader network of people, and hence took longer. Computers, faxes, satellite communication, and systems such as the CNN organization create heightened pressure on leaders and on their sense of their own significance and the rapid-fire value of what they do. One result is that whereas once the rich were able to enjoy their leisure while the poor had to toil at length, now the situation is reversed. The working hours of the modest are in steady decline, but powerful, wealthy people are on call nearly all the time. Portable telephones carried into the restaurants of the rich may ring at table — in that environment, like a red blister on the face of a beauty. A friend who makes tens of millions trading currency and commodities will, when the action is hot, dine with a signal box beside his fish fork in case he must return to his phones to shift yen to sterling or oil to copper or cash to debt. He can command more resources, but it takes more time. Increased working hours may reduce the appeal of great jobs, should they move decisively beyond the human scale in which a mortal can maneuver.

They Are Not Quality Circles

Let me deal with what may seem like a paradox in this discussion of the pleasure of power and the power of pleasure. I have said that dominant individuals enjoy physiological and psychological benefits of their positions, and that these have their roots in the formative prehistory of our own and other species, most obviously the other primates. Well then, does this mean that everyone else is miserable, with defective bodily systems, with hopeless outlooks on the world and the future?

It depends on the system. In dictatorships, harsh, mean-spirited monarchies, or otherwise despotic governments, it is clearly or potentially the case that many people will on many public occasions be obligated to act in ways that deprive them of a sense of dignity and autonomy. People will have to do things that serve the state or the existing system of power without sensitive reference to the needs or desires of the population at large.

But this is obviously explosive, as the astonishing shifts in the USSR in the fall of 1991 made clear. In more benign forms of organization, people who are not absolute leaders enjoying absolute power may nonetheless take part in deciding many of the conditions of their lives and work, and they will take pleasure in doing so. At the very least, people enjoy the company of other people. Solitary confinement and ostracism I have already identified as utterly severe punishments, and there is now good analysis of the importance of basic social interaction in offering people a sense of empowerment and connection.[23]

I want to take the example of a familiar social group to show

how dignified membership is itself a valuable asset. The quality circle is now a standard feature of much industry, particularly in Japan, where it was introduced by the American statistician W. Edwards Deming. Essentially, this circle is just a group of people doing a particular job who meet to discuss how they can do it better. It has been an extraordinarily successful device in Japan and has yielded high-quality products and ways of making them that are efficient and well suited to the individuals involved.

What turned this simple arrangement into a surprisingly effective instrument was that it avoided the critical error of American management theory, which formed the basis for industrial activity in the United States. In my book *The Manufacture of Evil* I called this error a shift in emphasis "from man to management." I showed how this extraordinarily influential change was associated with the emergence in the United States of the idea of management itself. This idea was essentially an American invention of around the beginning of the century (it was actually spearheaded by military engineers, many from West Point).

In turn this resulted in schools of management and business that developed explicit notions of standard operating procedure. These depended on strong principles applied by the senior managers to the sections down the line. The top dogs were enlightened, had good theory, and knew their accountancy and their charts of organization. In any event, where there were unions, they had to take a somewhat adversarial stance with the employees on whom they were relying to execute their carefully crafted plan. And even where there were no unions, there remained an adversarial relation, because of the premise that it was the role of managers to manage, of executives to execute plans, but of workers to work.

But what the quality circle is all about is not only, or not even, productive efficiency. It is more about equality than quality. Here again, "the medium is the message." People are asked their opinion, which they give, and it is evidently useful. But in accomplishing this they are also taking part in a social group the importance of which is recognized by the organization. They receive the message that they are important, their opinions matter, that they are more than operatives of the lordly plans of their anointed superiors. They are allowed to take an adult role of capable contribution to the survival and prosperity of their group. They are able to enjoy what Upper Paleolithic people had to do to carry on and were reproductively rewarded for doing: operate, cooperate, communicate, and share. This is more fun than being told what to do in the hellish manner of the assembly-line worker Charlie Chaplin plays in *Modern Times.* The quality circle functions in modern times by successfully using ancient principles of cooperative social contribution. Very simply, it works. Work becomes a source of social pleasure as well as material resources. Even if the boss is healthier and sleeps better, the employee in the equality circle also feels pleased and rewarded. He or she does not suffer functional ostracism. No one doubts that people should be able to vote about their political lives, and the equality circle is an important analogue of the vote in life on the job.

The quality circle works very well. But I have to confess I find it astonishing that evidently no one has stressed its essentially social nature. This relates to my basic hypothesis in this book, which is that the carrot is at least as important as the stick. In American management theory, the manager is the stick, the carrot is the paycheck, but neither is as effective as the rigors of international business demand they be, because they fail to enlist fully the zest for cooperative effectiveness that had to be, and was, the hallmark of our evolutionary success. In the Upper Paleolithic, laziness was unwise. People do best the work they want to do most.

Marx Was Wrong

Groucho Marx was wrong in general when he announced that he didn't want to be a member of any club that would have him as a member. Perhaps he spoke accurately for himself, which may explain the arch and frequently rancorous comedic connection he had to the world around him. But most people appear to sort themselves into social networks so that they experience a reasonably comfortable balance between where they fit in a system and where they have, for various reasons, decided they should or could fit. Not only do people not generally want to go where they are not wanted, but they will try to place themselves within social milieus in which their sense of their own status is confident — not too high, not too low. What the Cornell University economist Robert Frank has called "choosing the right pond" is an endless process in which people try to sort themselves within comfortable hierarchies. They broadly confine their status concerns to a sharply limited universe.[24] Therefore Ivy League football players become as ambitious and committed about their games as the broadly superior players of other colleges who receive athletic scholarships and are much more likely to aspire to careers in professional football. The greater skill of one group evidently does not diminish the enthusiasm and avidity of the other.

As Frank asserts, "we sort ourselves into leagues."[25] Leagues are important because they permit competition that is agreeably fair. This ubiquitous human pattern reveals what is presumably a "comfort zone" in how people respond to many of the differences between them. It implies they try to even these out within some broad bands of minor difference. Leagues define differences that should be interesting and stimulating and cannot be crushingly unequal. Like the weight categories of boxers or age grades of schoolchildren, leagues allow expression of differences in competence but within a relatively narrow range that is seen to be fair. Leagues allow people to have fun playing games with people who will neither overwhelm them nor collapse in embarrassed incompetence. They permit people to have pleasure in a defined scheme of competition the outcome of which is regarded as sufficiently agreeable so that everyone will play again another day.

Leagues may be one of the least appreciated but most useful of human arrangements in large populations.

Amateur golf is particularly interesting in this context. In effect individuals play against the course and their own histories and not one another — they try to improve their own scores but don't have to compete with other people, who might be depressingly better than they or woefully worse. The so-called handicap evens things out. The conviviality of the foursome or the duo can be maintained. This may indeed be one reason for the extensive popularity of golf, to say nothing of the fact that like the suburb (where most courses are located), it offers immersion in landscape — the savanna.

The game of golf has succeeded in solving the problem that

marked differences in competence can create — that they become differences in status and hence can have, as we have seen, appreciable impact on how people feel both mentally and bodily. But when individual competence is measured against an impersonal standard, even fierce but unequal competitors can enjoy their afternoon of eighteen holes of golf.

In a metaphoric if not real sense, golf is also the ultimate example in sport of the success of the Protestant ethic, which of course has greatly to do with individual effort and destiny. Golf's origin in especially stern Scotland may be pertinent here, as well as its popularity with business executives, many of whom are by definition competitive and ambitious for accomplishment. Too many of them too intent on besting each other at play would hardly provide pleasure. There would be one winner and eleven or three or six players with a sense of failure.

But the handicap system turns the contest into a kind of league that is personally manageable and not overwhelming. First the golf association assigns each player a handicap rating that is based on his or her play over a period of time at a particular course. Each course has its own weighting of difficulty, and the player's score and the course difficulty are combined to define the individual's handicap, which he or she carries to courses anywhere. The rating reduces the difference between "par for the course" and the individual player's performance. Thus the handicap (what a harsh word for a factor in a game) reduces the pressure and sustains the fun. It represents a way of making the game interesting without wholly demoralizing a player who has no possibility of achieving a par score without the boost of a handicap. Without the handicap system, golf would be too depressing to too many players. It wouldn't enjoy its extensive popularity. A similar scheme exists in trapshooting, too; poor shooters are allowed to stand closer to the target in competition with better ones.[26] Again, differences in competence do not become translated into differences in status. No one need feel badly bested, disconsolate over an inferior score, or suffer from a depleted store of serotonin or testosterone or simple good humor.

There is a comparable arrangement in professional sports, most particularly basketball, that permits lowest-ranked teams the first right to recruit the highest-ranked rookies. This is an effort to create parity between teams for the sound commercial reason that games between sharply unequal teams are broadly unamusing. Severe subordination is very uncomfortable and spectators all-too-painfully identify with it. This is also why the most absorbing games are close, tightly fought, and most exciting when the outcome is upsettingly and even agonizingly uncertain. Even if such discomfiting games are tense, they are seen as fair.

Identification with people enduring subordination is at the root of the widespread phenomenon of "rooting for the underdog." This is why athletic victories such as Jesse Owens's at the Berlin Olympics carry such strong emotional messages and provide such rich satisfaction. Fairness matters. Sorting into leagues moderates the social distress of sharp inequality and minimizes displeasure.

The Iron Law of Hierarchy

Low status and powerlessness are obviously uncomfortable conditions, even physiologically. It is no big news that high status and power are healthful, comfortable, and pleasurable. The work or social function of particular groups largely doesn't matter: the status distinctions emerge anyway. They exist in groups of whatever kind, from garden clubs, to street gangs, to orchestras with soloists and dramatic conductors, to seminaries where some are holier than others and holier than thou, to the military and other official hierarchies with highly refined power schemes. And as William Whyte wrote in *The Organization Man*, "the more exquisite distinctions are, the more important they become."

Finally, and most extremely, there is the remarkable hierarchy of the caste system of India and several other societies. There, contemporary status is fixed in the mists of antiquity by the caste into which one is born. Change in the status of particular castes takes generations of careful and thoughtful attention to climbing the social ladder. The statuses remain vitally, viscerally important, extending not only, of course, to whom one is able to marry but even from whom food may be accepted; observant Brahmins may not accept food from lesser castes. Until recently, the lowest-caste Untouchables lived within what was effectively a bubble of quarantine because of assumptions about their presumed cellular inferiority. Despite numerous and quite draconian government laws to the contrary, they continue to suffer stigma and profound disadvantage. In general, when differences of status become sanctified by religion, entrenched over generations, or visibly symbolized by race or ethnicity, they become wrenchingly difficult to reduce.

But with evident ease they cause much agony and also vicious acrimony. Status differences are that unpleasant to those deprived by them. And when the private pain of subordination becomes a general one, shared by others and made concrete by common conversation and common cause, violence and bloodshed can and do result. The physical danger and pain of combat, privation, even of death, appear at least for a time to fade in meaning. By contrast, there is a collective surge of desire for restitution of equity or for revenge, or at least a vivid exposition of desperate anger. What happens in the brain and body is so important and potentially so painful it can lead to widespread mayhem. The pain of disadvantaged status interpreted and amplified by the brain may, can, and does yield extreme displeasure. It can animate the most dangerous behavior in the world.

The Harem Door Is Ajar

A central question remains: If very basic human patterns reflect our evolutionary experience, and if power is pleasurable and powerlessness unpleasant, why is this? How did this get into the system? Was Henry Kissinger enunciating an evolutionary reproductive principle when he announced that "power is the great aphrodisiac"? And for which sex?

We have to return to first biological principles to try to reply.

The evolution of the species depends half on the characteristics of the males who successfully fertilize females, who donate the other half. These characteristics then come to predominate in the gene cocktail that has become the basic human recipe. Sexual intercourse, which yields offspring, is pleasurable. It is fair to assume as a corollary that so are those actions that lead successfully to such intercourse, particularly with partners defined as desirable by the community. Sexual selection . . . produces natural selection . . . produced us. Therefore, what leads men and women to seek sex with each other — what Charles Darwin quaintly called "charm" — becomes part of our important equation.

I have already described how intercourse is potentially much more consequential for women, particularly where contraception is unavailable — which was, of course, the underlying reality for virtually all of human history, and still is for the rest of nature. Modern work on human and animal biology indicates that this fact is accompanied by much greater female selectivity than male.[27] With more at stake, females choose more carefully. They are generally slower and more reluctant to enter into sexual activity, not because females are inherently less interested in sex, but because they are far more willing to discourage many potential candidates and encourage only a few.[28] As the mother of a friend of mine told her, "men are like buses — another one always comes along." But once primate females, including humans, determine their reproductive goals, they pursue them aggressively and decisively.[29] And women display extensive skillfulness at securing a partner once a suitable candidate has been identified.[30]

Males go to great competitive lengths to secure preeminence in the male group they care about most. This is often converted into obvious sexual blandishment. Again, the most dramatic example is the peacock, who spends a vast amount of his life's energy growing and maintaining his outrageous tail. The size and appearance of the tail looms large in the drab peahen's decision about which cock to accept for intercourse. Though there are some subsidiary professional arguments about the status of the basic theory, there seems little broad doubt that the hen concludes that the cock's willingness, capacity, and dominance — which are finally expressed by his tail — help her predict, or gamble, that he is likely to serve as a more effective parent than his less colorful, more modest competitors. This generates both genetic and behavioral consequences.[31] In various versions, it is obviously central to the entire course of human social life, and there is no question that human males engage in sharp, continuous effort to demonstrate by some equivalent of the peacock's tail that they are worthy candidates for female attention.

Once again, there is a sharp difference between the sexes here. Of recorded human cultures, some 84 percent are polygamous,[32] with the overwhelming majority allowing males more than one female rather than vice versa. If power is an aphrodisiac, it is far more so for men than women. In about 10 percent of the societies that permit more than one spouse at a time, relatively powerful males secure access to more females than less powerful ones do.[33] Such access is often sexual, though this is, of course, not the only expression of power. William Irons of Northwestern University conducted a precise and early study of polygamy among the Turkomans of Iran.[34] It showed how their eager and culturally valued pursuit of wealth resulted in significantly more numerous offspring among the wealthy males than among the poor ones. This is a general pattern: "In every case for which the data are at all adequate . . . cultural success — whether defined in terms of power, prestige, or wealth — is correlated with reproductive success, at least for males."[35] The most overtly and drastically sexual version is the harem of the powerful Muslim rulers, who are permitted by their religion and subsidized by their wealth to enjoy marriage to a number of women at once. Less dramatic but as durable is the modest polygamy of wealthy traditional West African men whose "co-wives" coexist according to a set of rather clearly articulated rules. Or it may take the form chosen by an unusually wealthy and intrepid English financier who maintains a woman and family in both London and Paris, or H. L. Hunt, who apparently fathered two large families, conveniently in the same Dallas neighborhood. The director of *Burke's Peerage*, in a bizarre attack on gossip columnists, has listed the large documented number of illegitimate children spawned by English monarchs. For example, Henry I had 21; Stephen, 3; John, 8; Henry VIII, 1 (though, of course, he had many legitimate wives); Edward IV, 2; James II, 6; Charles II, 14; and William IV, 11.[36]

Actual fecundity is not the only symptom of polygamy. Sexual access may be enough on its own. Some men who dazzle women, such as Jack Nicholson or Warren Beatty or Mick Jagger, are colorfully chronicled, if not also widely envied, by other men, who seem impressed by the populous array of eager females willing to enjoy the blandishments of love with a famous stranger.

Master and Mistress

Another version of polygamy is the widespread institution of the mistress. In classical terms, she is supported by a male at some appropriate level of economic suitability while his domestic and reproductive life is shared with another woman; the mistress may not become a mother, so in this case there is no additional reproductive advantage for the male. Or the arrangement may be elaborate, formal, and elegant, as the one described by American anthropologist Lisa Dalby in her detailed inside study of the geisha system in Japan.[37]

Far rarer — if only because until they are widowed, women usually control less wealth than men — is a lover kept on a permanent basis by a woman functionally married to someone else. A more banal case is of the coyly termed "serial polygamy" of many industrial communities — the practice whereby divorced men, far more often than their ex-wives, marry sharply younger mates, frequently to raise additional children.[38] There are some data to suggest that more frequently than ever, successful or affluent or simply avid women now enter into similar relations. This may portend a more substantial move toward sexual similarity in the polygamy game.

But this remains mainly a statistical suggestion, not a broad social movement. Nevertheless, it appears likely that with increased economic status and occupational confidence, women will be increasingly willing and able to choose partners on sexual, erotic, and emotional grounds rather than economic ones. They will be able to enjoy opportunities for pleasure rather than succumb to the obligations of economic restraint. The 1980 US Census revealed that women who earned more than $25,000 per year were four times more likely to divorce their husbands than those who earned less than this amount. The reasons are obvious, and the consequences will inevitably affect the overall rate and nature of sexual choice among both men and women. Economic power will be translated into erotic opportunity.

In a variety of ways, that happens already. There is a relationship between power, sexual pleasure, and short-term sexual control — as is reflected in prostitution, or even in "escort services," which may or may not provide sexual services. Here again there is an overwhelming difference between the sexes. Men are the main purchasers. Females are the main suppliers. Among homosexuals, too, far more men than women employ other people for sexual purposes. Men are far more coercive, mercenary, and demanding than women in sexual employment of other people's bodies. Since sex is in some central way part of people's potential menu of pleasures, it becomes significant that so many males and so few females find it worthwhile — or pleasurable — to purchase pleasure frankly and overtly in the many and diverse marketplaces that exist for it. How much this will change with women's increased economic and psychological freedom remains to be seen.

Waterloo, Private Loo

I have tried to describe and to understand how and why possessing and using power gives people pleasure. People will often have power over you because they enjoy it, not because they hate or disdain you or are consciously trying to exploit you. You may have power over people not because you want to violate their dignity or abuse their purses, but because you are meeting a challenge, advancing a purpose, gaining some freedom of action — because you are taking part in a central fact of life.

Not incidentally, when you are powerful you may be experiencing a range of situations that are colorful, heady, dramatic, and irreversibly consequential. In certain circumstances, your every breath, every word, every frown, every signature, every handshake, every trip across an ocean, will make a difference. Skilled and concerned assistants will evaluate in deep night whether the crisis is grave enough to justify a call to wake you. Those who have to treat with you will prepare dossiers about your life and nature, as if you were a chemical element. They will know and care far more about you than you about them. And depending on the nature of your power, you may have to make decisions that will reverberate for many people; there is a deep practicality to power and the folderol and passion that surround it.

Even the real dangers of the job — terrorists, kidnappers, cranks — are translated into a drama of all-too-obviously discreet guards, walkie-talkies, security sweeps, and an ongoing pageantry of fierce concentration on the One in Power.[39] I once had dinner with a visiting head of state who was being guarded by the United States Secret Service, and when we discussed our plan to enjoy a Spanish lobster restaurant nearly next door to my home, he said he would tell his keepers where we would dine only as he left his hotel. If they had the whole afternoon to sanitize the bistro, they would turn the place upside down, interview every hapless diner, seek the life history of the pot washer and Diego the bartender, and otherwise convulse a venue I chose precisely because of its congenial ease of use.

This dramatic centrality of power has psychological implications, sexual ones, obviously political and economic ones. Large modern communities containing mighty groups and astonishing military and economic power have magnified remarkably the impact that individual people can have on the world around them. These people may enjoy such efficacy enormously — we can suspect they do, judging by the lineup of candidates for their jobs waiting at the door. But even if these latter-day titans enjoy novel power, they remain Upper Paleolithic tribe members. They may have done well for themselves, and even for the world, but they still remain bound by banal reality. Do you know why the CEO of the Disney Corporation, who earned over $11 million in 1990, has a private toilet adjoining his elegant and assertively spacious office? Because he still has to pee during working hours. Some things never change. At least he has his own hydrant.

CONCLUSION

"Elephant? Elephant? What Elephant?"

A DURABLE show-business story is about Jimmy Durante, the beloved American entertainer, who also regularly advised, "Accentuate the positive." The routine occurred on the huge stage of the old Hippodrome in New York: Durante wanders onto the stage leading a stolen elephant. A stern policeman approaches him and asks him where he got the elephant. Durante answers: "Elephant? Elephant? What elephant?"

I find myself equally surprised to have been leading an elephant for a while, during this performance of a book. The elephant is, of course, the rather extensive claim that contemporary human communities, particularly in the industrial world, have without really meaning to, devalued the pleasures they could enjoy. They have also missed an opportunity to understand the nature of human nature because of their systematic inattention to the fun of life.

This assertion sounds naive. But much of the phenomenon seems naive too, from an evolutionary and biological perspective. For example, I have described the prestige enjoyed by hard work as opposed to casual indolence. I have puzzled over the far greater honor that is given in both religious and moral contexts to suffering as opposed to play. Religious icons and leaders are forever having to endure dreadful fates such as martyrdom, whereas individuals who lead smooth and enjoyable lives marked by ease and pleasure are far less likely to be written up in religious or even just ordinary history books. They are hardly likely to be provided the star casting in history accorded to hapless characters who lie on nails or have arrows stuck into them or are burned at the stake or killed in struggle for a divine principle or related goal. While the rich and famous, who may also be happy, certainly receive a disproportionate amount of public attention, their moral meaning and the undertow of their historical significance is minor by comparison with souls like Gandhi or Joan or Thomas à Becket, whose work is about life's darkness.

This recurrent fascination with suffering is strange and haunting. Yet it is also possible that the lean gene that makes us easily get fat physically may, analogously, bias us to "accentuate the negative" in moral terms.

This presents a startling problem. Is it possible that humans have the equivalent of a lean gene for pleasure as well as for butterfat? Then does this mean that we must lead lives as resistant to fun as to hollandaise sauce? Is pleasure simply too dangerous to be either treated lightly or embraced with avidity? What could this mean for public policy (a question I posed in the Introduction)? And what does it mean for private policy, for the lives of individual people and their intimates (which has been a theme running throughout these pages)?

Furthermore, is this even the kind of question that a scientific approach can help answer? Or should it be left to artists and cardinals and comedians and chefs to ponder? No. Here I second E. O. Wilson, who warmly asserts his hostility to the obscurantist belief that "cold, clear Apollonian methods will never be relevant to the full Dionysian life of the mind, that single-minded devotion to science is dehumanizing."[1]

I can even take this another step, given the thesis of this book. Let's say that the glad play of Dionysus and the firm directedness of Apollo are of equal weight in both understanding human purposes and advancing them. In fact, this is the point: all work and no play would have made *Homo sapiens* an unlikely candidate for survival in our elegant and amusing — and vastly successful — form.

But it's important how play is defined. I have been less interested here in the kind of play that occurs at Club Med or the World Cup (though I have nothing other than respect for the remarkable ballet of activity that produces both diversions) than in what happens around a café table in a small village nowhere near the festive sea. That is, I am convinced that the principal trove of luxurious pleasure is a vast range of undramatic experience of daily living, of daily thinking, of daily talk, of midday conversation with a pet, of daily cuddling, of daily enjoyment of fresh and fragrant air and some seedless grapes.

Pleasure can be very ordinary indeed.

From Fun to Function

The industrial model of life has relegated such unheralded banalities to the background of the pleasure arts, because they cannot be entered into a daily diary of appointments, because they are largely free, or at least cheap, and because they lack an earnest outcome such as a product or a score. Because they have no obvious commercial protagonists, they are unlikely to show up as part of the gross national product. A sociological axiom is "If people define a situation as real, then it becomes real in its consequences." What has happened — to put it grandly (and why not?) — in the social sciences and in the industrial system that created them is that social life has been defined as mainly productively oriented, so that even behavior is a product. Here is the independent contractor I described earlier, hard at work.

By contrast, mere domestic experience has far less value. For example, this may be why first-time parents are, as I have already suggested, often taken aback by how much fun they have with their child. They are puzzled by the failure of their community or anyone in it to have in advance advertised with confidence and cheer this zillions-year-old pleasure center they received more or less for free. In confused but pleased surprise, they post signs in their car's rear window boasting "Baby on Board." They are unprepared for the clarity of parental love and even for the banal pleasure of doing what is necessary to get through the day and night. One day, I realized that I valued a full dishwasher ready to be run because it reflected food activity at home and all the warm social flurry that this requires and sustains. I felt the way I did as an adolescent Maupassant when I proudly wrote *"The End"* after an earnest short story.

The essence of my project in this book has been to assert and establish the moral, scientific, and political authority of pleasure. I have tried to recapture it from the world of commerce, and monetized transaction, to which it is tending, and return it to the life of intimacy. One of my goals has been to offer a decent and responsible intellectual context within which people can consider the nature and extent of their pleasures. Their evolutionary heritage as sentient social beings entitles them to a balance sheet of fun as well as an agenda of function. The relative prosperity of the industrial world compels its members to decide how much they want to play rather than produce, and how much they wish to be absorbed in reproduction rather than production. The heartbeat is the same in the artist and the accountant. They are both equally involved with amortizing the elephant. Each is owed a say in what happens with resources and with time.

As for communities, let us add to their job description an obligation to decide if they are as generous about pleasure as they are attentive to pain and prudent about resources. Who loses points or votes when people don't have time to babble with their kids, or even to have children? Is nobody responsible for ugly-looking public places with sharp edges, and is it nobody's problem when the draft-beer neighborhood bar is recycled into a fifty-story building whose major convivial spot is a revolving twenty-dollar-a-plate pasta restaurant on the roof? And should anyone care?

Part of the problem, and hence a possible source of the solution, is that the conduct of life itself has ceased to be defined as obvious fun because it is ordinary, necessary, and goes on so long. That is, how can something be entertaining when it is also a kind of obligation, such as choosing a mango or giving a tourist directions or polishing a mirror? In a community unsure about what pleasure is and who may enjoy it, the most accessible pleasures become those that announce themselves, often with a price tag. These are publicly certified, the personal equivalents of "Christmas specials" on network television. Pseudo-event and the illusion of pleasure unite, and the consumer-victim smiles uneasily. Are we having fun yet? Let's look at the program guide to see if that last performer was the fabulous star from France.

The Celebration of Necessity

Now would be a useful time for Spinoza to ride to the rescue with a paraphrase of his notion that freedom is the recognition of necessity. I have been describing a kind of pleasure — sociopleasure — that is the celebration of necessity. But domestic activity doesn't show up in the GNProduct. However, it might well in the GNPleasure. The overall problem is, of course, that there is no GNP number for pleasure and there is no obvious and easy way to generate one. It is not even clear there should be one, if only because of what depressing measure of human fun a covey of bureaucrat economists reflecting political pressures and economic interests might generate.

My concern is not the statistical number but the behavior it claims to represent. In this sense, contemporary numbers defile and belittle contemporary behavior. If I want to entertain some friends and spend a day preparing food for them, my effort is largely lost to the numbers game that governments call the economy. If I call in a caterer, then my payment to that person becomes part of the GNProduct. But my day's activity as amateur cooker is part of the GNPleasure, and certainly part of mine. Similarly, the rapid expansion of the fast-food industry, which was a significant engine of "economic growth" in the 1970s and 1980s, essentially involved replacing the work family members or chums did for each other with the work of paid strangers.

This is an old economic problem — of two people who take in each other's laundry and so add to the GNProduct by charging each other for services they would otherwise provide themselves for free. Now they generate an economic statistic. But it is only about the new value of something that had no statistical value before — there was just a bunch of dirty clothes made clean. Yet such statistics increasingly dominate what people think about the economies they are part of and that, in a real sense, also color how they feel.

In an odd, almost aesthetic transposition, "store-bought" goods and services seem to become more pervasive than ever. Home delivery of even elaborate foods becomes increasingly common in large cities; one can easily derive the impression that more people in Manhattan eat delivered Chinese food than is consumed in Ch'eng-tu. Countless dinners course through the ubiquitous pipeline of delivered pizza. I have already noted the expansion (and profitability) of ready-made foods in supermarkets, to say nothing of the long-standing popularity of frozen dinners and comparable approximate renditions of what Mama used to make. But at the same time that more food is being industrially prepared, products boasting that they are "homemade" are attractively salable. And though virtually all such products are made in factories, they are never advertised as "factory-style" or "factory-made." The mythic pleasure is about home. The reality is industry. Think of kissing a machine.

The Bureaucratization of Intimacy

My complaint is neither original nor particularly thoughtful in economic terms. What may be useful is my specific emphasis on the pleasure people derive from private activities they undertake for and with other people. This is an important reflection of our natural skills, because the essentially cooperative and active history of our species has been largely in the domestic sphere.

But the increasingly obvious trend is for elements of domestic action to be turned into economic work — laundry, noodles, choosing home interiors. Even acutely intimate personal advice comes from a paid therapist, not an astute aunt. People hire other people to help them do exercise, organize their time, arrange their cupboards, and determine which color suits to wear. Expertise becomes ever more refined and intimate. More things cost "cash money." While more and more people have secured extended rights to public activity such as voting, receiving education, and, to some extent, medical care and the like, at the same time there appears to have been a decline in the realm of private experience and competence that people feel they can comfortably command. Fewer things people do themselves and for themselves are evidently pleasing. This is a strange new authoritarianism, neither of church nor of state, in the domestic sphere.

Antinatal Uncle Sam

One clear indication of this trend is that the more affluent the society in which people live, the more difficult they feel it is to contemplate, bear, and raise children. Hence, the historically low birthrates of nearly all the wealthy industrial societies. This may occur for two primary reasons. First, there is the dread issue of "life-style,"[2] the support of which appears to be more important than the life of which it is just one aspect. And, second, there is the reluctance of young people to spring for having children in a culture that is either antinatal or, at best, neutral about reproduction. They find it difficult, unnecessary, or undesirable to do what organisms have always done in the world: convert resources into offspring. (Along with some other rulers concerned about static or declining population, the government of Japan has recently introduced significant bonuses for people who have children, obviously hoping to sweeten the resource pie for reluctant parents. This has not succeeded, at least in its early stages. Much public response has been negative, particularly among women, many of whom see the initiative as a threat to the long-restricted occupational freedom they are seeking.[3]) And the "birth dearth" is no respecter of social or ideological systems, either. For example, East Germany and West Germany had equally low birthrates while the country was divided, even though there were vivid differences between political and economic life in the separate territories. And traditionally Catholic countries such as Italy and Spain showed the lowest rates of birth in the European community — about 1.3 children per female. (Demographers consider that replacement of the population requires about 2.2 children per woman.)

People who do not press to "convert resources into offspring" are unlikely to accept Spinoza's point and try to translate necessity into freedom. They will ignore my humble proposal to celebrate necessity into pleasure. Nevertheless, the reproductive process has yielded experiences and relationships we humans have found pleasurable throughout our history. People who opt out of the process or who feel unable to enter it appear to be unfortunate victims of a novel historical situation. It may be the social equivalent of the erotic decision about celibacy — certainly, not having children is far more consequential than not having sex.

My concern is not solely, or even mainly, with a decrease in the number of experiences of parenthood in a community. I wonder about the impact of denying people the range of intimate private social encounters on which families rest. The most successful zoos are those in which animals live in agreeable conditions that allow them to reproduce generously. What does the low and often negative birthrate of industrial societies imply in this context? Again, when gross national production declines for two quarters, many economists define this as a depression. By this standard, GNR — gross national reproduction — has been in deep depression for years.

Non-parenthood is not only a step along the road to celibacy but is also a new if subtle form of unemployment. In my opinion it reveals sharply reduced access to the classical menu of personal pleasure that has nurtured us through our deep history. And even when governments try to increase the birthrates of their population, it's often because they want to be stronger in military terms, or have fuller markets, or be larger than a competing ethnic group, or simply be proud of their sheer numbers. The most understandable and congenial reason may well be their lowest priority (if they think of it at all): that it offers their citizens more opportunity for more pleasure with more people for whom they care deeply.

Not only is there a decline in the forming of families. In the families that do exist, more members work more assiduously. Employment comes to dominate domestic lives more than ever. Even though weekly hours on the job appear to be in modest general decline (except for the high-status high achievers I mentioned earlier), the fact that nearly all husbands and wives work drastically alters the opportunity to linger in languorous meadows of unscheduled time. Fatuous contortions about creating "quality time" threaten to turn whatever hours are available into premeditated assaults on the peace of mind of all concerned.

Outside institutions, usually connected with employment, pull people in disparate ways and according to different schedules. A consequence is that in some families appointments must be made to share meals, shopping, or whatever. The bulletin board has become as important to many middle-class households as to offices, clubhouses, and bowling leagues. Telephone answering machines have features that allow family members to speak "memos" to one another without interfering with the sacred stream of messages from faithful callers. A special red light glows. With the aid of electrical devices, the bureaucratization of intimacy has been achieved.

Nevertheless, some faint objections are evidently still heard in the land from people who resent being asked on personal dates by the secretaries of their hosts or courtiers.[4] It appears to irritate people when the personal touch becomes an impersonal gesture and when an expression of the heart is revealed as an element of organizational strategy. There is even some revival in the use of fountain pens by people in business, because as small a hands-on gesture as a personally signed letter is some antidote to the effortless perfection of computer-generated, laser-printed communication. And even forms of genuine civility and collegiality can be traduced by the conditions of work; for example, it is always somewhat interesting to watch the struggle, as if between two drugged reptiles, when business lunch companions argue over whose expense account will be pillaged for their mutual bill.

Hardly ever are bureaucracies thought to be pleasurable. Very simply, the more human activity is turned over to formal organizations marked by the bureaucratic style, the less pleasurable people's lives will be. It is that plain. Yet the March of the Officials seems invincible. What is a lad or lass to do? What is a community to do?

Pleasure: The Private Policy

The practical problem inescapably arises: how can people increase the amount of pleasure they enjoy while being socially responsible members of the real world? How can they look forward to both fun and decent conditions during their rather clearly allotted span of years at work and, more indeterminately, in life itself? At what point does a relatively wealthy community say to itself, "We have so many objects, so many facilities, so many structures — when is it time to enjoy rather than replace them or create more?"

Here the "is/ought" philosophical problem stares us in the face: because we have evolved pleasure systems in the past and they exist now, does this mean that we ought to employ them, that there is not only a natural right to pleasure but an obligation to seek it? By the same token, because we are able to experience pain, does this mean we ought to?

One issue must be confronted immediately — the particular value a person or a cultural group places on pleasure. Ascetic religious groups such as the Shakers were committed to the most limited of aesthetic embellishments — hence, the brilliant simplicity of their furniture and other artifacts — and also to no sexual pleasure — hence, the inevitable extinction of this drastic experiment in the management of genital pleasure. Other groups permit their members to employ more mixed approaches. Accordingly, Mediterranean Catholics are encouraged by their religious environment to enjoy elaborate visual and musical stimuli while only the priesthood must be officially committed to sexual emptiness. More informal tribes, such as tycoons, may be drawn with immense energy, avidity, and accomplishment to both sexual and aesthetic pleasure. Some individuals are pleased by interacting with people, while others are more drawn to solitary artistic experience.

Obviously, my answer to the "is/ought" question — and my own point of departure — is that pleasure is valuable both as a guide to useful activity and as a natural, and indeed virtually necessary, enhancement of the life span. My opinion is that people who advise us that pleasure is bad or sinful or unnecessary should endure a substantial burden of proof for their dolorous case. They have a lot to answer for — more than those who recommend lives burnished by enjoyment, if also mediated by sense as well as sensibility.

Nevertheless, I don't think it is correct to assume that ought derives from is. Just because cancer exists does not mean it is therefore desirable. But, if something clearly and recurrently does exist, even something like cancer, it is merely practical to respond to it seriously, to confront it naturalistically, at the same level of biological reality at which it occurs. It will do no good to attribute cancer to devils or sin or astrological movements. We have to look at the genes or cells or environmental insults that stimulate it. The same with pleasure. It is a phenomenon as natural as life itself. It cannot be explained away as an artifact of Original Sin or as human weakness or as the devil's misdemeanor or as an irrelevance, lustrous but shallow, in the lives of worthy people.

Are We Having Fun Yet?

What can individuals do in their own lives to permit themselves satisfying and seemly access to pleasure? Here's an example of — in my opinion — what *not* to do. I once gave a lecture on the politics of West Africa, from which I had recently returned, to a group of Peace Corps volunteers about to go there. At a reception I chatted with a senior official who was administering the program. During our conversation he described the busy round of activity he invariably conducted and told me something that has remained prominently on my list of life tactics to avoid. Each day, he earnestly told me, he made certain to spend at least fifteen minutes doing something he thoroughly enjoyed, even if it was only taking a stroll out of his office when the cherry blossoms were at their most generous in Washington, DC. Or he would read a few sections of a book that entertained him. He glowed with pride at how adroitly he was able to outwit a system he had willingly joined, by stealing from it his daily fifteen-minute portion of careful devotion to life's pleasure.

This struck me as a remarkable compromise at best, and at worst, as the result of a deeply flawed analysis. This individual had a challenging job that gave him influential contact with one of the most celebrated and innovative programs of the Kennedy administration. He dealt with lively Americans of good spirit and citizens of recipient countries eager to improve living conditions for their fellows. Why was that not a pleasure? My assumption was that it was, or very readily could be. But the unfortunate fellow appeared to misunderstand his life severely, and, indeed, the nature of employment as well. He had somehow concluded that work was not a pleasure. Pleasure was a bonbon to be snatched from the compulsory imposition that was essentially his whole professional activity. His life appeared to rest on a debilitating category problem.[5] Whether he enjoyed his work or not, the conceptual reckoning he evidently brought to bear on it sold his pleasure short. His solution was small-minded, it was boring, it could make you laugh because of its solemn high foolishness. But it was also a depressing symptom of a privileged life lived without the color of fun.

Perhaps this was simply another version of the syndrome I have already described, of hard-work-as-redemption. Certainly, he was not alone in approaching his work with mournfulness; that approach is hardly unusual in industrial communities. There are surely many reasons for this. Undoubtedly, the most important is simply that many people's jobs *are* unpleasant, *are* dangerous, *are* hardly worth the money they yield, *are* undignified and demeaning, *are* exploitative, *are* demoralizing. Many people do have to work in terrible places and organizations. They have to work for and with unpleasant people who appear to be the administrative equivalent of sexual sadists. If the workplace is no longer relentlessly Dickensian for most people, neither is it automatically an arena of effortful fun.

But don't despair, because this isn't inevitable or permanent.

If You Don't Ask . . .

Subway conductors have to announce every station, on every train, every day. Some appear to enjoy it and complete their potentially tedious work with some energy and an informative interest that communicates itself to passengers. Others mumble the set sentences listlessly and succeed in depressing themselves as well as listeners. Different people do the same jobs in different ways. Here is the opportunity to establish a firm claim that jobs should provide pleasure as well as resources and useful accomplishment. As early trade unionists discovered, if you don't ask, you don't get. There is no reason why enjoyment of work should not be as negotiable a currency as payment for work, even though it is a subtler one. After all, break periods, vacation time, task rotation, and similar attributes of many labor agreements are quite explicitly tuned to the enjoyment of work rather than to its monetary rewards alone. Let's recall the "equality circle" that yields both effective work and satisfaction because of its implicit affirmation of dignity and membership. Small idea, large potential consequence. There is no reason to accept that this innovation exhausts human capacity to add human value to the process that creates economic value.

Sign Language in the Sawmill

Once pleasure is treated as an entitlement as reasonable and serious as safety or consistency of employment, then agreeable ways will be found to foster it in the workplace. These need not be costly, and if past experience is a guide, they will in fact lead to improved work and more enduring identification of employees with the purposes of their enterprise and hence its effectiveness. For example, the Four Seasons hotel chain promotes active interaction between its employees and managers and assumes all employees are entitled to interesting tasks and an open line to their superiors. When the company takes over an existing hotel, either to own or to manage, its first renovation investment is in the employees' locker facilities and the second is in their dining room. A consequence of this and other similar procedures is that the turnover rate in the company is half the industry average — a major competitive advantage in a high-turnover industry pointedly dependent on the quality of personal contribution to the experience of hotel guests. Another result is that the hotel chain has been consistently rated highly by travelers and sustains higher occupancy rates than its competitors in its markets even though it is often also the highest-cost hostelry in town.

In organizations performing complicated work, skilled and complicated people are necessary to work in them. But they won't if these workplaces are unpleasant, demoralizing, reduce the effective autonomy of people, and fail to acknowledge that a person who contributes a day of time and work is rendering a large commitment indeed. People who make clear demands on themselves for good work done in a decent manner — these are precisely the ones organizations will need and want — will also make demands on their places of employment for accomplishment and pleasure. One very simple demand is for human contact. As we have seen, the quality circle not only enshrines this but turns it directly to potentially useful ends. You can catch a clue to the importance of social contact at tollbooths. This appears to be a stupefying place to work. Yet often tolltakers conduct lively conversations with each other between cars, over the alley, despite the grim circumstances. Had I the skill I would like to write a play for people in that setting. People want to communicate. In the very noisy lumber mills of British Columbia, and presumably elsewhere, employees have created a hand sign language of their own so that they can carry on a conversation even though no one can hear a word.[6]

Of course, there are sectors of the industrial way of life that are worse than others. It is difficult to turn coal mining into anything resembling playing jazz or landing helicopters. Eviscerating poultry is deadly boring and evidently potentially dangerous for the musculature of the hand and arm. Various clerical tasks are crabbed and of minuscule flexibility and amusement. And there are systems such as the Soviet and Chinese in which individuals may have little choice of which work they are permitted to do; there may be little connection between what educated people are schooled to do and what they are then hired for. Or, in countries such as India, there may be too many graduates — for example, of college — for the relatively few justifiable jobs there are. As a result, government employment becomes the desired point of occupational rest because it is secure and can be expanded more as a function of patronage and the tax base than of real work that has to be done.

None of these organizational facts make it easy — or in many circumstances even politically and personally safe — for individuals to assert the claim for occupational pleasure I advocated earlier. These are people who are among the legions for whom this book and its argument are largely irrelevant because their main concerns are survival, avoidance of hazardous official whimsy, and ensuring some tolerable scheme of personal life. It is grim that some human beings have to spin out the trajectory of their life span in a manner that they feel is worthless, or harmful to themselves or others, or unrelated to the ambition for craft or drama that they may have had as dreaming children or earnest students. These unfortunate people suffer from a palpable form of malnutrition. Like people who lack food, they not only do not receive enough from their world, they can't contribute enough either.

This pathology is simple, but it is consequential. The situation is not, however, irremediable. The circle of space and action surrounding an individual person is a good starting point for influencing the larger system. But such influence and the change it can induce will not take effect if individuals and groups of people do not believe in their evolutionary entitlement to pleasure. Nothing will change if people continue to assume that gloom and monotony are the inevitable and even somewhat respectable attributes of work. There are legion ways in which people can and do make their work and its environment pleasurable. For example, in offices in large buildings where only senior or influential people have windows on the real world, an elaborate set of "open plan" warrens constitutes the physical form of the workplace. It is always interesting to see the array of photographs, objects, bits of artwork, and the like, that mark individual territories in an otherwise indistinct and impersonal setting.

This isn't much, but it's a start and a step. People want their eyes to see sights they enjoy. A statement, some assertion, and a sense of place. Once upon a time, this was discouraged or even forbidden. But try to restrict this entitlement now.

The Uses of Nostalgia

A well-known psychological principle is that people remember good times more readily than bad. Happy words find a sturdier place in the human memory bank than sad ones.[7] It is clear that people somehow manage to forget the intensity of pain involved in childbirth, dental work, and the like, or even the psychological painfulness of unsuccessful courtships, disrupted relationships, or comparable traumas, which for most people happen many more times than once. Neurotransmitter secretions called endorphins, and possibly other substances, physically limit the cortical experience of pain. They are presumably a significant reason for forgetting or downplaying physiological pain. They may also have a role in affecting psychological distress — alleviating psychopain as well as facilitating psychopleasure.

This is substantial. It appears that nature has evolved if not a bias in favor of pleasure, at least a physiological mechanism to ensure that the experience of pain does not paralyze an organism so severely that it is unable to take action to escape the danger that the pain reveals. Perhaps the fascination with suffering I mentioned earlier is a way of trying to remember what we also want to forget — and there may even be a physiological mechanism to help us do so.

The haze of fuzzy memory called nostalgia offers an interesting possibility: that there is a cortical bias in favor of the support and pursuit of pleasure. The benign nature of much reminiscence suggests that the frictions of reality become smoothed by the glaze of retrospect. The good old days probably existed in only a very partial manner. Nevertheless, the myth of that golden age of the past continues to loom as a lively and spectral feature of how human beings think about their lives.

In my study of the biology of hope, I called optimism "nostalgia for the future." Perhaps this notion may be adaptable to find how to accomplish Mr. Durante's objective — to "accentuate the positive." Is it possible to enjoy experiences that have been heretofore defined as banal and unamusing? Is it possible to accomplish immediate nostalgia while celebrating necessity? Shopping can be pleasing or abrasive. So can driving, so can planning cupboards, so can negotiating a trade treaty, so can navigating a steamer, so can steaming some mussels in a liquor of wine, onion, garlic, and a rumor of hot red pepper. The approach, as well as the journey, matters. Children enjoy what they are doing if they think it is similar to what their heroes do — play baseball, dance ballet, uphold law and order. They are good at dramatizing the meaning of what they do and hence they enjoy nostalgia for the present, if only because the past is neither a burden nor a beacon to them. Therefore they appear to enjoy themselves vivaciously and quite fully. This is one of the qualities it is thought adults are obligated to lose, or at least are likely to lose, with age.

Why? First, what is wrong with age? It is a certificate of competence and implies a library of experience. Second, it is surely not inevitable that adults lose their fun. The common culture of adult surliness and chronic mild occupational depression is not immutable. Neither is it written in metal that vacations deliver decisively more fun than normal life and that genuine celebrations revolve principally around defined private and public occasions. Sometimes it is clear how even daily celebration can be achieved. For example, on technical grounds much if not most wine that is drunk within a few years of production does not need to have cork stoppers. It could as well be stored in screw-top bottles. But wine producers find it difficult to sell even wine of modest *ordinaire* quality without corks. One theory about this is that people who drink wine are inclined to be snobs and insist upon the cork folderol. That may animate some people on some occasions. But far more than that, I think people enjoy the ceremony of pulling the cork — even better if it is champagne, which makes a fine, explicit pop — because the cork ritual defines that what follows will be fun. Accentuate the positive, just like the man said.

This may seem a small matter. But lives are composed of small matters. Anyway, a similar cordial principle may apply also to large events, such as being a parent or having a garden, or writing an essay on tax policy, or repairing an air-conditioning system. Not only is big the summary of small, but — as in charming cities with intimate neighborhoods, such as Paris or Geneva or San Francisco — the essence of the whole lies in the nature of the parts.

Public Policy: A Just Measure of Pleasure

Let me turn to one final issue.

The historian and critic Michael Ignatieff described in *A Just Measure of Pain* how the English created various policies during the industrial revolution in order to punish criminals, vagrants, and other people defined as disturbers of the social order.[8] While there were controversies and changes in the plans, they nonetheless resulted in particular forms of penitentiary building, and particular attitudes toward punishment and rehabilitation. For example, before the late 1700s, incarceration was relatively unimportant since it was only temporary — a stopgap until the accused could be tortured, executed, or banished. What Ignatieff calls "a theater of guilt" became the principal occasion for the community's physical retribution against its interlopers. However, because of an expanded notion of serious crime, and growing complexity in commerce and the power of property owners, this became an unduly volatile matter. Executions and torture could as well stimulate antipathy to the sovereign power as satisfaction with the vengeance exacted on the gallows or the rack. Hence, there developed substantial penitentiaries such as Pentonville, and associated theories about the kind of pain and extent of it that were thought best for the criminals and the community at large.

I am interested in this only because it is an example of how communities can set themselves to deal on the level of public policy with how much physical and psychological pain people should endure, and for what purpose. Certainly, an animating impulse of aggressive proponents of capital punishment and "law and order" is to inflict one or another kind of pain on malefactors.

If there can be policy about pain, why not about pleasure? Is it possible to generate an idea of "a just measure of pleasure" that even a complicated and heterogeneous community could broadly accept? Is it even worth trying?

This is obviously an exceptionally complex matter. Any answer to the question will depend on the nature of the community offering it. Strict Muslims may decide that the most pleasurable way of life is one in which worldly enjoyment is wholly subservient to the most stringent regulations of the Koran — this may yield the richest experience of all. For some aggressive penitents, a life of suffering and pain is both fiercely meaningful and ultimately redemptive.

A Russian central planner in 1950 could conclude that the most important social pleasure was intrinsically connected with increasing production, to which private consumption had to be subordinated. The short-term pleasure it might provide had to be strictly and justifiably curtailed.

A prerevolutionary marquis of Clermont-Ferrand might assert that his highly disproportionate wealth and luxury were necessary symbols and bulwarks of the social order itself. Even if the peasantry suffered real and comparative deprivation, this would be far greater were the overall system, of which the marquis's gilded ballroom was an integral part, to founder in an orgy of greed and indecisive anarchy.

The Greek Orthodox children in dark uniforms marching silently in line through their quarter of Jerusalem reflect a sense of the link between obedience, piety, and childhood that reveals a suspicion of pleasure when snatched by children. This is quite a common view; even in relatively open communities, a bias exists in favor of children remaining quiet in class and seated, though it may be pertinent that among all the other primates, learning takes place amid movement and noise. And, revealingly, movement and noise are what characterize "recess" — that frivolous time of respite from the real and stern endeavor of instruction. Montessori schools even call the play of children their work.

Even if it wanted to, there is no obvious way a community could decide how its citizens enjoy a certified ration of pleasure. This would require an unusual amount of agreement about what pleasure is — and we have already had ample account of its varieties and their advocates. If the community wanted its government to supervise pleasure, it would almost invariably fall to bureaucrats and not comedians or bakers to write the specifications, and there is hence good reason to fear that the spirit of the endeavor will be lost in the whereases and subclauses that often terminally blight even well-meaning official action.

There would also be the problem of equity, as with any entitlement. Should depressed patients receive more access to whatever pleasure facilities the community has? Will a pleasure-means-test reveal that Joe is always jovial while Josette is just gloomy? Well then, what then? Should people without musical talent be given lessons because they need them badly while people who can carry a tune on a high wire are deemed already enriched enough? How can the fun be shared out of making major decisions about where to build bridges, which countries to threaten with war, which deadly disease to select when allocating scarce research money?

Let's Hear It for the Town Fool!

Good questions and difficult ones, but there may be answers. Perhaps the most obvious triumph of policy has been in architecture and urban planning, pursuits in which serious and effective efforts in various places and at various times in history have yielded delightfully pleasurable environments in which to work, live, and hang out.[9] There has been an often one-sided contest between the hard finances of real estate and the fugitive feelings of people not necessarily able to articulate what they like and why. Nevertheless, there *are* some buildings and places that are more agreeable than others. Invariably, particular people had to decide to create them. They may have been private citizens or governments or more likely a mixture of both. But somehow, pleasing decisions were made.

Again, even ideology appears not to make a decisive difference. Perhaps in theory it should. However, urban planning in new communist Moscow or Beijing could not be less pleasant, while Rockefeller Center remains both a capitalistic and an architectural triumph. And while many US interstate highways, and particularly the older parkways, may be beautiful environments for driving, the free economies generating strip development on more modest roads have bewildering visual displeasure to answer for.

Something other than ideology or even bureaucracy is involved. During the colorful 1960s when I lived in Vancouver, the Canada Council, which was then the main federal agency supporting the arts and social sciences, inventively funded a local citizen who applied to be Town Fool. And Town Fool he was. He dressed in a fool's costume, stationed himself at the main Courthouse steps during the working day, or at other busy spots in town, and asked fool's questions, gave fool's answers, and in general performed a spirited function for the community. Of course, there was controversy about such a foolish endeavor. Yet people would smile when they saw him. It gave the city a sense of puckish pride, and both citizens and visitors were charmed. There seemed to be some serious sense in publicly sponsoring a real Fool in addition to the theater fools in Shakespeare at Stratford-on-Avon in Ontario and elsewhere in the country. I don't know what happened to Vancouver's Town Fool and to the idea. But he created, and the government officials created, a moment of modest but pleasing luminosity. There is no reason to believe this is impossible to repeat in a different way, or in many different ways. They can also be quite ordinary.

Folk Artists of the Industrial System: Various

For example, we can begin with one simple consideration: many physical products of the industrial system are in effect art objects that many people use — the Coke bottle, the Taurus car, the Thonet bentwood chair, le Creuset cookware. Yet there is hardly any major appreciation of industrial design in the industrial countries; it remains an almost cultish enthusiasm, though this is slowly changing. Meanwhile, I frequently ask students to name five poets. Nearly all can do so. Then, five industrial designers. Hardly any can name even one. Yet virtually none of them read poetry except in courses that are often mandatory, whereas all of them regularly evaluate, buy, and use industrial objects from cars to sneakers to spoons. This appears to reflect some kind of inchoate public belief that the products of the earnest industrial system cannot also be artful and entertaining (perhaps because the system itself can't be). One result is that neither at school nor at home do youngsters have an opportunity to develop an informed and appreciative connection to the actual equipment of their lives. Industrial designers are genuine folk artists in the industrial way of life. There is no reason they and their work should fail to deliver not only appreciation of the utility of effective function but the fun of elegant form.

This is an example, just an example, and a small one at that. But it reflects a much larger issue, which is that the formal theory of the community is that art is in the museums, the opera houses, even the cinemas (but not the movies). It is less and less significantly a feature of the intimate or domestic sphere. There are some major and significant exceptions to this. One is, of course, the preparation and enjoyment of food, as discussed in chapter 5, "Big-Mouth." There is the whole swirling subject of clothing and fashion, and, as well, the intricate and endlessly absorbing matter of the interior decor of homes and workplaces. Certainly, there are museums and forms of instruction about these subjects. But with the exception of fashion designers, there is little knowledge of the individual creators who fashion the stuff of daily life and of the determining conditions under which they do their work. This is a form of illiteracy.

There are three other forms of obvious pleasure — sports, popular music and dance, and television and film — that pleasantly animate many people in many communities. I have not discussed them adequately because they do not need it. They are considered entertainment, also part of an industry, but a different one than others. They are considered popular culture, as if other forms are unpopular or not popular. They involve countless people for countless hours in a wholly absorbing way. This they accomplish largely without benefit of academic instruction or support, but, of course, with a great array of sportswriters, promoters, disc jockeys, hype artists, and the like. These people chronicle the public's urgent aesthetic preoccupation with those entertainments whose snap and ardor are largely ignored by the academic and literary community. The popular arts are substantially ignored and even denigrated by the academy in part because they lack a formal traditional role in the pageant of high cultural endeavor. Of course, they figure in the white-water discussion of "the canon" of appropriate fixtures in the inventory of cultural and historical importance. But this is hardly for the joy or provocation they stimulate as it is for their ethnic, racial, national, ero-political, or some other lusterless category of demographic accountancy.

Nevertheless, the popular arts provide enormous pleasure to vast congregations. They literally unite the world in an electronic community that individual people privately elect to join. Here are genuine folk artists of the industrial age, providers of pleasure on a scale unsurpassed in the human story.

The Great French Snake Oil Spill

What accounts for the ability of some artists to generate a robust and willing response from people in a variety of nations, tribes, religions, and ages? Is there the communicator's equivalent of the universal solvent or universal code? Is there some natural knack that is as widely appealing in the arts as sugar is to taste? There is no reason this can't be so, and there are some good ones why it may be true. One clue is that films, television, and popular music have been especially successful, quite astonishingly so, when they are Made in the USA. There are dozens of reasons for this that have to do with the irreverence of American culture, its newness as an establishment, its large internal market and external marketing experience and power, its drastically heterogeneous educational system, the experimental and democratic nature of its political and social structure, and the stubborn, often oblivious confidence of its cultural producers. But to my mind a largely unexplored but fundamental reason is the fact that of all the nations in the world, the United States has heretofore most accurately and enthusiastically represented and encompassed the range of human ethnic and cultural experience.

In essence I am suggesting that in any international comparison, American popular culture most effectively, recognizably, and interestingly reflects the human gene pool back to itself. First because of its embrace of immigrants as a formal political policy — the welcoming Statue of Liberty is no idle construction — and then because of the extraordinary variety of its ethnic strains, an American permissiveness and tension have yielded the predominant art forms — pleasure forms — of the twentieth century. The cultural contributions range from the dour austerity of New England Puritans with their firm, clear shapes, to the aggressively communal music and dancing of Slavs and Irish, to Cajun rambunctiousness, to the authentic frontal sentiment of country music, to the urgent African dance and song with which slaves first allayed their ghastly plight and later communicated its meaning to the world. As the novelist and Ellington biographer Albert Murray has commented, "singing the blues makes you feel better, that's why you do it."[10]

For reasons intrinsic to the alchemy of art, audiences feel better too.

America was the primary and most aggressive immigrant country. One consequence has been that its most talented and spirited artists have in a host of fields created, magnified, and distributed a variegated story of human experience. The story has found its rich international echo in the hundreds of tribes and nations from which the Americans originally came. This has been consistently the case since electronic communication made it possible for vivid and rapid artifacts to circle the world.

It is unreasonable and unnecessary to think this is mere accident. Obviously, there are economic and political reasons I've already mentioned that explain this in part. Nevertheless, people cannot be forced to go to movies or buy music or watch television they don't like — not if they have a choice, and not for long. Here, the market speaks. Perhaps some of its listeners don't appreciate the message, particularly as it affects the more traditional classical arts. Nevertheless, the evidence seems indisputable that if the body politic of the planet has a psychopleasure center, it is the United States.

I exaggerate somewhat, but defensibly. Certainly, the United Kingdom has generated a happy chorus of music, film, dance, opera. But in the United Kingdom there was, for one example, real and symbolic resistance (which still persists, if in diminished intensity) to the authority of new pleasure, particularly when it was created by the baby-boomers. For example, when the Beatles first emerged as an intractably lucid and effective musical force, heaps of condescending scorn greeted the musicologist Wilfred Mellers, who was the first intrepid writer to send a communiqué (in the *Times* of London, no less) about their technical musical skill and their likely durability as artists.

Similarly, in France, while there was for a time an effective film industry, its clotted intellectual life appears to have suffocated many of its potentially creative artists. Evidently, along with many French scholars, they succumbed to the stupefyingly pretentious and nihilistic obfuscation of "deconstructionists" such as the two Jacques, Lacan and Derrida. They became lost in a shepherd's pie of confusion about the relationship between the snap of experience and the obligation to describe and analyze it as if it really existed.

Many academic Americans, too, were coated by this snake oil spill — literary critics such as De Man and anthropologists such as Marshall Sahlins, Clifford Geertz, and Donna Harraway.[11] But this was fortunately a small matter, because it affected only a small cadre of people with its dull and marinating glaze — a group that lacked the intertribal openness, exuberance, and candid empiricism that makes public impact in the media of communication. On this score, the Left Bank is in left field while the widely intoxicating product of Vine and Hollywood travels very well indeed. People choose it. They are willing to pay for it. They like it. It pleases them.

Market might does not make aesthetic right. Nevertheless, what people choose to embrace offers an unavoidable lesson about human pleasure.

The Elephant's Attractive New Clothes

I have tried to find a link between campfires, Judy Garland, the Place Vendôme, playing patty-cake with a baby, the scent of gardenias, kisses, and a good read. I've sought a law of pleasure that might unite such an array of phenomena and more besides. In so doing, I tried to unite the deep past and the vast present. The bridge I have used is the human nature that is carried from one generation to the other by the genetic codes that mark us as a distinct species. One important message inscribed on those Commandment Codes may in fact be the law of pleasure — that pleasure is a legitimate and influential, even imperative, component of normal life. Furthermore, pleasure may reveal to contemporary people aspects of the evolutionary process that formed us.

Pleasure grows out of the deepest roots of human beings. The pursuit of it is ceaseless, inventive, and vigorous. Therefore it has to be respected for both the force it is as well as the factor it is likely to remain in human affairs. When churches, governments, schools, ideologues, and the like want to reduce or channel or prohibit pleasure altogether for whatever reason they fashion, it requires unceasing, costly, and extensive action. Often, many people must be forced into action to enforce the great inhibitory scheme.

Remarkably, it appears that many if not most governments, for example, are often ready, willing, and somewhat able to do this. They use the money entrusted them by taxpayers to impose various restrictions on the pleasures available to these same taxpayers. Much of this rather common social control is unnecessary. There need be no inevitable contest between order and desire. Over thousands of generations, a balance has been struck between the dancer and the judge and between sense and the senses. It has worked and it has prevailed.

Here is an important issue with ancient roots. In my opinion new findings and perceptions about the role of pleasure in human physiology and social life suggest that its censors are in fact violating a law of nature. Sensual and aesthetic freedom may be as much a political concern as freedom of speech and of political endeavor. An emerging agenda of human rights must expand to include pleasure more explicitly than heretofore.

There is new evidence. Therefore there have to be new responses.

O Sweet Nature

I have described a substantial feature of human biology. And it is benign. For decades the role of biology in the discussion of human behavior has been associated with what has been perceived as the darker side of life — with hierarchy and inequality, with aggression and violence, with that fabled struggle of nature dripping red in tooth and claw. Only recently has the picture begun to brighten. Now we know about the power of altruism, the positive nature of social bonds, the durability of the matrilineage in sustaining complex groups, the fact that fanaticism and xenophobia have another face of group loyalty, commitment, and sometimes self-sacrifice.

Our human nature is not principally a mean and gloomy force generating regressive lapses from a sunlit community planned with the crisp excellence of modern thought. It is partly that, because the mortal coil presses not only for death but also for other mean outcomes which, by and large, people prefer to avoid. Nevertheless, we inherit the quiet pond as well as the irritating, unnecessary mosquito who lives there. We benefit from the durable, animated generosity of people with loving family ties at the same time that we suffer from the exigent cruelty of racists or bigots. We enjoy the elixir of organic health at the same time that we are aware of the body's frailty. With special ferocity we grip life in preference to its hated alternative. This is the most obvious clue to the power of enduring. Here is the clearest claim on the living people: celebrate! With ripe fruit, conversation, velvet, cellos.

The force of biology is expressed in shifting, sinuous, ineluctable ways. Isaac Bashevis Singer won the Nobel Prize in literature and was widely interviewed in the press. In a New York discussion he made a remarkable comment when asked if he believed in free will. "Do I believe in free will? Of course. I have no choice."

Certain large themes of human existence are difficult to avoid. They ring in the ear. Pleasure resonates as an imperative. There is no choice but to expect it, experience it, enjoy it. We could not have survived the dark nights and bright days of our immense story without it. It was a guide, a lure, a road sign to an oasis. Its enjoyment summarized good and successful choices and its experience was a confirmation. It was and is central to our deepest accountancy, finally as clear-cut as the mysterious certainty of soaring music. Pleasure as guide, pleasure as proof, pleasure as tonic, pleasure as festivity, pleasure as fun and as triumph.

There's no choice. We have to have pleasure.

Yes.

Notes

INTRODUCTION

1. Theodore D. Kemper, *Social Structure and Testosterone* (New Brunswick, N.J.: Rutgers University Press, 1990). My Rutgers colleague Richard Nurse tells me that at the Pennsylvania residential high school he attended, the wife of the headmaster was discovered adding saltpeter to the food — the substance supposed to reduce male sexual drive. In which food group was this?
2. Alan Riding, "Paris Schools Add a Course," *New York Times*, February 6, 1991.
3. Wassily Leontieff, personal communication. A skillful and pioneering effort to address this imbalance is Cornell University economist Robert Frank's *Passions within Reason* (New York: W. W. Norton, 1988).
4. I am grateful to Jack Raymond for this significant historical point.
5. Kevin Cahill, Leonard Bernstein's physician and friend, recalls that Bernstein's first composition after he moved to New York was, desperately, called *Sin City*. The composer sent the piece to his mother. Cahill notes the common problem that both Jewish and Irish young folk experienced in coming to terms with the matter of pleasure and the fact of religious and public censoriousness about it. He remembers in particular the lessons in anatomical theology he and his chums received about the moral consequence of touching particular parts of women's breasts. If touched, certain places and proportions generated mortal sin, others merely venial. This is almost indescribably fabulous.
6. Nevertheless, there is the grim German word *Schadenfreude* — the pleasure people derive from the unhappiness of others.
7. Natalie Angier, "Busy as a Bee? Then Who's Doing the Work?" *New York Times*, July 30, 1991.

CHAPTER ONE

1. See Ronald Melzack and Patrick D. Wall, *The Challenge of Pain: Exciting Discoveries in the New Science of Pain Control* (New York: Basic Books, 1983).
2. For a full discussion, see Sidney Mintz, *Sweetness and Power: The Place of Sugar in Modern History* (New York: Viking, 1985).
3. John Hinge, "Marketing," *Wall Street Journal*, November 16, 1990. The addition of substantial amounts of caffeine to many soft drinks presumably also accounts for their appeal.
4. Paul Rozin, "Sweetness, Sensuality, Sin, Safety, and Socialization: Some Speculations," in *Sweetness*, ed. John Dobbing, (New York: Springer-Verlag, 1987).
5. Jane Brody, "New Data on Sugar and Child Behavior," *New York Times*, May 10, 1990.
6. *The Economist*, August 5, 1989, p. 58.
7. Richard Gibson, "Low-Fat Burger Being Tested by McDonald's," *Wall Street Journal*, November 15, 1990; Anthony Ramirez, "Low-Fat McDonald's Burger Is Planned to Answer Critics," *New York Times*, March 13, 1991.
8. The best general discussion of the relationship between diet and evolution is S. Boyd Eaton, Marjorie Shostak, and Melvin Konner, *The Paleolithic Prescription: A Program of Diet and Exercise and a Design for Living* (New York: Harper and Row, 1988).
9. Francis X. Clines, "Miners Win a Cornucopia," *New York Times*, July 21, 1989.
10. Matthew L. Wald, "The Bleakest Business Address in America," ibid., May 1, 1989.
11. Rose E. Frisch, "Fatness and Fertility," *Scientific American*, 258 (March 1988): 88–95.
12. Nancy Friday, personal communication.
13. David Buss, "Sex Differences in Human Mate Selection Criteria: An Evolutionary Perspective," in *Sociobiology and Psychology*, ed. C. B. Crawford et al., (Hillsdale, N.J.: Erlbaum, 1987). See also David Buss, "Sex Differences in Human Mate Preferences: Evolutionary Hypotheses Tested in 37 Cultures," *Behavioral and Brain Sciences* 12, no. 1 (1989).
14. Camille Paglia, *Sexual Personae: Art and Decadence from Nefertiti to Emily Dickinson* (New Haven: Yale University Press, 1990).
15. Frisch, "Fatness and Fertility."
16. Michel Foucault, *The Use of Pleasure*, vol. 2 of *The History of Sexuality*, trans. Robert Hurley (New York: Vintage Books, 1986), p. 10.
17. Benjamin Barber, personal communication.
18. John Kenneth Galbraith, *Economic Development in Perspective* (Cambridge: Harvard University Press, 1963), p. 43.
19. Simon Schama, *The Embarrassment of Riches: An Interpretation of Dutch Culture in the Golden Age* (New York: Knopf, 1987), pp. 125–188.
20. T. D. Allman, "Blind Vision: Qadaffi's Libyan Dream," *Vanity Fair* 52, no. 7 (July 1989), pp. 92–136.

21. Joseph H. Wright, Jr., personal communication. (He was the director at the time.)
22. Colleen McDanell and Bernhard Lang, *Heaven: A History*, (New Haven: Yale University Press, 1988), p. 92.
23. Ibid., p. 307.
24. Quoted ibid., p. 347.
25. Ibid., p. 309.
26. Ibid., pp. 59–63.
27. Ibid., p. 152.
28. Quoted ibid., p. 171.
29. Ibid., pp. 206–227.
30. Ibid., p. 263.
31. Ibid., pp. 297–330.
32. Diane Ackerman, *A Natural History of the Senses* (New York: Random House, 1990), p. 63.
33. Stanley Tigerman, *The Architecture of Exile* (New York: Rizzoli, 1988).

CHAPTER TWO

1. Colin Morris, *The Discovery of the Individual* (New York: Harper Torchbooks, 1973).
2. Melvin Konner, MD, "Where Should Baby Sleep," *New York Times Magazine*, January 8, 1989.
3. Alison Bass, "Should Newborns Sleep Alone?" *Boston Globe*, March 14, 1988.
4. Nicholas Cunningham and Elizabeth Anisfield, "Carrying, Like Touching, Is Beneficial to Babies," *New York Times*, February 24, 1988.
5. Lewis Lipsitt, "Please Don't Touch the Children," *Providence Sunday Journal*, June 29, 1986.
6. Deborah Barnes, "Need for Mother's Touch Is Brain-Based," *Science* 239 (January 8, 1988): 142.
7. For a comprehensive early review, see Ashley Montagu, *Touching: The Human Significance of the Skin* (New York: Columbia University Press, 1971).
8. Ackerman, *Natural History of the Senses* (see chap. 1, n. 32), p. 79.
9. For a lively account, see Delta Willis, *The Hominid Gang: Behind the Scenes in the Search for Human Origins* (New York: Viking, 1989).
10. A spirited exploration is Robin Fox, *The Search for Society: Quest for a Biological Science and Morality* (New Brunswick, N.J.: Rutgers University Press, 1990).
11. For a skeptical but thoughtful view of this issue, see Richard Potts, "Untying the Knot: Evolution of Early Human Behavior," in *Man and Beast Revisited*, ed. Michael H. Robinson and Lionel Tiger (Washington: Smithsonian Institution Press, 1991).
12. In his remarkable novel *Perfume*, Patrick Susskind describes the life of a French orphan who has a masterful ability to create perfumes and identify odors but whose body itself gives off no smell whatever. In due course the indi-

vidual becomes, effectively, a tyrant, who is nevertheless spared by a vengeful mob because of the unknowable appeal of his lack of odor. The novel is, I think, a fable about Hitler, with smell serving as the unexpected defining characteristic of this wholly unexpected real figure. It is also a technical marvel because of the author's ability to focus narrative attention on a narrow, relatively unexplored, but vital sensory mode. And one with political power at that.

13. Dean D. DiMaio, personal communication.
14. Horst D. Steklis et al., "Progesterone and Socio-Sexual Behavior in Stump-tailed Macaques *(Macaca Arctoides):* Hormonal and Socio-Cultural Interactions," in *Hormones, Drugs, and Social Behavior in Primates,* ed. H. D. Steklis and Arthur Kling (New York: Spectrum, 1983).
15. Lorus and Margery Milne, *The Senses of Animals and Men* (New York: Atheneum, 1964; pb ed., 1972), and Ackerman (see chap. 1, n. 32).
16. Marcia Barinaga, "How the Nose Knows: Olfactory Receptor Cloned," *Science* 252 (April 12, 1991).
17. See my earlier work *The Manufacture of Evil: Ethics, Evolution, and the Industrial System* (New York: Harper and Row, 1987).
18. Jim Frazee, "Iss It Oslo, Oschlo, Ozlo, or Osslo?" *New York Times,* October 28, 1989.

CHAPTER THREE

1. Ralph Norgren, "Central Neural Mechanisms of Taste," in *Handbook of Physiology: The Nervous System 111,* ed. I. Darian-Smith (Bethesda, Md.: American Physiological Society, n.d.).
2. Joseph B. Travers, Susan P. Travers, and Ralph Norgren, "Gustatory Neural Processing in the Hindbrain," *Annual Review of Neuroscience* 10 (1987): 595–632; Paul Rozin and T. A. Vollmecke, "Food Likes and Dislikes," *Annual Review of Nutrition* 6 (1986): 433–456.
3. See chapter 1, note 3.
4. Paul Rozin, "Sweetness, Sensuality, Sin, Safety, and Socialization: Some Speculations," in *Sweetness,* ed. John Dobbing, (London: Springer-Verlag, 1987).
5. In his *Principles of Psychology,* William James gave an early, still generally pertinent definition: "Instinct is usually defined as the faculty of acting in such a way as to produce certain ends without foresight of the ends and without previous education in the performance."
6. According to Brendan Gill, this was so in Irish-American communities in the northeastern United States in the early part of the century (personal communication).
7. Barbara Ehrenreich, *The Hearts of Men: American Dreams and the Flight from Commitment* (New York: Anchor Press/Doubleday, 1983).
8. Heather Remoff, *Sexual Choice: A Woman's Decision* (New York: Dutton/Lewis, 1984); and see chapter 1, note 14.
9. Quoted in Michael Moffatt, *Coming of Age in New Jersey: College and American Culture* (New Brunswick, N.J.: Rutgers University Press, 1989), p. 216.

10. Camille Paglia, "Rape: A Bigger Danger Than Feminists Know," *New York Newsday*, January 27, 1991.
11. Wade C. Mackey, *Fathering Behaviors: The Dynamics of the Man-Child Bond* (New York: Plenum Press, 1985).
12. Robert Ardrey, the much-underrated commentator on these matters, made this general point long ago in *The Social Contract* (New York: Atheneum, 1970).
13. Joseph Slater, personal communication.
14. Jack Raymond, personal communication.
15. Jack Mendelson et al., *Alcohol: Use and Abuse in America* (Boston: Little, Brown, 1985), p. 83.
16. A very thorough account is Ronald K. Siegel, *Intoxication: Life in Pursuit of Artificial Paradise* (New York: Dutton, 1989).
17. Ronald K. Siegel, "An Ethologic Search for Self-Administration of Hallucinogens," *International Journal of the Addictions* 8, no. 2 (1973).
18. N. Taylor, *Plant Drugs That Changed the World* (New York: Dodd, Mead, 1965).
19. Siegel, *Intoxication*, p. 379.
20. George Koob and Floyd Bloom, "Cellular and Molecular Mechanisms of Drug Dependence," *Science* 242 (November 4, 1988): 716.
21. Siegel, *Intoxication*, p. 99.
22. C. Robert Cloninger, "Neurogenetic Adaptive Mechanisms in Alcoholism," *Science* 236 (April 24, 1987): 410.
23. Ibid., p. 719.
24. Calvin Martin, personal communication.
25. Cloninger, "Neurogenetic Adaptive Mechanisms," p. 410.
26. Associated Press, "Drinking Problems Rise among Young Women," *New York Times*, October 13, 1988; Geraldine Youcha, *A Dangerous Pleasure: Alcohol from the Woman's Perspective* (New York: Hawthorn, 1978), p. 15.
27. Youcha, *A Dangerous Pleasure*, p. 15.
28. Gina Kolata, "Study Tells Why Alcohol Is Greater Risk to Women," *New York Times*, January 11, 1990.
29. Linda Marsa, "Addiction and IQ," *Omni*, October 1989.
30. It is interesting that even in England, with its strict licensing laws, a pub in the Covent Garden area of London was permitted to be open specifically to serve the night workers in the area's fruit, vegetable, and meat markets. They needed a point of transition too, from work to personal, and the pub was the necessary arena for this.
31. Stephen David and Michael Rigby, "Booze and Britain," *The Sunday Times* (London), June 26, 1988.
32. Susan Diesenhouse, "Drug Treatment Is Scarcer Than Ever for Women," *New York Times*, January 7, 1990.
33. "Russia's Anti-Drink Campaign: Veni, Vidi, Vodka," *The Economist*, December 23, 1989, p. 50.

34. Peter Passell, "Faulty U.S. Logic in Cocaine Policy," *New York Times*, March 9, 1988.
35. Jeffrey Steingarten, personal communication.
36. Diesenhouse, "Drug Treatment."
37. Herbert Kleber, "No Quick Fixes for Drug Addicts," *New York Times*, January 26, 1990.
38. Ibid.
39. "Rien ne va plus," *The Economist*, December 15, 1990, p. 24.
40. Edward Jay Epstein, *Agency of Fear: Opiates and Political Power in America* (New York: Putnam's 1977), pp. 24ff.
41. Daniel Patrick Moynihan, "Epidemics," in *Letter to New York*, Washington, D.C., July 1, 1988.
42. Ibid., p. 28.
43. Ibid., pp. 33–34.
44. Ibid., p. 201.
45. See also Jefferson Morley, "Contradictions of Cocaine Capitalism," *The Nation*, October 2, 1989.
46. Franklin E. Zimring and Gordon Hawkins, "Bennett's Sham Epidemic," *New York Times*, January 25, 1990.
47. Eliot Marshall, "Drug Wars: Legalization Gets a Hearing," *Science* 241 (September 2, 1988): 1157–1159.
48. Ethan Nadlemann, "The Case for Legalization," *The Public Interest* 92 (Summer 1988), p. 10.
49. Dr. Daniel Fernando, personal communication. (He has studied street use of needles in the New Jersey drug trade.)
50. This is all more fully explained in *The Manufacture of Evil* (see chap. 2, n. 17).
51. Mynda de Gunzburg, personal communication.
52. Robert Bolles and Michael Fanselow, "Endorphins and Behavior," *Annual Review of Psychology*, 1982, p. 96.
53. Ethan Nadelmann, "Drug Prohibition in the United States: Costs, Consequences, and Alternatives," *Science* 245 (September 1, 1989): 939–947.
54. "The Line in Legal Drugs," *The Economist*, June 4, 1988, p. 15.
55. Flora Lewis, "The Opium War," *New York Times*, October 29, 1989.

CHAPTER FOUR

1. Robert Trivers, *Social Evolution*, (Menlo Park, Calif.: Benjamin/Cummings Publishing, 1985), p. 287.
2. A recent study of the dangers of such initiations is Hank Nuwer, *Broken Pledges: The Deadly Rite of Hazing* (Atlanta: Longstreet Press, 1990).
3. Robert Jay Lifton, *The Nazi Doctors: Medical Killing and the Psychology of Genocide* (New York: Basic Books, 1985).
4. Kenneth Noble, "From Liberian War, Tales of Brutality," *New York Times*, July 9, 1990.

5. Otto Keifer, *Sexual Life in Ancient Rome* (New York: Dutton, 1935), p. 84.
6. J. P. V. D. Balsdon, *Life and Leisure in Ancient Rome* (New York: McGraw-Hill, 1969), pp. 298–301.
7. Elliott Gorn, *The Manly Art: Bare-knuckle Prize Fighting in America* (Ithaca, N.Y.: Cornell University Press, 1987), p. 76.
8. Ibid., p. 141.
9. Joyce Carol Oates, "On Boxing," *New York Times Magazine*, June 16, 1985.
10. Gorn, *The Manly Art*, p. 205.
11. J. Crook, J. Haskins, and P. Ashdown, eds., *Morbid Curiosity and the Mass Media* (Knoxville: University of Tennessee/Gannett Foundation, 1984).
12. Edmund White, *States of Desire* (New York: Bantam Books, 1981), p. 52.
13. F. González-Crussi, "The Dangerous Marquis de Sade," *The New York Times Book Review*, March 27, 1988. Camille Paglia (see chap. 1, n. 14, and chap. 3, n. 10) has also discussed in an interestingly idiosyncratic and vibrant manner the reception of de Sade's work and his role in the history of attitudes toward sexuality.
14. Marla Powers, *Oglala Women: Myth, Ritual, and Reality* (Chicago: University of Chicago Press, 1986), p. 72.
15. James Madison, *The Federalist*, no. 51 (1787), in *The Federalist Papers*, rev. ed. (n.p.: Fairfield, 1961), p. 160.
16. Melvin Konner, *The Tangled Wing: Biological Constraints on the Human Spirit* (New York: Harper and Row, 1983), p. 288.
17. See chap. 3, n. 8.
18. Sylvia Ann Hewlett, *A Lesser Life: The Myth of Women's Liberation in America* (New York: William Morrow, 1986); Mikhail Bernstam and Peter Swan, "The State as the Marriage Partner of Last Resort: New Findings on Minimum Wage, Youth Joblessness, Welfare, and Single Motherhood in the United States 1960–80," unpublished report of Domestic Studies Program, Hoover Institution, Stanford University, Palo Alto, Calif., n.d.
19. Nancy Burley and Richard Symanski, "Women Without: An Evolutionary and Cross-Cultural Perspective on Prostitution," in *The Immoral Landscape: Female Prostitution in Western Societies*, ed. Richard Symanski (Toronto: Butterworth, 1981).
20. Quoted in Natalie Angier, "Hard-to-Please Females May Be Neglected Evolutionary Force," *New York Times*, May 8, 1990.
21. White, *States of Desire*, p. 51.
22. Peter Brown, *The Body and Society: Men, Women, and Sexual Renunciation in Early Christianity* (New York: Columbia University Press, 1988), p. 20. This is an astonishingly authoritative and helpful book.
23. Quoted in John Money, *The Destroying Angel: Sex, Fitness, and Food in the Legacy of Degeneracy Theory, Graham Crackers, Kellogg's Corn Flakes, and American Health History* (Buffalo, N.Y.: Prometheus Books, 1985), p. 105.
24. L. R. Hiatt, "On Cuckoldry," *Journal of Social and Biological Structures* 12 (1989): 53–72; Trivers, *Social Evolution* (see n. 1 above), p. 204.

25. Martin Daly and Margo Wilson, *Homicide* (New York: Aldine, 1988).
26. Lionel Tiger and Joseph Shepher, *Women in the Kibbutz* (New York: Harcourt Brace Jovanovich, 1975).
27. Powers, *Oglala Women*, pp. 71–72.
28. John D'Emilio and Estelle Freedman, *Intimate Matters: A History of Sexuality in America* (New York: Harper and Row, 1988), p. 187.
29. Ibid., p. 185; Paglia, "Rape" (see chap. 3, n. 10).
30. Donald Symons, *The Evolution of Human Sexuality* (New York: Oxford University Press, 1979), pp. 82–83.
31. Franz de Waal, *Chimpanzee Politics: Power and Sex among Apes*, (New York: Basic Books, 1982), p. 167.
32. Suzanne Chevalier-Skolnikoff, "Male-Female, Female-Female, and Male-Male Sexual Behavior in the Stumptail Monkey, with Special Attention to the Female Orgasm," *Archives of Sexual Behavior* 3 (1974): 95–116.
33. Gerald Eskanazi, "Athletic Aggression and Sexual Assault," *New York Times*, June 3, 1990; see my study *Men in Groups* (New York: Marion Boyars, 1987) for discussion of the general phenomenon of male bonding under these circumstances.
34. William Davenport, "Sex in Cross-Cultural Perspective," in *Human Sexuality in Four Perspectives*, ed. Frank A. Beach (Baltimore: Johns Hopkins University Press, 1977), p. 149.
35. Of prurient options there are an increasing number. Ironically, some pornographic renditions of heterosexual episodes may offer a relatively comprehensible and clear insight into sexual practices that please women. If for no more crass reason than to extend the duration of the sexual acts that performers are hired to depict, straight pornography appears to show a menu of fairly extensive and sophisticated techniques for offering sexual pleasure to both males and females. While I do not imply that such depictions are stimulated by pedagogic ardor, the very fact of their existence becomes a demystification of sexuality and could sanction forms of (for example) oral sex, which research projects suggest women enjoy, although naive men may not understand this or be willing to cooperate.
36. Thomas Gregor, *Anxious Pleasures: The Sexual Lives of an Amazonian People* (Chicago: University of Chicago Press, 1986), pp. 34–36.
37. Nisa, the subject of Marjorie Shostak's Bushman biography, equably enjoyed both. See Marjorie Shostak, *Nisa: Life and Words of a !Kung Woman* (Cambridge: Harvard University Press, 1981).
38. Money, *The Destroying Angel*, pp. 40–47.
39. An interesting if controversial neurophysiological explanation for this can be found in Helen Fisher, "Monogamy, Adultery, and Divorce in Cross-Species Perspective," in *Man and Beast Revisited* (see chap. 2, n. 11).
40. Vernon Reynolds and Ralph Tanner, *The Biology of Religion* (New York: Longman, 1984).
41. See I. M. Lewis, "Faith and Fertility," *Times Literary Supplement*, August 31,

1984; and also, my own review "Survival of the Faithful" in *The Sciences* (March–April 1985): 61–63.

42. Peter Hebblethwaite, "Holier Than Thou," *New York Times Book Review*, November 4, 1990.
43. Kenneth Woodwarde, *Making Saints* (New York: Simon and Schuster, 1990).
44. Chapter 5 of *The Manufacture of Evil* (see chap. 2, n. 17).
45. Betsy Israel, "Sex and the City Girl," *7 Days*, November 2, 1988.
46. Ibid., p. 25.
47. Paula Ardaheli, personal communication. Her Rutgers University doctoral dissertation explores Iranian sexuality in a fascinating manner.
48. Elaine Pagels, *Adam, Eve, and the Serpent* (New York: Random House, 1988), pp. 128, 130, 132.

CHAPTER FIVE

1. Alan Davidson, "Funeral Cookbook," in *A Kipper with My Tea: Selected Food and Essays* (San Francisco: North Point, 1990).
2. Harold McGee, *On Food and Cooking: The Science and Lore of the Kitchen* (New York: Charles Scribner's Sons, 1984), p. 564. This is a magisterial book, and also entertaining.
3. The importance of communicable disease in influencing social and even religious behavior is frequently underestimated. For an excellent review of the history of the subject, see William MacNeill, *Plagues and People* (Garden City, N.Y.: Doubleday, 1976).
4. Lionel Tiger, *China's Food*, with photographs by Reinhart Wolf (New York: Friendly Press, 1986), p. 76. See the chapter "Find the Dofu in This Picture."
5. Wendell Berry, *What Are People For?* (San Francisco: North Point Press, 1990), p. 136.
6. See also S. Boyd Eaton, Marjorie Shostak, and Melvin Konner, *The Paleolithic Prescription* (New York: Harper and Row, 1987).
7. I am indebted to Jeffrey Steingarten for first drawing my attention to the information that French cardiovascular experience is, relatively speaking, very favorable among industrial countries — the third best — even though the French diet includes comparatively high intake of cholesterol and animal fat in general. Steingarten considers the limited attention paid to this fact to be a reflection of the draconian attitudes to the pleasures of the table within the nutritional and medical establishments, which may not be changing.
8. R. Curtis Ellison, "The French Paradox: Is Wine Preventing Heart Disease in France?" Eighth International Conference on Gastronomy, American Institute of Wine and Food, Los Angeles, 1991.
9. Anthony Ramirez, "When Fast Food Goes on a Diet: McDonald's Cuts Fat. Will It Lose Profits?" *New York Times*, March 19, 1991.
10. Jane Brody, "Huge Study of Diet Indicts Fat and Meat," *New York Times*, May 8, 1990.

11. Eugene Anderson, "'Heating and Cooling' Foods Re-examined," *Social Science Information* (SAGE, London, Beverly Hills, and New Delhi) 23 (1984): 4–5.
12. M. F. K. Fisher, "Serve It Forth," in *The Art of Eating* (New York: Vintage, 1976), p. 78.
13. Michael Ghiglieri, *East of the Mountains of the Moon: Chimpanzee Society in the African Rain Forest* (New York: The Free Press, 1988).
14. Nelson Bryant, "High Seas Reprieve of Atlantic Salmon," *New York Times*, April 21, 1991.
15. Erving Goffman, personal communication. It is less clear that this applies across racial lines, though certainly the segregation by race in country clubs approaches totality in many communities.
16. See note 5 above.
17. An interesting and unexpected discussion of this is offered by the philosopher José Ortega y Gasset in his *Meditations on Hunting* (New York: Scribners, 1972).
18. Pat Shipman, "Scavenging or Hunting in Early Hominids: Theoretical Framework and Tests," *American Anthropologist* 88 (1986): 27–43; Robert Blumenschine, "Early Hominid Scavenging Opportunities: Implication of Carcass Availability in the Serengeti and Ngorongoro Ecosystems," *British Archeological Reports International Series* 238 (1986).
19. Robert Blumenschine, "Characteristics of an Early Hominid Scavenging Niche," *Current Anthropology* 28, no. 4 (August–October 1987): 383–407; James O'Connell, Kristen Hawkes, and Nicholas Blurton Jones, "Hadza Scavenging: Implications for Plio/Pleistocene Hominid Subsistence," *ibid.* 29, no. 2 (April 1988).
20. An informative study is Michael Moffatt, *An Untouchable Community in South India: Structure and Consensus* (Princeton: Princeton University Press, 1978).
21. Eric Block, "The Chemistry of Garlic and Onions," *Scientific American*, 252 (March 1985): 114–119.
22. Claude Lévi-Strauss, *Les Structures Elémentaire de la Parenté* (Paris: Presses Universitaires de Paris, 1943).
23. T. Douglas Price and Erik Brinch Petersen, "A Mesolithic Camp in Denmark," *Scientific American* 256 (March 1987): 112–119.
24. Jean S. Aigner, "Early Arctic Settlements in North America," *Scientific American* 253 (November 1985): 163.
25. S. H. Katz and M. M. Voigt, "Bread and Beer," *Expedition* 28, no. 2 (1986).
26. John Noble Wilford, "The Earliest Wine: Vintage 3500 B.C. and Robust," *New York Times*, April 30, 1991.
27. Hugh Johnson, "Wine in Western Civilization" (Paper presented at the Eighth International Conference on Gastronomy, American Institute of Wine and Food, Los Angeles, 1991).
28. Marvin Shanken and Thomas Matthews, "What America Thinks about Wine," *The Wine Spectator*, February 28, 1991.
29. Ibid., p. 26.
30. Susan Lehman, "Ready, Aim, Ready," *Spy*, September 1990.

CHAPTER SIX

1. Felicity Barringer, "What Americans Did after the War: A Tale Told by the Census," *New York Times*, September 2, 1990.
2. Dirk Johnson, "Population Decline in Rural America: A Product of Advances in Technology," *New York Times*, September 11, 1990.
3. But their choice in practice may not have been their choice in theory. In a Gallup poll of Americans in 1989 (four of five of whom were urban residents when interviewed), 34 percent preferred small towns, 24 percent suburbs, 22 percent farms, and 20 percent the city. (Ibid.)
4. Gordon Orians, "An Ecological and Evolutionary Approach to Landscape Aesthetics," in *Meanings and Values in Landscape*, ed. E. C. Penning-Rowsell and D. Lowenthal (London: Allen and Unwin, 1986).
5. Rachelle Garbarine, "Converting Rooftops into Playgrounds," *New York Times*, September 7, 1990.
6. Roger S. Ulrich, "Human Responses to Vegetation and Landscapes," *Landscape and Urban Planning* 13 (1986): 29–44.
7. Roger S. Ulrich, "View through a Window May Influence Recovery from Surgery," *Science* 224 (April 27, 1984): 420.
8. Roger S. Ulrich, Ulf Dimberg, and B. L. Driver, "Psychophysiological Indicators of Leisure Consequences," *Journal of Leisure Research* 22, no. 2 (1990): 154–166.
9. Benjamin DeMott, *The Imperial Middle: Why Americans Can't Think Straight about Class* (New York: Morrow, 1990).
10. Quoted in Fernand Braudel, *The Structures of Everyday Life: Civilization and Capitalism, 15th–18th Century*, vol. 1 (New York: Harper and Row, 1981), p. 229.
11. F. González-Crussi, *The Five Senses*, (New York: Harcourt Brace Jovanovich, 1989), p. 83.
12. Esther Fein, "Millionaire's Bad Fortune: Why Is K.G.B. Calling?" *New York Times*, March 5, 1991.
13. Raymond J. O'Brien, *American Sublime: Landscape and Scenery of the Lower Hudson Valley* (New York: Columbia University Press, 1981), p. 5. This work provides an excellent and full discussion of the topic.
14. Quoted in Humphrey Jennings, *Pandemonium: The Coming of the Machine As Seen by Contemporary Observers, 1660–1886* (New York: The Free Press, 1985), p. 114.
15. Lionel Tiger and Robin Fox, *The Imperial Animal* (New York: Henry Holt, 1971; rev. ed., 1989); Jared Diamond, "The Worst Mistake in the History of the Human Race," *Discover*, May 1987, p. 64.
16. Jane Holtz Kay, "Applying the Brakes," *The Nation*, September 17, 1990.
17. Albert M. Wojnilower (Untitled luncheon talk delivered at the International Monetary Fund/World Bank Meetings, Washington, D.C., 1990).
18. Leo Bustad, "An Overview of Our Relations," in *Man and Beast Revisited* (see chap 2, n. 11).

19. Quoted in Bernard Rudofsky, *The Prodigious Builders: Notes toward a Natural History of Architecture with Special Regard to Those Species That Are Traditionally Neglected or Downright Ignored* (New York: Harcourt Brace Jovanovich, 1977), p. 17.
20. William H. Whyte, *City: Rediscovering the Center* (New York, Doubleday, 1989), pp. 10, 55, 21.
21. *The Independent*, March 5, 1991.
22. Whyte, *City*, p. 21.
23. It was never clear to me why the Catholic church decided to conduct its services in the vernacular when the Latin, which no one understood, was so well integrated into the nonverbal musicality of the ritual. Perhaps this has accelerated the decline in Catholic church attendance. (For example, the English Roman Catholic church lost 14 percent of its worshipers between 1979 and 1989 — mainly people under twenty.) After all, people don't go to church for information. And in any event, the service is virtually the same, week after week. What is the point of comprehending the repeated words? Maybe understanding the service is driving people away.
24. Out of fairness to the New York subway system, I am bound to record that I use it frequently, in preference to most forms of surface transport. The subway car is the poor man's helicopter. I am not here being critical of the system. However, it is not normally considered perfect for concertizing. Of course, it isn't. But the music often makes a difference. Perhaps, also, even ugly noise, such as of a train rolling by, unites a crowd in some way that perhaps insects would understand better than bipeds. To paraphrase Marshall McLuhan, who said that "light is information," perhaps man-made sound is social information too.
25. See Whyte, *City*, p. 35.
26. For description and discussion of the event, see the excellent biography by Otto Friedrich, *Glenn Gould* (Toronto: Lester and Orpen Dennys, 1990; New York: Random House, 1990), pp. 102–105, and Leonard Bernstein, "The Truth about a Legend," in *Glenn Gould Variations*, ed. John McGreevy (Garden City, N.Y.: Doubleday, 1983).
27. They meant "ape," really, since that's what chimps are. "Monkey" sounds funnier, however — and "ape" is more likely to be used as threatening or sinister epithet.
28. Desmond Morris, *The Biology of Art* (New York: Knopf, 1962).
29. The best general study of this subject is Ellen Dissanayake, *What Is Art For* (Seattle: University of Washington Press, 1988). John Pfeiffer provides an excellent overview of the archaeological record that pertains to this in *The Creative Explosion* (New York: Harper and Row, 1982).
30. Jean-Louis Flandrin, "Distinction Through Taste," in *A History of Private Life*, vol. 3, eds. Phillipe Aries and George Duby (Cambridge, Mass.: The Belknap Press/Harvard University Press, 1989), p. 302.
31. "The Solitary Dancer," *The Economist*, November 3, 1990, p. 103.
32. For a discussion of this, see Dean MacCannell, *The Tourist: A New Theory of the Leisure Class* (New York: Schocken Books, 1976), especially chapter 8.

33. Sebastian de Grazia, *Of Time, Work and Leisure* (New York: Twentieth Century Fund, 1962), p. 3.
34. Or a book. See Penelope Gilliatt, *To Wit: Skin and Bones of Comedy* (New York: Scribner's, 1990).

CHAPTER SEVEN

1. See the insightful study by Earl Shorris, *The Oppressed Middle: Politics of Middle Management* (New York: Anchor Press/Doubleday, 1981).
2. Benjamin DeMott, "In Hollywood, Class Doesn't Put Up Much of a Struggle," *New York Times*, January 20, 1991.
3. John Porter, *The Vertical Mosaic: An Analysis of Social Class and Power in Canada* (Toronto: University of Toronto Press, 1965).
4. Bill Maxwell, "To Black Frats: Grow Up," *New York Times*, May 11, 1991.
5. Richard Sennett, *The Hidden Injuries of Class* (New York: Random House, 1972).
6. A student of mine who worked at the Princeton University admissions office in the 1970s quit because as many as a third of the available freshman class openings were set aside for allocation to children of Princeton graduates. Presumably, there have been significant changes in the admission policy at Princeton and elsewhere since then. Nevertheless, the practice was not openly broadcast then, and there is little reason to expect it would be now, if it, or a modification of it, still applies. Greed for preferment is intergenerational, and there is always understandable sympathy for the visceral claims of family.
7. Michael McGuire, Michael Raleigh, and Gary Brammer, "Sociopharmacology," *Annual Review of Pharmacology and Toxicology* 22(1982): 643–661.
8. Douglas Madsen, "A Biochemical Property Relating to Power-Seeking in Humans," *American Political Science Review*, 79 (1985): 448–457.
9. A. Roy, J. De Jong, and M. Linoilla, "Cerebrospinal Fluid Monoamine Metabolites and Suicidal Behavior in Depressed Patients: A 5-year Follow-up Study," *Archives of General Psychiatry* 46 (1989).
10. Fox, *The Search for Society* (see chap. 2, n. 10), provides a valuable analysis of this fundamental issue in social science.
11. Michael McGuire and Michael Raleigh, "Behavioral and Physiological Correlates of Ostracism," in *Ostracism: A Social and Biological Phenomenon*, ed. Margaret Gruter and Roger Masters, (New York: Elsevier, 1986).
12. Robert H. Frank, *Choosing the Right Pond: Human Behavior and the Quest for Status* (New York: Oxford University Press, 1985), p. 23.
13. Madsen, "Biochemical Property."
14. Michael Raleigh et al., "Serotonergic Mechanisms Promote Dominance Acquisition in Adult Male Vervet Monkeys," *Brain Research*, in press.
15. Roger Masters et al., "The Facial Displays of Leaders: Toward an Ethology of Human Politics," *Journal of Social and Biological Structures* 9 (1986).
16. Alex Coppen, "The Role of Serotonin in Affective Disorders," in *Serotonin and Behavior*, ed. J. Barchas and E. Usdin (New York: Academic Press, 1973).

17. Michael McGuire, personal communication.

18. A peripherally related anecdote was told to me by the influential Australian biologist Glenn McBride, who is an expert on fowl. He was asked by Australian egg producers to solve a problem they faced when they began to create groups of chickens that laid especially large eggs. Why waste food and space on indifferent producers? they reasoned, so they proceeded to weed out the paltry poultry. The difficulty was that instances of unusual and fatal violence developed within the groups of selected layers. It seems that the animals producing large eggs were also dominants, and they found it intolerable to be with other dominants, who did not subserve them. Hence, the mayhem. The poultry farmers flew the coop and went back to using more "natural" groups.

19. Joseph Price, "The Dominance Hierarchy and the Evolution of Mental Illness," *The Lancet* 2 (July 29, 1967): 243–246. With equal prescience Price identified what could be evolutionary bases of other mental illness — and there has been considerable subsequent work that suggests the soundness of his perception.

20. Michael McGuire, personal communication.

21. Jack M. Long, et al., "The Effect of Status on Blood Pressure during Verbal Communication," *Journal of Behavioral Medicine* 5, no. 2. (1982): 165–171.

22. Raleigh et al., "Serotonergic Mechanisms" (see n. 14 above), p. 23.

23. See Gruter and Masters, *Ostracism.* A searching and rich discussion is "The Biology of Social Participation," chapter 7, in Roger D. Masters, *The Nature of Politics* (New Haven: Yale University Press, 1989).

24. Frank, *Choosing the Right Pond.*

25. Ibid., p. 9.

26. I am grateful to Tom Benenson for this information.

27. An up-to-date and authoritative discussion is Helena Cronin, "The Peacock Rises from the Ashes: The Death and Life of Sexual Selection," in *Advances in Evolutionary Biology*, ed. Evelyn Keller and Elisabeth Lloyd (Cambridge: Harvard University Press, 1991).

28. Timothy Perper, *Sex Signals: The Biology of Love* (Philadelphia: ISI Press, 1985).

29. Sarah Blaffer Hardy, *The Woman That Never Evolved* (Cambridge: Harvard University Press, 1981).

30. Remoff, *Sexual Choice* (see chap. 3, n. 8).

31. Jerome H. Barkow, *Darwin, Sex, and Status: Biological Approaches to Mind and Culture* (Toronto: University of Toronto Press, 1989), p. 58.

32. Pierre ven den Berghe, *Human Family Systems: An Evolutionary View* (Amsterdam: Elsevier, 1979).

33. Fisher, "Monogamy, Adultery, and Divorce" (see chap. 4, n. 39).

34. William Irons, "Natural Selection, Adaptation, and Human Social Behavior," in *Evolutionary Biology and Human Social Behavior: An Anthropological Perspective*, ed. Napoleon A. Chagnon and William Irons (North Scituate, Mass.: Duxbury, 1979).

35. Barkow, *Darwin, Sex, and Status*, p. 206.

36. Harold Brooks-Baker, "Kitty Kelly Could Rock the Royals," *New York Times*, April 25, 1991.
37. Lisa Dalby, *Geisha* (New York: Random House, 1985).
38. Fisher, "Monogamy, Adultery, and Divorce," provides an informed and intellectually lively discussion of this and associated matters.
39. I am grateful to John Chancellor for describing his extensive personal experience of political leaders and how they respond to the uneasy mixture of provocative fear and exhilarating power.

CONCLUSION

1. E. O. Wilson, *On Human Nature* (Cambridge: Harvard University Press, 1978), p. 10.
2. I apologize for using this phrase, but in this context it appropriately expresses a contemporary confusion between a life and the style of a life. (At Rutgers I tell my students at the beginning of term that I assume they are all skilled enough to pass, but that they nonetheless will be summarily failed if they cheat, plagiarize, or use the phrase "life-style.")
3. Steven Weisman, "In Crowded Japan, a Bonus for Babies Angers Women," *New York Times*, February 17, 1991.
4. Enid Nemy, "The Invitation Is Personal But . . . ," *New York Times*, March 31, 1991.
5. Such pigeonholing can also involve what is otherwise thought to be pleasure. In a memoir about the opening day of the fishing season, a fisherman commented that "angling in general in America is largely rural and Protestant. Even fly fishermen believe that failure is the natural outcome of any human endeavor, and that anything that's too easy or too comfortable isn't as good for the soul as it could be" (John Gierach, "Opening Day, a Private Ritual," *New York Times*, April 13, 1991).
6. Martin Meissner, personal communication.
7. Margaret Matlin and David Stang, "The Pollyanna Principle," *Psychology Today*, March 1978.
8. Michael Ignatieff, *A Just Measure of Pain: The Penitentiary in the Industrial Revolution, 1750–1850* (New York: Pantheon Books, 1978).
9. For example, see Melvin Charney's skillful description of the planning of a garden to complement not only a public building but the history and texture of the city in which it is located: "A Garden for the Canadian Centre for Architecture," in *Canadian Centre for Architecture: Building and Gardens*, ed. Larry Richards, (Cambridge: MIT Press, 1989).
10. Albert Murray, personal communication.
11. For a more specific survey of how this somewhat morbidly amusing subject relates to social science, see the new introduction in Tiger and Fox, *The Imperial Animal*, rev. ed. (cited in chap. 6, n. 15).

Acknowledgments

I am grateful to the Harry Frank Guggenheim Foundation for grants in 1988 and 1989 that decisively accelerated this project. For a similar reason and others too I am grateful to Dean Richard McCormick of the Faculty of Arts and Sciences at Rutgers University. I am also in congenial debt to Vice President Kenneth Wheeler of Rutgers and Dieter Steklis, who coolly chairs the Department of Anthropology. Dean Catherine Stimpson of the Graduate School has with unfailingly intricate amusement shared her judgments about pebbly academic politics and the mystifyingly earnest announcers of disparate intellectual certainties.

I am in debt to a cotillion of colleagues who with unselfish warmth have been willing to comment on this project, send reprints, block obvious overinterpretation, and in general have been patient members of the invisible college that essayists may be fortunate to enjoy. With the simplicity that frank helplessness often requires, I merely but gratefully list their names here: Flavio Accornero, Susan Heller Anderson, Steven Aronson, Benjamin Barber, Janet Bascom, Tom Benenson, Kevin Cahill, John Chancellor, Ann Charney, Mel Charney, Marie Collins, Karen Colvard, Barbaralee Diamonstein-Spielvogel, Wilton Dillon, Andy Fisher, Nancy Friday, Gordon Getty, Vicki Goldberg, Margaret Gruter,

Oscar Hechter, Rocco Landesman, Robert Jay Lifton, Ingemar Lindahl, Lewis Lipsett, Roger Masters, Ed McCabe, Michael McGuire, Ronald Melzack, Barry Miles, Ralph Norgren, Jane Pasanen, Michael Robinson, Allan U. Schwartz, Jeffrey Steingarten, Heather Strange, Gay Talese, Robert Ulrich, Rosa Urena, Alex Walter, Helen Whitney, Al Wojnolower.

Preparing a book often appears an endless matter. But in this case my correspondents at Little, Brown have been perfectly cordial and helpful. Ronald McElwain transported the molecules of manuscript in fine weather and foul but always in good cheer. Sanda Lwin and especially Becky MacDougall were always astutely but firmly solicitous about the needs and obligations of an author. I owe the largest debt to Fredrica S. Friedman, who is at once a thriving modern publishing executive and at the same time a classical editor who translated her commitment to the reader and the argument of the book into a detailed commentary of an extensiveness for which, surely, the word processor was invented. And for the sake of historians of modern publishing, I am happy to record the wholly eccentric fact that my entire benign cooperation with F.S.F. was not once catalyzed by a publisher's lunch.

All the good people I have gratefully cited here, and any I have unwittingly forgotten, are guilty only of generosity of spirit and professional skill. My responsibility is complete for whatever portion of corned hash I have made of what they shared.

Index